PRAISE FOR *SHADOW WORK*

"Where have all the sales clerks/bank tellers/travel agents gone? Long time passing, along with the secretaries, waitstaff, ticket agents, and so many more. Those jobs still exist, but now you, the so-called customer, are doing them—without pay, of course, and on your own time. As Craig Lambert shows in this mordant, mischievous book, our no-service gig economy gives new meaning to the phrase 'free market.'"

—HENDRIK HERTZBERG, STAFF WRITER, *THE NEW YORKER*

"Increasingly, time is our scarcest resource. Craig Lambert's important book will change how you think about your days. Shadow work is a new and vitally important concept for understanding the new economy. Lambert's arguments need to be carefully considered by all who ponder our economic future."

—LAWRENCE H. SUMMERS, FORMER U.S. SECRETARY OF THE TREASURY,
PROFESSOR AND PRESIDENT EMERITUS, HARVARD UNIVERSITY

"Without any debate or conscious choice, during the last couple of decades technology has radically changed the premises and nature of everyday life and work. We may know this, more or less, but reading *Shadow Work* still triggers multiple 'D'oh!' moments. Craig Lambert lucidly, thoughtfully, and provocatively connects the dots of this profound, pervasive, and unfinished social and economic transformation."

—KURT ANDERSEN, AUTHOR OF *TRUE BELIEVERS* AND HOST, STUDIO 360

"Shadow work is all the things we do—from assembling our own furniture to booking our own travel—that has become the new normal. And like everything that becomes the new normal, it is invisible. Lambert's ambition is substantial: to make that invisible visible. His hope is that once we see where we are, we can make some choices about where we want to go. A deft writer; a compelling case."

—SHERRY TURKLE, AUTHOR OF *ALONE TOGETHER: WHY WE EXPECT
MORE FROM TECHNOLOGY AND LESS FROM EACH OTHER*

"Think you know how you spend your days? Think again. *Shadow Work* is a visionary book that will change the way you look at—well, just about everything."

—ANDY BOROWITZ, *THE NEW YORKER*

"Craig Lambert combines his gifts as sociologist and detective to solve that perennial mystery: where has all our time gone? In *Shadow Work* he reveals how we unwittingly perform labors that companies used to do, but have offloaded onto us. Reading *Shadow Work* will be full of 'Aha!' moments for readers. It's delightful, surprising, witty, and smart."

—DANIEL GOLEMAN, AUTHOR OF *EMOTIONAL INTELLIGENCE*

"Who knows what larceny lurks in the heart of our economy? Lambert knows."

—ROY BLOUNT JR., AUTHOR OF *ALPHABET JUICE*

"I've been enjoying Craig Lambert's work for decades in *Harvard Magazine*. He can make any topic clear, readable, and fascinating. And here he's got a great story: the excess "shadow work" we've all taken on in the modern age. From the first page, he'll have you looking at your life, and the world, in a whole new way."

—MIKE REISS, EMMY-WINNING WRITER, *THE SIMPSONS*

"An insightful and original book that lit up areas of daily life I'd never looked at before. Lambert does a brilliant service by explaining where our vanished, old-fashioned free time went, and why."

—IAN FRAZIER, AUTHOR OF *TRAVELS IN SIBERIA*

"This book will revolutionize the way you look at how you spend your time—doing countless hours of unpaid work for The Man. Like Malcolm Gladwell, Craig Lambert brilliantly reveals the hidden currents of contemporary life."

—DANIEL KLEIN, CO-AUTHOR, *PLATO AND A PLATYPUS WALK
INTO A BAR: UNDERSTANDING PHILOSOPHY THROUGH JOKES*

"With precision, wit, and erudition, Craig Lambert identifies the invisible drains on our leisure time—and on our mental and emotional freedoms. None of us signed up for all of this pro bono overtime for corporations. How can we quit? This book shows the problem's economic and social causes—and even better, suggests an escape route."

—VIRGINIA HEFFERNAN, AUTHOR OF *MAGIC AND LOSS: THE PLEASURES OF THE INTERNET*

"Craig Lambert has written a wonderful book that is so persuasive about the unpaid work we do, I feel I should be paid to finish this sentence and. . . ."

—PATRICIA MARX, STAFF WRITER, *THE NEW YORKER*, AUTHOR OF *LET'S BE LESS STUPID: AN ATTEMPT TO MAINTAIN MY MENTAL FACULTIES*

"Craig Lambert has written a lively, smart, fun-to-read account of The Way We Work Now. In the new do-everything-for-yourself world, we've become responsible for doing all the chores; outsourcing is so over. *Shadow Work* will explain why we've forgotten what leisure is—and make you want to leave your Starbucks coffee cup on the counter."

—JAMES ATLAS, AUTHOR OF *BELLOW: A BIOGRAPHY*

"An appealingly different view of employment based on what people actually do and not just statistics."

—KIRKUS REVIEWS

"Do we work to live or live to work? Do we accumulate wealth to achieve a meaningful life, or is life made meaningful in the crass accumulation of wealth? Is time money, or is it life? These are some of the deeper issues probed in this deceptively modest but ultimately profound work. A skillful, wide-ranging exploration of the changing nature of work, the erosion of leisure, and the excessive commodification of time in modern society, rendered in an accessible, wryly elegant style that engages on every page."

—ORLANDO PATTERSON, JOHN COWLES PROFESSOR OF SOCIOLOGY, HARVARD UNIVERSITY, WINNER OF THE NATIONAL BOOK AWARD FOR NONFICTION

"*Shadow Work* is a game changer. Craig Lambert opens our eyes to how we are enticed and then burdened into doing work that years ago was done by others—work that isolates us from community. He allows us to appreciate why children can no longer play because soccer Moms have taken over the sandlots. Adults enjoy leisure on paper and believe they have organized the perfect life. Only Lambert again and again provides fresh detail to show that we aren't living it. This book will be a favorite of book clubs as the new generation tries to recover what the past generation has just lost—their free time!"

—GEORGE E. VAILLANT, PROFESSOR OF PSYCHIATRY, HARVARD MEDICAL SCHOOL, AUTHOR OF *TRIUMPHS OF EXPERIENCE*

"Even though you may be busy with shadow work, make time to read this book! Craig Lambert helps to raise our levels of awareness of how, without noticing it, we have become slaves to countless tasks and chores. *Shadow Work* can help us leave this modern form of slavery behind so that we can begin to live more deliberately, fully, freely."

—TAL BEN-SHAHAR, AUTHOR OF *HAPPIER*

"*Shadow Work* is an eye-opening expose of the countless subtle ways in which corporations and other large organizations are conscripting all of us to donate our invaluable time and labor to advance their economic and other goals, without our consent and often even without our awareness. By bringing this serious problem out of the shadows, this important book makes an essential contribution toward countering it."

—NADINE STROSSEN, JOHN MARSHALL HARLAN II PROFESSOR OF LAW, NEW YORK LAW SCHOOL AND FORMER PRESIDENT OF THE ACLU

"With brio and precision, Craig Lambert exposes what we've suspected all along but never really tallied: that our lives in this era of automation, instead of being freer and more independent, have become hostage to endless multitasking. We book our own air travel, pump our own gas, even play the role of cashier at the supermarket, and each of these jobs erodes our available leisure time. Lambert's goal, so eloquently framed, is to 'make the unconscious conscious,' so that awareness can help us better use the precious time we have."

—JOHN ADAMS, COMPOSER, WINNER OF THE PULITZER PRIZE FOR MUSIC

SHADOW
WORK

SHADOW
WORK

the unpaid, unseen jobs
that fill your day

CRAIG LAMBERT

COUNTERPOINT
BERKELEY

Library of Congress Cataloging-in-Publication data is available.

ISBN 978-1-61902-525-7

Cover design: Kelly Winton
Interior design: Megan Jones Design

COUNTERPOINT
2560 Ninth Street, Suite 318
Berkeley, CA 94710
www.counterpointpress.com

Printed in the United States of America
Distributed by Publishers Group West

10 9 8 7 6 5 4 3 2 1

To my parents, L. William Lambert and Ruth K. Lambert

contents

introduction

L IFE HAS BECOME busier. Somehow there seems to be less time
in the day, although days remain indisputably twenty-four
hours long. In truth, *time* isn't vanishing, only *free* time is. How
can this be? We are living in the most prosperous era in human history, and prosperity supposedly brings leisure. Yet, quietly, subtly,
even furtively, new tasks have infiltrated our days, nibbling off bits
of free time like the sea eroding sand from the beach. We find ourselves doing a stack of jobs we never volunteered for, chores that
showed up in our lives below the scan of awareness. They are the
incoming tidal wave of *shadow work.*

Shadow work includes all the unpaid tasks we do on behalf of
businesses and organizations. Most of us do not recognize it or
realize how much of it we are doing, even as we pump our own
gas, scan and bag our own groceries, execute our own stock trades,
and assemble our Ikea furniture. Scores of shadow tasks have infiltrated our daily routines, settling in as habits as we drive our kids
to school or make our lunch at the salad bar. We are not slaves in
ancient Greece or peasants in medieval Europe, but nonetheless we

1

are working for nothing. Shadow work has introduced a new element to the modern lifestyle: middle-class serfdom.

Shadow work is not a marginal nuisance snipping spare moments away from the edges of life. It is a fire-breathing dragon, operating 24/7 throughout the industrialized world. This very moment, millions of people are performing shadow work: It's as common as traffic signals, Facebook, or weight-loss advice. Those ubiquitous computers smuggle in tons of shadow work, leaving us to delete spam, book travel, and manage dozens of usernames and passwords. Gift cards, which give *you* the job of choosing and buying a gift for yourself, come wrapped in shadow work. Punching through endless phone menus and waiting through recorded announcements—with the inevitable "Please listen carefully, as our menu has changed," which begs for the reply, "No, your menu hasn't changed in two years, and I'm *not* going to 'listen carefully' to this robot voice"— constitute shadow work, as does filling out your tax return.

Recycling? A sound practice, certainly, but also more shadow work. As with recycling, many of us in some cases willingly *choose* shadow work, but most of the time, it can feel like a raft of tasks that corporations and organizations once handled but are now pushing back onto the consumer.

Volunteering for charitable or nonprofit organizations like the Sierra Club or Disabled American Veterans isn't shadow work, but a *gift*. Volunteers do unpaid work on behalf of an organization; they contribute their time to the cause just as others may donate money. Shadow work can be many things, but it is always a *transaction* of some sort, not a gift freely bestowed. Though volunteers may derive personal satisfaction from what they do, as with all real gifts, there is no quid pro quo: The transactional element is absent.

This book is a field guide to shadow work: what it is, where it came from, how it affects your life and our world—and how to deal with it. The book offers lenses that, like binoculars, will help you spot shadow work in the wild. Shadow work has many results— some useful, some troubling, others simply disruptive or annoying. Quite often, it seems like an imposition—a corporation helping itself to your free time. Yet shadow work can also enable you to control the pace and execution of some jobs, whether you are pumping gas at the filling station or booking a trip to Prague at Kayak.com. "I love booking my own travel," says Charles, a public relations executive in Washington, D.C. "I look directly at the menu of flights available and choose exactly what I want. That's so empowering. When our firm used a big travel agency, they always got it wrong." Shadow work may save you time, when you scan and bag your own groceries at the supermarket, for example, or save you money, such as when you sidestep a large brokerage fee by selling your own stocks online. Some shadow work serves a social good: Recycling conserves natural resources and means less trash dumped into landfills.

Yet, unquestionably, it gives us more to do. Minor tasks like returning our supermarket shopping carts to a holding pen or busing our own Starbucks tables have become routine. "Why am I doing this?" asked Daniel, a philosophy professor in western Massachusetts, wheeling his empty shopping cart to the collection area. "What happened to those teenagers who used to collect these things? I kind of liked watching them push about twenty carts, all nested together, across the parking lot." The routines also embrace major time hogs like chauffeuring our kids to school as unpaid school-bus drivers, or completing extensive medical histories (for the umpteenth time) when applying for health or life insurance. Shadow work is steadily lengthening the to-do lists of people whose days are already crammed. It ushers in a paradoxical twenty-first-century era in which individuals gain more autonomy while surrendering more control of their lives.

I ADAPTED THIS term from the 1981 book *Shadow Work* by Austrian philosopher and social critic Ivan Illich. For Illich, shadow work included all the unpaid labor done in a wage-based economy, such as housework. In a *subsistence* economy, work directly answers the needs of life: gathering food, growing crops, building shelters, tending fires. But once money and wages come into play, we encounter a whole range of tasks that do not address our basic needs. Instead, such jobs enable us to earn money to *buy* necessities and, if possible, luxuries.

That is *paid* work, not our subject here. This book will identify and describe the *unpaid* jobs (like commuting) that an industrial economy spins off for its citizens. Such jobs go unnoticed because they take place in the wings of the theater while we are absorbed in the onstage drama of our lives. They exist in the shadows. Yet they are every bit as real as anything in the spotlight.

They also expand the realm of our work, which is already large. Let's face it: Though love may be our highest value, the thing we spend most of our time on is *work*. Excepting sleep, humans devote more of their lifetimes to work than any other activity. No one spends forty, fifty, or sixty hours per week eating, exercising, having sex, or even surfing the web—at least, no sane person does. "I spend more time with the people I work with than I do with my family," says Andrew, who manages two health clubs in suburban Michigan. "In a way, they are a second family."

Work is the main event. It is central to our economy and our society, and it makes family life possible. It underpins our finances and our sense of purpose in life. Given work's overriding importance, it is imperative to recognize the profound, far-reaching transformation that shadow work is having, and the way it is redefining our very notion of work. We will track down shadow work in its natural habitats, which are the familiar environments of daily life: the home and family, the office, shopping, restaurants, travel, and the digital world of computers and the Internet.

SHADOW WORK HAS upended a number of fundamental, long-established patterns. The traditional marketplace, for example, brought together producers and consumers: Producers delivered goods and services and sold them to consumers for cash. Shadow work is rewriting this agreement. Now the customer not only pays for her purchases but also joins the seller's team to help produce them. In the bulk-food section of a Whole Foods supermarket, for example, she handles the packaging: scooping her cherry-almond granola into a plastic bag, closing it with a twist-tie, then labeling it with an SKU (stock keeping unit) number to identify her package for the cashier.

Shadow work is erasing the distinction between work and leisure. Recently, some organizational analysts have argued that the women's-magazine staple of "work/life balance" is already obsolete, as there is no longer any meaningful distinction between "work" and "life." Smartphones trill and vibrate with calls or texts from the office at virtually any time, adding hours to the workday. "I was playing tennis with my son at my club around eight o'clock at night, when my boss texted me, asking me to elaborate on something in a report I'd written," says Ron, a financial analyst in a Chicago suburb. "That was nothing unusual. It didn't bother me, though maybe it should have." The standard of living in modern industrialized countries easily surpasses that of any historical society. Yet, despite our unprecedented wealth, pure leisure time is, incredibly, becoming scarce, partly because shadow work often shows up uninvited, a party pooper at the cookout.

There are social and psychological effects that ripple through a society suffused with shadow work. People are becoming isolated from each other as shadow work has them flying solo on tasks that once included human contact and cooperation. When we book our European vacation on Expedia.com, we no longer banter with our travel agent about where she has been in Alsace or on the Amalfi Coast, or where she suggests going in Andalusia. "My travel agent, Nina, used to book me into these little country inns, places where she knew the owners personally," recalls Sheila, a Toronto anesthesiologist. "She'd tell me their names and ask me to say hello. Nina's retired now, and that kind of thing just doesn't happen anymore." When we scan our own groceries at the supermarket, we don't get to ask the cashier about the job offer she has after graduation. The relentless march of robotic technology not only thins out human contact but can also sideline the illiterate, the elderly, the poor, and those lacking the dexterity to deal with high technology.

The technological and corporate worlds have adopted a farm word, *silo*, for units isolated from each other. Shadow work is a force that can make people more self-sufficient, while at the same time sealing them off in silos. Doing something with a robot feels quite different from doing it with a fellow human, and the siloing of individuals via shadow work is having a significant and cumulative impact on the texture of community life.

THIS BOOK WILL shine a fresh light on your activities. It will identify instances of shadow work in your everyday routine and flag others you may not yet have noticed. Such recognitions put you in a position of *choice*—at least, when there is a choice.

Take commuting. Commuting—the job of *getting to* the job— is an unpaid task done to serve the employer. It has become so woven into American life that we scarcely recognize it for what it is. Yet commuting is very expensive, time-consuming shadow work. The commuter must either brave crowded public transportation, or own, insure, maintain, and fuel a car—and drive it— just to make the round-trip from home to workplace. In 2005, ABC News reported that the average American commuter travels sixteen miles, one-way, to work. At current federal auto mileage reimbursement rates of 55 cents per mile, that thirty-two-mile round-trip costs $17.60 daily, or $88 per week and $4,400 per year. The average daily commute takes fifty-two minutes both ways, or about 217 hours per year—more than *five forty-hour weeks* of unpaid travel time. Jobs that allow employees to work from home save them thousands of dollars annually and also free up untold hours now spent on the road—time you might devote to, well, productive work.

Given these costs, some workers might try to telecommute at least a day or two per week. Others set up a flexible work schedule that shifts their commute away from rush hour traffic, saving fuel and time. Cutting back on the shadow work of commuting can enhance quality of life.

Very few commute by air, but business travelers fill the airports, and shadow work is making incursions into flying. For example, consider how the terrorist attacks of 9/11 immediately triggered greatly increased security at U.S. airports. In the fall of 2001, the United States established what amounts to a second Department of Defense, the Department of Homeland Security, which includes the Transportation Security Administration (TSA). This bureaucracy handles security screening at transportation sites, including airports. Such screening lengthens travel time significantly and also hands passengers a dose of shadow work as they pass through all the hoops of security screening. These have come to include not only x-ray inspection of luggage and carry-ons but a requirement to remove shoes, jackets, and belts for security purposes, to pull out laptop computers, and to submit to metal-detector scans and even strip-searches.

Recently, the TSA launched a program called TSA Precheck to expedite this process for "low-risk travelers," such as U.S. citizens and military members with "clean" records. Such VIPs are allowed to walk through security in a precheck line while wearing their jackets, belts, and shoes. (Membership has its privileges. No stripping!) The kicker is that to qualify for TSA Precheck on *every* flight (some lucky ones now get selected by chance), a traveler must pay a nonrefundable $85 application fee, make an appointment to appear in person at a TSA location to be fingerprinted, and then be cleared to receive a known traveler number (KTN). The KTN is valid for five years. Precheck has not yet existed for five years, but does anyone think the government will renew KTNs at no charge?

Understandably, after 9/11, passengers worldwide were willing to cooperate with screening to increase their safety. Before those attacks, the convenience of boarding an airplane while wearing a jacket, belt, and shoes was available to everyone, with no $85 fee for the privilege. Changing norms added shadow work—or a fee to *avoid* shadow work—to travelers' routines.

Sometimes it is shadow work or nothing. In other situations you might discover an alternative—even one with a price. (After all, it's only money.) Perhaps a friendly chat with the skycap at the airport, rounded off with a generous tip, will make for a more enjoyable flight than checking your own bag at a kiosk. Maybe you'll delegate that 1040 form to a tax preparer. Or put your daughter on a school bus to ride with her peers instead of chauffeuring her to school. On the other hand, you might *choose* shadow work by selling your own house—saving the broker's commission and learning something about the real estate market. Shadow work can both add new tasks and open up possibilities.

FOUR MAJOR FORCES underlie the flood of shadow work. The first is *technology and robotics*. Internet travel websites, for example, enable shadow-working consumers to do the job of travel agents by booking their own flights. Secondly, the vast expansion of publicly available information has brought about the *democratization of expertise*. The average person can now retrieve knowledge once monopolized by experts—and thus do shadow work such as downloading a legal template from the Internet to write a contract without a lawyer. Third, the skyrocketing value of data has given rise to an *information dragnet:* institutions constantly trawling to collect data in whatever way possible. The dragnet foists on consumers a whole array of shadow tasks that involve both supplying personal information and managing the reams of data that the information economy pushes into their computers and smartphones. Fourth, constantly evolving social norms affect behavior. An emergent norm like parental overengagement in children's lives can fertilize an entire meadow of shadow work with previously nonexistent tasks.

IT IS QUIXOTIC to oppose the winds of change. We cannot outlaw shadow work. No government regulation will hold back a social current that the economy continues to reward. Yet shadow work is simply an evolutionary development, and like all evolutionary trends, it has many potential pathways. Becoming *aware* of shadow work—what it is, what it looks like, where to find it, and what its consequences are—is the first step toward mastering it. Once we grasp the phenomenon, we may be able to steer it in productive and desirable directions.

Despite its disruptive effects, we must avoid seeing shadow work simply as a *problem*. "Problem solving" is an intellectual trap that confines our thinking to the parameters of the perceived "problem." Instead, we should consider the advent of shadow work as an *opportunity*. As robots and consumers absorb jobs, they also liberate the rest of the workforce for creative tasks not so easily mechanized or delegated—for precious jobs, in other words, that require thinking humans.

My intention here in one respect resembles Sigmund Freud's goal for psychoanalysis: *to make the unconscious conscious*. This book offers a new way to view the familiar facts of daily life. Like a telescope, binoculars, or a magnifying glass, it may reveal surprising aspects of things that have been right in front of your eyes. The narrative will explore the rewards, bonanzas, and pitfalls that stud the little-known road of shadow work. We have no choice about traveling that road; my aim, in this book, is to at least provide its travelers with a map.

one: middle-class serfdom

If he had been a great and wise philosopher, like the writer of this book, he would now have comprehended that Work consists of whatever a body is obliged to do and that Play consists of whatever a body is not obliged to do. . . . There are wealthy gentlemen in England who drive four-horse passenger-coaches twenty or thirty miles on a daily line, in the summer, because the privilege costs them considerable money; but if they were offered wages for the service, that would turn it into work and then they would resign.

—MARK TWAIN, THE ADVENTURES OF TOM SAWYER

I N HIS 1876 novel *The Adventures of Tom Sawyer*, Mark Twain created a character who ranks among the pioneers of shadow work. In the book's most famous episode, Tom Sawyer's guardian, Aunt Polly, commands the young boy to spend Saturday whitewashing "Thirty yards of board fence nine feet high." To make matters even worse, Saturday dawns as a beautiful summer day, "bright and fresh, and brimming with life. There was a song in every heart, and if the heart was young the music issued at the lips." Wanting nothing more than to play with his friends, Tom turns glumly to the whitewashing job—until inspiration strikes. His friend Ben Rogers happens by, announces that he is going swimming, and taunts Tom: "But of course you'd druther *work*— wouldn't you?"

Tom asks Ben what he calls work and astonishes Ben by admitting that he likes whitewashing: "Does a boy get a chance to whitewash a fence every day?" "That put things in a new light," writes Twain, and Ben stops nibbling his apple. Tom continues whitewashing, but with the demeanor of an artist: "Tom swept his brush daintily back and forth—stepped back to note the effect— added a touch here and there—criticized the effect again," with Ben getting more and more absorbed. Before long, Ben is whitewashing instead of Tom, and even hands over his apple for the privilege.

For the rest of the day, Tom carries out "the slaughter of more innocents" as he convinces an endless succession of boys that the chance to whitewash is so desirable that they must pay for it. By mid-afternoon, the job is not only done but "Tom was literally rolling in wealth," having collected a kite, twelve marbles, a tin soldier, six firecrackers, and a kitten with one eye, among other coveted possessions. "If he hadn't run out of whitewash," writes Twain, "he would have bankrupted every boy in the village."

Tom Sawyer achieved his amazing success simply by redefining *work*. He convinced the boys that whitewashing was a fun project with an artistic aspect, not a monotonous chore. Work became *play,* and so the boys, who instinctively loved play, eagerly embraced whitewashing that Saturday.

To redefine something changes how we perceive it. The concept of *shadow work* can redefine many things we do. These are tasks we may never have categorized as *work*—even though many people have been paid for doing them. Over the last twenty years or so, the phenomenon of shadow work has grown up around us rapidly. To understand its significance, we can use a touchstone that indicates how we lived before its arrival.

LIFE BEFORE SHADOW WORK

The Sunoco station where Dad and I went to fill up our family's car on Saturday mornings sat atop a small rise on the highway in Denville, New Jersey. The coverall-clad gent who pumped the gas, Ralph, was in his late sixties. His smile shone out from a well-lined face. Engine grease had become part of his fingers. You could look at Ralph and tell he was a *good* mechanic.

He was mostly retired from hands-on auto repair, though Ralph advised the younger men and would still crank a ratchet wrench on occasion. He pumped gas with casual skill. He'd raise the hood of our 1949 Plymouth, pull the dipstick and check the oil, and then clean the windshield and rear window with a squeegee. When I was seven, in 1955, gasoline cost 29 cents per gallon, and Dad paid in cash, of course. I loved the smell of gasoline. That scent is a sweet memory, an aroma that modern vapor-recovery systems removed from the gas-station experience.

Today, I do Ralph's job. I pump the gas, pull the dipstick, check the oil. I squeegee the windows. Never mind that I have a Ph.D. and work as a writer. Unlike Ralph, though, I don't get paid by the gas station. I fill the tank of my *own* car on an amateur basis. It's not like I have a choice. Where I live, in Massachusetts, gas pump attendants have pretty much disappeared.

WELL, LOTS OF things have changed since the 1950s. Various jobs have gone extinct, bequeathing chores like gas pumping to the rest of us. Let's briefly revisit American society in the mid-twentieth century to benchmark how our world of work has evolved since then.

In 1955, most mothers, like mine, stayed at home, kept house, cooked meals, and cared for the children. This was the "women's work" that wives and mothers had traditionally done. They never earned wages for doing housework, of course, unless they were doing it in someone *else's* house. But "women's work" always anchored family life, and since the Industrial Revolution, it has enabled men to work for money *away* from the homestead. Though housework went unpaid, the institutions of marriage, family, and even the economy could not have survived without it. The most important work we do may not be for cash. Housework is the original and most fundamental form of shadow work.

By and large, 1950s fathers earned the family's income. They *went* to work. There were hardly any home offices, except when dentists or doctors added them to their houses. Nobody telecommuted: People commuted with cars and trains, not fiber-optic cables. In offices, "support staff"—secretaries, typists, office managers, messengers, janitors—helped the rest of the staff produce by taking care of routine tasks. In today's home office, those jobs are all your own, and support staff have thinned out in downtown offices, too.

To shop in the 1950s, you went to something called a *store*. It would have been redundant to call it a "bricks-and-mortar" store because there was no other kind. Yes, there were mail-order catalogs, but online commerce was not even a dream. Door-to-door salespeople like the Avon lady, the Fuller Brush man, or the *Encyclopedia Britannica* sales force were the face of home shopping—that and Tupperware parties. Salespeople who visited your home, like the ones in stores, were thoroughly trained and brimmed with knowledge about their merchandise. They could answer any question you had; it was their job to provide the "research" you now do for yourself when you shop online or even in big-box stores, where finding a salesperson can be like spotting a scarlet tanager in a city park. At the supermarket, the cashier would "ring you up" (the mechanical cash register actually made a *ka-ching!* sound) and take your money. You did not tip the cashier for accepting your payment. Self-service checkouts did not exist.

All that stuff we brought home from stores produced tons of trash. We threw it all out. The trash got dumped in landfills choked with the refuse of a consumer society. There was no recycling.

In the 1950s, we didn't eat out much. For all but the well-to-do, going to a restaurant was a special experience. The few fast-food chains in operation were local or regional, not national. When you did eat out, you rarely served yourself anything. In restaurants, waiters and waitresses brought your food to the table—including salads, as there were no salad bars. At the end of the meal, you just paid, got up, and walked away. Busboys cleaned up your table.

Lacking Internet commerce, you had to go to the local drug-store or newsstand to buy embarrassing items like condoms, dia-phragms, Preparation H, pulp-fiction paperbacks, or raunchy magazines. At-home pregnancy tests did not yet give women the privilege of being the first, and perhaps only, person to know the state of their fertility. Living in a small town deepened the pri-vacy issue, because the people behind the counter probably knew you and your family, and maybe even understood exactly why you were buying this particular incriminating item.

IN THOSE DAYS, people did their banking by going *inside* the bank building. You made your deposit or bought your savings bond from a teller at a window, waiting in line for your turn if the bank was busy, as there were no ATMs. The teller could cash a check for you and, unlike an ATM, could give you bills other than just $20 bills, or even a roll of dimes for phone calls. (Public phones were available in phone booths, before cell phones privatized the telephonic experience and made it ubiquitous.) The Dover Trust, where my father was president, also offered flourishes unavailable at ATMs; during the holidays, for example, a retired local music teacher played Christmas carols on a small organ in the bank's lobby.

Today, many customers never enter a bank: They bank online at their computers. They are their own tellers, bookkeepers, and loan officers, with a flat-screen display for a bank lobby. Holiday music, if any, comes through earbuds from an iPod, not a live musician who takes your request for "Silver Bells." And their invisible virtual bank, unlike my Dad's granite one, is always open. (Or it is until their computer—or their bank—crashes.)

Stores did not stay open twenty-four hours a day. They closed at night. You could not buy cough medicine, Cheerios, magazines, or lottery tickets (there were no state lotteries, anyway) whenever you felt like it. You had to tailor your habits to the merchant's hours. This confined you to a certain schedule. Yet it was also a relief. You had downtime to escape the ceaseless thrum of the consumer economy. That off switch no longer exists, so it can feel like you are always somehow in the marketplace. Day and night, you are either producing or consuming—and if not, you *could* be. Today there's no rest from work and consumption.

The global economy roars on like ceaseless background noise: Wall Street traders rise before the sun to check prices on the Börse Berlin or the Tokyo markets. They are at *work,* but the individual investor who Googles a pharmaceutical stock at 2 AM, then clicks onto Scottrade's online brokerage to buy 400 shares of it when the market opens, is not; he is doing *shadow work.* His stockbroker used to handle the tasks that he now performs.

Scottrade and other online brokerages enable investors to buy or sell securities for transaction fees as low as $7, a small fraction of what full-service brokers charge. Taking on this shadow work does place the full responsibility for the investment on your shoulders. But luckily, online investing need not be rocket science. The

main thing that vanishes in the self-serve mode is the sense of working with a partner, a broker with whom to discuss your moves.

Talking about investment decisions with *any* intelligent adult
is probably a good idea (particularly if you are married to them).
But talking with a stockbroker will probably not improve your
portfolio's performance. The professional "expertise" of stockbro-
kers is largely, alas, a case of the emperor's new clothes. Statistical
research has repeatedly shown that over the long run, the vast
majority of professional stock pickers and money managers generate returns on investment that fall short of indexed mutual funds.
In other words, having *no one* in charge of your money generally
works better than hiring a Wall Street gunslinger. (Magazines like
Money publish annual lists of the "top five mutual fund managers," and their numbers do in fact surpass the returns of the index.
The problem is that next year, *the list is completely different.*)

Yes, there *are* great investors, and some, like Warren Buffett
of Berkshire Hathaway and Peter Lynch of Fidelity, have become
legends. But Wall Street data indicate that no more than 20 percent
of professional money managers have consistently beaten market
indices. We know the genius of people like Buffett and Lynch
now, because their track records have established it. But identifying gifted investors at the beginnings of their careers is a much
dicier call, one that very few of us can make. Statistically, you have
only a one-in-five chance of getting it right—and you're betting big
money on the outcome.

Hence, you might well opt for the shadow work of being your
own broker. At low-cost mutual fund houses like Vanguard, you'll

save a lot on fees and probably end up with better results, while minimizing time devoted to the task, For most of us, this kind of shadow work is a wise option.

IN THE 1950S, compared to now, kids spent more time with other kids and less time with their parents. A school bus took me to school and back, along with a score of youngsters from my neighborhood. We picked up a couple dozen more along the forty-five-minute route. It was a long and highly sociable trip. That daily school bus ride, repeated year after year, meant that the boys and girls on board got to know each other very well. In our neighborhood, we played together daily after school.

In those halcyon days, holidays and weekends were your own, to enjoy as you saw fit. When you worked, you *worked*. When you played, you *played*. The two did not mingle. No text from the office interrupted an evening softball game or a weekend picnic by the lake. You toiled by day in the factory or office. Nights and weekends were your own, a sacrosanct time to relax in your backyard. In 1955, we enjoyed a more leisurely pace of life, and a sense in our small northern New Jersey town that, in some way, we were all in this together.

IN THE 1950S, tasks like pumping gas, typing letters, researching products, checking out groceries, composing salads, disposing of cans and bottles, handling bank deposits, and driving the kids to school were handled by pump jockeys, secretaries, salespeople, cashiers, waitresses, garbage men, tellers, and bus drivers. Today, *you* have inherited these jobs. They have become shadow work.

In fact, much of the work we do outside our jobs is shadow work. The twenty-four-hour economy has brought the workplace home for those whose jobs could be affected by, say, a market meltdown in Singapore. Smartphones tether people to colleagues for whom work may *always* be the top priority. When your boss texts just as you sit down to a restaurant meal with your husband at 8 PM, are you at work or not? In many fields, expectations have shifted to make such intrusions normal. New customs can open the door to more work—and more shadow work.

The erosion of leisure time, like all erosion, happens steadily, one grain of sand at a time. Its *persistence* confers its power: Those sand grains keep disappearing all day long, every day of the year. They are leaving the hourglass of your lifespan.

Similarly, the ocean of shadow work never rests. Had these extra jobs appeared all at once, there'd have been howls of protest. But the pecking away of unnoticed seconds, one at a time, draws not a murmur. It's a bit like Silicon Slim, a cyber-thief portrayed in a satirical song, from John Forster's CD *Entering Marion*:

*Well, you've heard of Jesse James and you've heard of
    Robin Hood
Here's a ballad of a bad man who was every bit as good
This guy held up Chase Manhattan unarmed and all alone
With just a trusty home computer that was hooked up to
    his phone
In the dead of night he'd access each depositor's account
And from each of them he'd siphon off the teeniest amount*

And since no one ever noticed that there'd even been a crime
He stole forty million dollars, a penny at a time.

The human olfactory system adjusts to a foreign smell after it has persisted a while. The nose and brain acclimate even to a repulsive new odor and stop perceiving it, just as we no longer notice the wallpaper in our dining room. In like manner, we adapt to the quotidian nature of shadow work. It becomes routine. Bit by bit, we get habituated to pulling a nozzle to dispense our own frozen yogurt, or manning one to pump our gasoline.

To get millions of people to do shadow work, it's imperative to avoid consumer *choice* in the matter by making sure the new job never comes up for a vote. The antidote to this is *awareness*—which, sometimes at least, will let you decide for yourself. You might want shadow work at times. A task like a home pregnancy test, for example, offers advantages: It's easy—and less costly, more convenient, and more private than dealing with a medical lab. In contrast, deleting spam in your inbox involves shadow work without conferring any advantages or offering any easy alternative.

WORK: A LOVE STORY

Work is to Americans what wine is to the French: an unquestioned good. We regard work as the foundation of our material prosperity. Employees in the United States work longer hours than those of the vast majority of industrialized nations. They also receive—and use—fewer weeks of vacation than their peers in most other developed economies. In America, we worship at the temple of work.

In her book *The Overworked American*, economist Juliet
Schor describes how, after a century of declining work hours
that ran from roughly 1850 to 1950, Americans' time on the job
steadily *increased* in the postwar era. Her data go back to the relatively leisurely Middle Ages, when thirteenth-century peasants put
in 1,620 hours a year. They worked twelve-hour agricultural days,
but only 135 of them per year, which averaged out to a workweek
of just over thirty hours. Alternatively, we could tally up their
work year as seven months of sixty-hour, five-day weeks—with
five months off.

Machinery got people working a lot longer, partly because
indoor factory jobs could ignore the natural cycles of the seasons.
In the United States of 1850, the Industrial Revolution had amped
up labor to an astonishing all-time high of 3,650 hours, based on
seventy-hour weeks and fifty-two weeks per year. Work was ceaseless. Over the next century, with the rise of labor unions and other
factors, Americans began to get weekends off and paid vacation
time. But Schor calculated that in the latter part of the twentieth
century, their annual hours on the job rose from 1,876 in 1969 to
1,949 in 1987, an increase of 163 hours or about an *extra month
of full-time work per year* for each person. Schor cites a 1988
Harris Poll finding, in a parallel development, that Americans' leisure time had fallen nearly 40 percent—from twenty-six weekly
hours to seventeen—in the fifteen years since 1973.

New York Times reporter Steven Greenhouse, in *The Big
Squeeze*, his 2008 book on the plight of the American worker,
notes somewhat fewer work hours by 2006—a decrease to 1,804,

a lower level than in 1969. Even so, that amounts to "three full-time weeks per year more than the average British worker, six more weeks than the average French worker, and nine more weeks than the average German worker," he writes. Furthermore, "The U.S. is the only advanced nation that does not legislate a minimum number of days of vacation," he adds. "The average in the country is twelve days of vacation a year, with 36 percent of Americans reporting that they do not use all the vacation days to which they are entitled."

Economic necessity isn't always what drives this juggernaut of work. Take, for example, William Gross, head of the Pacific Investment Management Company. One might think that a sixty-eight-year-old man who makes $200 million per year and lives in Laguna Beach on the southern California coast would have time to relax. Not so. A *New York Times* report of 2012 places Gross at his desk at 5:30 AM, after greeting his colleague Mohamed El-Erian on the way in—El-Erian has been there since 4:30. Gross used to slip away sometimes for a little golf in the afternoon, then return to the office. No longer. "To some extent, I wish that I could go over and hit golf balls like I used to at 3:30," he told the *Times*, "but I have not hit balls in three and a half years."

In personal affluence and dedication to his job, Gross is extraordinary, but his ingrained work ethic fits the mainstream ethos. Many young investment bankers, entrepreneurs, and lawyers put in fourteen-hour days and skip vacations to accumulate wealth they don't have time to enjoy. This goes far beyond economics: Deep social and cultural forces underlie our nearly religious belief in work.

These figures, of course, do not include shadow work, which goes unrecorded. We can only speculate about how much extra labor it contributes. One thing that's clear is that paid employees, from janitors to professional athletes, can organize to protect their common interests and negotiate collective bargaining agreements that limit and govern the amount and kind of work they do. White-collar workers are less often unionized but do operate within a set of established standards that are often set down by trade and professional associations. Shadow workers have no such protections. They are a politically and socially unorganized throng of people who do not know each other, do not associate together, and lack any vehicle for coordinated action. (Their one powerful tool is the boycott, but even boycotts usually require organized leadership.) Thus, for the most part, shadow workers have no one to represent their interests or to push back against the continual introduction of new shadow jobs.

IN A SERIES of experiments published in *Psychological Science* in 2013, researchers investigated the balance between work and leisure. They placed subjects at computer terminals with headsets on. They could listen to pleasing music ("leisure") or choose to have blasts of harsh noise ("work") interrupt the music. Listening to the harsh noise twenty times earned one group (high earners) a chocolate; the other group of subjects (low earners) had to hear the noise 120 times to earn their chocolate; this corresponds to a lower hourly wage.

Subjects could not eat their candies until the next phase of the experiment and couldn't take any uneaten chocolates home with them. Reviewing the study for Canada's online magazine *Hazlitt,* Nicholas Hune-Brown noted that the researchers said their study "'simulates a microcosmic life with a fixed life span.' First you choose between leisure and work, then you consume what you've earned. As in real life, you can't take it with you."

Surprisingly, the subjects didn't just earn as much chocolate as they could enjoy and then go back to listening to music. Instead, the high earners collected 10.74 chocolates on average but ate only 4.26, leaving most of what they'd suffered for on the table. Low earners brought in a little less chocolate than they could eat but heard about as many harsh sounds as the high earners. Hune-Brown concludes that "both groups weren't considering the optimal results, but rather how much work they could bear. Instead of trying to create the most enjoyable experience, they unthinkingly worked as much as possible, stockpiling useless treasure." The researchers called this phenomenon "mindless accumulation" and compared overearning to overeating. They described both as specifically modern problems, brought on by the material overabundance of contemporary life.

Indeed, in today's world, work seems to trump all other values. In some social groups, it nearly monopolizes human attention and, along with its by-product, money, bids to become the *only* value. Let's examine a few indicators of the emphasis we place on work.

In professional sports, one of the highest compliments sportscasters pay athletes is to praise their "great work ethic." Amateurs *play* sports for fun, but professionals do so with a great *work* ethic. Talent may be God-given, but an athlete chooses a work ethic.

Choosing hard work is a sign of virtue: Morally, we equate work with fortitude—that is, strength of character. (Ironically, in the United States, it would also require some strength of character to resist the social norm and *not* work so hard.)

We admire parents who work two or three jobs to support their families: Their willingness to put in long weeks shows a capacity to sacrifice free time and/or pleasures to sustain others. Usually, though, we do not analyze what *motivates* people to work, and it's not always altruism or admirable personality traits. There are, for example, those who simply prefer to be out of their homes and away from spouses and children. ("I'm taking on this new job so I can spend *less* time with my family.") Some moonlighters just want a higher standard of living, regardless of what it costs in human terms; perhaps their children would prefer fewer TV sets and digital toys but more time with Mom and Dad. There's also the "last man standing" ethos that reigns in some businesses—film production, for example. It encourages workers to put in extremely long hours just to show they are working harder, or at least longer, than their colleagues. Regardless of motive, it's off to work we go.

Short of true *workaholism*—an extreme condition that dominates someone's life like obsessive-compulsive disorder or anorexia nervosa—work commands universal respect for its own sake. Our reverence for work sets the stage for our unthinking embrace of shadow work. We don't merely admire work, we worship it, and things that are worshipped tend to become sacred. The sacred is beyond criticism or reproach, so we accept whatever shows up under its sanction.

RELIGION HAS, FOR centuries, intertwined itself with work. Americans' worship of work came over on the *Mayflower* with the Puritans, who esteemed work far above pleasure. Recall Thomas Macaulay's remark that the Puritans objected to bearbaiting not because it tormented the bears but because it gave pleasure to the spectators. Max Weber's sociological classic *The Protestant Ethic and the Spirit of Capitalism*, a series of essays written in 1904 and 1905, linked the ethic of hard work and worldly success to certain aspects of Protestant theology, such as the Calvinist view that secular prosperity indicated that one was predestined for salvation rather than damnation. Working hard honored God. Various Protestant doctrines discouraged or limited donations to the church (due to disapproval of icons and the potential for idolatry) or to the poor (as encouraging begging and laziness) and advised against the purchase of luxuries as sinful indulgences. Weber argued that the upshot was to encourage *investment* of one's wealth, spurring the development of capitalism.

Like all Protestants (and Christians generally), Puritans identified pleasure with sin. Take the classic "seven deadly sins," a list traceable to the monk Evagrius the Solitary (AD 345–399). The current Deadly Seven embrace anger, greed, sloth, pride, lust, envy, and gluttony. Yet these are simply aspects of human nature. One might interpret all except anger and envy as *pleasures* rather than sins—it is largely a matter of semantics. (Even envy could rank as a pleasure, if it includes watching *Access Hollywood*.) Translate greed, sloth, pride, lust, and gluttony as *ambition, relaxation, self-confidence, sexual passion, and appetite*, and sins suddenly become signs of vitality. Only the sinners, apparently, are really living.

But perhaps it is just a matter of degree: Pleasures are good in moderation, but to *overindulge* in them is sinful. Sounds reasonable, but this view willfully ignores our cultural values. Relaxation and rest, in *any* degree, never command the respect of industry and work. Love of self is nowhere honored like humility, and slender adults draw universally greater admiration than zaftig ones who sensually indulge their appetites. Sin is not a question of "balance" or moderation but a moral compass, and like all moral convictions, it reads out in black and white, not degrees.

Just as sins have never held the status of virtues, pleasures have never been valued as highly as work. Work earns a living: It makes money and supports the family. Work builds character. Work keeps you off the street and out of trouble. Work sustains the economy—productivity keeps the nation strong. We work not only for our own rewards: Work contributes to others. Teamwork bonds people together and teaches unselfishness. Work sustains and strengthens social ties, and so builds the community. Work gives meaning to life.

We could go on. Work embodies nearly all the virtues Western culture holds dear. For this reason we are, a priori, positively disposed toward anything defined as work. Some work earns money while other jobs, like household chores, do not, but all work is honorable. Philosopher John Locke even argued that work is the basis of property: By tilling a plot of land, you make it your own.

Our culture not only discredits pleasure but also enshrines the worth of pain. Sometimes pain even becomes something to aspire to: "No pain, no gain." The Roman Catholic Church approves of martyrdom and at times canonizes it. In Christian culture, the dominant symbol of love is one of a human sacrifice: the death by torture of an innocent human being. The crucifix not only surmounts altars, but its more abstract rendering, the cross, hangs around millions of necks in the form of pendants. Western society pays tribute to pain and often equates it with merit.

Perhaps one reason we revere work is that it often *does* give people emotional, mental, and spiritual pain. Empirical evidence shows that American workers are the most productive in the world but are also among the least happy in their jobs. A 2011 survey by the Conference Board found that only 45 percent of Americans felt "satisfied" with their jobs, the lowest rate since the survey began in 1987, and a significant falloff from the 61 percent recorded then.

For a lucky minority, work is a pleasure. In the fall of 2011, the NFL network showed a documentary, *Bill Belichick: A Football Life*, that went behind the scenes with the celebrated coach of the New England Patriots. Toward the end of the film, Belichick offers an overview of his job as he drives in the darkness to Gillette Stadium for his normal workday, which starts at 5 AM. He mentions a few of the drawbacks of his all-consuming career, like having relatively little time to spend with his family, but at the end he shrugs and says, "I don't know . . . beats working." He enjoys coaching football so much that it isn't *work*.

Work can be highly enjoyable, and play can become one's life-work, as it did for professional poker player Amarillo Slim, or for Steven Crist, a Harvard graduate who liked betting on horse races and became publisher of the *Daily Racing Form*. There are people whose love of dogs turns them into kennel owners, breeders, or veterinarians. You cannot distinguish work from play by simply sorting activities into one column or the other. You can find professional Frisbee players and accountants who love balancing books so much that they would do it even without a paycheck. It's not *what* you do but your *relationship* to it that defines an activity as play or work.

Things we do for their own sake—when the action is its own reward—are *play*. We are at play when we go for a family picnic on a summer day and toss a ball with our daughter: We do this just because it is fun. In contrast, *work* is something done as a *means to an end*: We don't work just to be working. (Or if we do, we are workaholics.) We may well enjoy our work, as many artists and athletes do, but Picasso painted to create a picture, Fred Astaire danced to make a movie, and Tom Brady throws a football to win games. In most cases, they also perform their work to earn money. We work to *accomplish* something. Maybe we'll have fun or express our inner selves in the process, but that is not why we do the activity. Work has a *goal*.

Yet, despite our love for work and the fact that we need work to remain individually and socially productive, in some ways, work seems to be drying up. World population has been growing for many a year, but more efficient forms of production have made many industries less labor intensive, so they need fewer workers. Companies are eager to trim payrolls. And a new contributor to structural unemployment has appeared in the form of shadow work.

CYBERNETIC UNEMPLOYMENT

Twenty-three-year-old Justine Forriez of Lille, France, near the Belgian border, who has a master's degree in health administration and served a two-year apprenticeship, was getting by—barely—on state aid and cash jobs like bartending and babysitting. She made $6.50 per day as a dog's caretaker. Forriez took a course in job hunting, met with ten recruiters, and sent out 200 résumés, but she was still unemployed. She painted watercolors in her spare time "to keep herself from going crazy."

She was featured in "Young, Educated, and Jobless in France," a 2012 story by Steven Erlanger of *The New York Times*. The piece pegged the unemployment rate for young adults at 22 percent in France, 36 percent in Italy, and 51 percent in Spain. Europeans call this cohort the floating generation. They float from internship to contract or part-time work, to more schooling, with no full-time job in sight.

The difficulty young people now have trying to begin careers looms as a serious economic dilemma. Structural changes in how work gets done, including the phenomenon of shadow work, may be shrinking the amount of paid work available. Widespread joblessness threatens to become a fixture of the social landscape.

In the modern economy, there is no bigger issue than jobs and the cost of maintaining a staff, and shadow work exacerbates the problem. For the vast majority of businesses, schools, and nonprofits, personnel is the largest budget item. This includes, of course, both salaries and benefits. (The latter were once called fringe benefits, though the term *fringe* disappeared when the category outgrew anything resembling a fringe.) Hiring, training, and supervising employees augment the cost of personnel, and another outlay kicks in when workers retire—pensions, annuities, and, for some employers, the gigantic healthcare costs that pile up from retirement until the end of life, which has become a lengthy period as life spans stretch into the eighties and nineties.

In recent years, salaries in real dollars have either remained static or dropped for most of the labor force. But the galloping cost of benefits—one rule of thumb pegs them at 40 percent of salary—has put steady pressure on employers. Healthcare expenses, in particular, have driven up this line item. In the United States, healthcare has become an enormous, seemingly uncontrollable sector, swelling relentlessly and growing far faster than the rest of the economy— much as cancer grows, without relationship to neighboring cells.

Short of a seismic change such as universal single-payer health insurance with price controls on drugs and procedures, the upward pressure on employee benefits will continue. The upshot is a strong incentive to replace full-time employees with part-time, outsourced, overseas, or contract workers, who receive no benefits. Better yet, simply lay people off—or hand off jobs to customers as shadow work.

Politicians and pundits who shake their heads at the stubbornness of high unemployment rates are either overlooking or ignoring the obvious. Our economic and political system is stacked to reward businesses for *discarding* employees, not *hiring* them.

There are three main strategies for cutting payroll; two are well-known. *Downsizing* is a classic: lay off workers and shift their jobs to the remaining, shrunken staff. Not long ago, a nonprofit education newsletter in Boston replaced all three of its full-time staff members with one new full-time editor and a part-time assistant, who were expected to carry on—with half the previous staffing level. The remaining employees have no choice but to work more. Supposedly they feel grateful to still have jobs. Downsizing is an in-house breed of shadow work created by thinning out both senior people and support staff.

Second, *automation* replaces employees with machines. This has gone on for centuries, at least since the Industrial Revolution and probably longer. Automation pervades manufacturing and many service industries. Robots do not draw salaries, belong to labor unions, or receive fringe benefits. They need maintenance but don't require vacation time, sick time, maternity leave, or, best of all, health insurance. Robots are impeccable "team players," with no personal agendas. They'll work round the clock and on weekends at their regular hourly rate. Hence, whenever financially feasible, businesses will substitute robotics for people.

The third, less-recognized way to cut staff is to *outsource jobs as shadow work.* Customers work hand-in-hand with robots as technologies like kiosks team up with them to complete transactions. The new check-in kiosk in the hotel lobby, for example, means one less person behind the desk. This pincer movement spins off unemployment that may be permanent, because technology, not the business cycle, drives it. Historically, automation has eliminated jobs at the point of *production*—for example, in factories. Shadow work instead deletes jobs at the point of *sale*—for example, at drugstore checkouts. There are no statistics yet on shadow work, so it is hard to say how much unemployment it causes. One thing we *do* know is that points of sale vastly outnumber points of production.

Shadow work thus represents a major—and hidden—force shrinking the job market. In particular, it is squeezing out entry-level jobs that have launched countless careers. These jobs at the base of the economic pyramid pay little but lay the foundation for everything that rises above them—and as with any structure, when the foundation crumbles, the superstructure may collapse as well. Entry-level jobs provide more than a paycheck. They are the sidewalk of the workplace, the platform that allows entry to all the businesses on Main Street.

Consider my father, who in 1937 began on the bottom rung of the ladder as a messenger in a small-town bank in New Jersey. In 1963 he became president, chairman of the board, and CEO after having been promoted through the ranks as a teller, bookkeeper, loan officer, and executive vice president. He understood every facet of banking by the time he took the helm of the Dover Trust Company. Contrast this with the preparation many banking executives get today: an MBA with specialization in finance and a penchant for high-risk derivatives. If these bankers had gone out on hundreds of mortgage appraisals like my dad did, seeing the actual houses for which they were lending money and meeting real, live borrowers, would the 2008 banking crisis have happened?

Starter positions, including summer and part-time gigs, are where young people learn how to hold down a real job. (That means a job with *wages*—not a volunteer job, not an unpaid internship, not an NGO project in a developing country.) This is where they learn to show up on time, appropriately dressed and groomed, with a professional attitude, and learn habits like cooperation, punching a clock, and service with a smile. But how does an aspiring banker work his way up from the teller's window if ATMs and shadow-working customers have displaced tellers? How does a secretary become the office manager and later an executive if shadow work eliminates support staff—so there *are* no secretaries?

For those without education and skills, these low-level positions often *are* their careers. If such jobs vanish, a throng of unemployed young people will find themselves with little money and too much spare time. This is a dangerous development in any society. Unrest and violence throughout the Arab world have erupted from streets teeming with young men lacking jobs—angry youths who congregate online through social media. Such mobs can become unruly. In 2003, the dissolution of the Iraqi army put 400,000 young men out of work, triggering a bloody insurgency that still continues. In today's global village, where citizens network and congregate in political flashmobs, we cannot risk creating an immense underclass of idle youth.

Yet this is exactly what we are doing. Young people aged fifteen to twenty-four make up 17 percent of the global population but 40 percent of the unemployed, according to the World Economic Forum. In 2013, their rate of joblessness (12.6 percent) was about triple the worldwide adult rate of 4.5 percent. Youth unemployment has reached 17.1 percent in North America, 21.4 percent in the European Union, 14.3 percent in Latin America and the Caribbean, 27.9 percent in North Africa, 26.5 percent in the Middle East, and 9 percent in East Asia.

In some countries, the better educated may be psychologically deflated as well, as they've been told that education guarantees a successful career. Many hold college and graduate degrees and even have "hard" skills like computer training, yet they must move back in with their parents. In the United States, students similarly float from internship to internship to degree program, as worthwhile salaried jobs remain scarce. Emily, at age twenty-eight, has moved in with her retired parents in downtown Boston. After earning a college degree in psychology from the University of Virginia, she hopped from one internship to another in fields including advertising and market research. She is now completing studies to become a licensed physician assistant, hoping that this recognized "hard" skill will finally begin a career for her.

Unfortunately, shadow work may be one obstacle that keeps this generation economically disabled. They can get stuck doing internships for years and find that they've only been spinning their wheels doing shadow work instead of building a career.

Yet all is not lost. While shadow work eliminates some jobs, it spins off others. For example, let's reconsider the robotic gasoline pumps that have replaced pump jockeys, those unskilled teenagers who once filled gas tanks. The advent of self-service pumps also *creates* new jobs, like designing, manufacturing, installing, and maintaining the robotic pumps. Furthermore, the charge-card data on gasoline sales gets uploaded via satellite to financial institutions, a process that needs technical and business oversight and employees to do it. Similarly, while Orbitz and Kayak.com reduce travel agencies' business by transferring shadow work to customers, such websites also produce jobs for web designers, software engineers, online marketers, and advertising executives.

Skilled jobs of this kind require education and technical training. Their salaries are a distinct upgrade over pump-jockey pay. But to cash in on the opportunities, we must renew our educational establishment, gearing it to the kinds of expertise the emerging workplace rewards. Traditional education has not yet caught up with the information economy; nor has it taken into account the incoming surge of shadow work. Online learning and teaching innovations can help connect students with windows that are being opened—sometimes by shadow work.

SHADOW WORK SAGA: The Don Quixote of the Oil Industry

In the late 1940s, a maverick filling station owner named Bill Henderson lived in Winnipeg, the capital and largest city of the Canadian province of Manitoba. Born in 1900, Henderson was the father of three girls and was a man with a restless, inventive mind. Though he had only a ninth-grade education, Bill had a filing cabinet full of patents; he was always seeking a better mousetrap. Bill's father had started the Henderson Oil Company decades earlier, and his son followed him into the petroleum industry. He sought ways to lower his prices to attract more customers to his filling station.

Like many innovators, Henderson was an individual entre-preneur, a small businessman who controlled his own operation. Henderson Thriftway Petroleum bore the family name, not that of Texaco, Esso, Shell, or Imperial Oil. In fact, he was a renegade gas man who constantly clashed with the petroleum giants who controlled the flow of product to the marketplace.

In 1949, gas in the United States averaged 26 cents per gallon, and in Canada it was even less, at 17 Canadian cents per imperial gallon, which is 20 percent larger than a U.S. gallon. Henderson found ways to whittle down that price, like eliminating middle-men by dealing directly with refineries when possible. Henderson had his own tanker trucks and imported gasoline from North Dakota and, later, from Blaine, Washington, directly south of the Canadian border. He also devised a dispenser with a handle and trigger that could draw a quart of oil from a bulk oil drum, elimi-nating the need for motor-oil cans. One of Bill's ideas changed the way people buy gasoline throughout the world.

Henderson believed that a new delivery method could reduce gasoline prices and lure customers. Between 1946 and 1948, he worked with electronics engineers to design a system that could transmit data about the price of gas and the number of gallons dispensed from a pump to an employee sitting in a tower above. A pneumatic tube running overhead to the tower could whisk cash up from the customer and return change. Self-service gasoline pumps were born.

Henderson Thriftway charged 3 cents per gallon less than the petroleum giants and immediately began taking business away from them. At prevailing 1949 prices, 3 cents was almost 20 percent less. "He sold an awful lot of gas," says Al Chalkley, Henderson's son-in-law, who worked with him. "He was so much cheaper than everybody else." Bill's seven-pump station stayed open twenty-four hours a day, seven days a week, and had a small attached store that sold chips and other snacks. Bill Henderson was well ahead of his time.

Drivers filled up at Henderson Thriftway both for low prices and the unique experience of pumping their own petrol, which wasn't available elsewhere; Henderson had patented his inventions. He later marketed the Henderson Electronic Control System, a fully solid-state electronic console that could authorize and monitor from two to twelve pumps and interface with credit-card imprinters and intercoms.

Pumping your own gas was kind of fun, although the technology was primitive. The trigger on the hand nozzle controlled the flow; there was no automatic cutoff. Releasing the trigger stopped the flow of gas. It was difficult to tell when the tank was full or almost so. An experienced pump attendant would recognize the distinctive sound a car's intake pipe made as the tank became nearly full, and release the trigger to stop the pump. Untrained customers didn't know this trick, so gas might overflow the tank, spilling down the side of the car and onto the ground or even splashing onto a customer's shoes and clothing.

Fire departments saw a safety hazard in letting people dispense their own fuel and insisted that the nozzles have a sensor to indicate a nearly full tank, linked to an automatic shutoff mechanism to prevent spillage. These were not major engineering challenges, and such improvements soon became available, removing an element of skill from the gas-pumping process and thus making it more accessible to untrained drivers.

Self-service was a success. Gas wars broke out in Winnipeg as competitors tried to match Henderson's low prices. He opened another station in Vancouver in 1957, again drawing whopping amounts of business away from competitors. Yet, as in Winnipeg, others soon mimicked his self-service model, trampling on Henderson's patents.

Big Oil corporations opened three gas stations on the corners across from his Vancouver outlet and lowered their prices to the point of selling at a loss. Petroleum giants like Imperial Oil could afford to do this at a single station for a limited time; the goal, of course, was to drive Henderson out of business, then raise prices freely with no fear of his renegade competition. Self-service was economical for the vendor, but unlike Henderson, the petrol giants were uninterested in passing on these savings to consumers.

Henderson even received anonymous death threats. No one knows if these originated with his competitors or were "just union guys trying to scare him off," as Chalkley suggests. Since self-serve pumping eliminated jobs, it is the kind of innovation that tends to provoke outcry from labor unions.

Furthermore, Imperial Oil and Shell had in-house lawyers to oppose Henderson when he sued for patent infringement or antitrust violations. Bill could not match their financial resources. He had beaten the oil giants in the marketplace but could not match them in the courtroom. By the mid-1960s, Henderson had closed his filling stations.

Over his career Bill gained and lost fortunes—he was "a millionaire two or three times over," Chalkley says. Henderson always had a roll of bills in his pocket and drove a yellow Thunderbird in the 1950s. He retired in Winnipeg, where his home overlooked the Red River. He was a congenial fellow who liked people; he had lots of friends and there were always parties at his place, the lights blazing. The parties went on until Bill died in 1976.

IN THE UNITED States, Frank Urich opened the first self-service station in Los Angeles, California, around the same time as Henderson got started, in 1947. It was an idea whose time had come, and the technology to make it a reality was available in more than one locale.

Full-service stations ruled the American market until the 1970s, but since then, self-service pumps have spread, becoming the dominant mode of gasoline delivery in the United States and Europe.

The transition happened in stages. At first, an attendant inside the service station controlled the pumps. In the 1970s and 1980s, customers typically had to prepay, giving the attendant, say, $20 before pumping that much gasoline. Those who wanted to fill their tanks, and so didn't know the final tab, might leave a credit card inside and return to sign the receipt.

This was a lot less convenient than sitting inside one's car while having the fuel pumped for you, then settling your bill at the car window. To compensate customers for the hassle, many stations offered two-tiered pricing, charging a lower rate for self-serve. The customer got paid indirectly for doing his or her own pumping.

The need for customers to enter the gas station buildings ultimately changed the gasoline retailing business itself. In the days of full-serve stations, customers remained in their cars or at best emerged to stretch for a moment and catch a breath of fresh air. But as self-service brought them inside the station to pay, the owners realized that they could sell their customers more than gas. In the old days, the station's "office" held little more than a desk, a cash register, perhaps a pay phone and a Coke machine. But a procession of self-serve customers paved the way for more vending machines and eventually changed the architecture of gas stations. Today, many have evolved into full-fledged convenience stores, selling a wide array of food and beverages, prepared sandwiches, and coffee and donuts, as well as automotive supplies like motor oil and windshield washer. Despite food author Michael Pollan's admonition "Don't fuel your car and your body at the same place," millions of drivers do exactly that.

From a social point of view, lumbering out of one's car to work a gas pump struck a blow at one's status. Instead of being served, one took on a fairly menial job. Pumping one's own gas equalized social classes and sexes. It stripped the customer of his or her privileges—and the loss of *her* privileges especially bothered some women. This new species of shadow work ran up against a venerable cultural norm: *Women don't do messy, manual labor*—at least not in public. Females did not work at service stations: pumping gas was *men's* work.

In 1982, actress and syndicated newspaper columnist Joyce Jillson published *Real Women Don't Pump Gas*. A companion to Bruce Feirstein's best-selling *Real Men Don't Eat Quiche,* Jillson's lighthearted volume seemingly voices a backlash against feminism, an attempt to reestablish the prerogatives of "real women," who reject the leveling of genders with a consequent loss of sexual polarity. But Jillson scarcely embraces any notion of feminine inferiority. She declares at the outset, for example:

> Thank God for Linda Evans, Kate Hepburn, and Miss Piggy. Real women, every last one of them. Women who wouldn't pump gas—and don't have to continually prove that they're men's equals—when in fact they *know* they're superior.

In the same chapter, Jillson lays out her philosophy in a conversation between two women at a filling station. The protagonist, Jennifer, guides her "sleek graphite Audi 5000" up to the self-serve pump at an Exxon station. We learn that Jennifer is a superwoman, a senior partner at Wall Street's biggest law firm who arranged the breakup of AT&T, put her husband through medical school, and can bake "the best quiche west of Paris." She has also just finished an hourlong workout on weightlifting machines. When her partner Kristin says, "I'll get the gas" and opens the passenger door, Jennifer is firm.

> "You'll do no such thing," Jennifer shot back, grabbing her arm and pulling her back into the car. "The time has come to draw the line. And the line, which we don't cross, is at

self-service gas stations. It's time to return to the days of
femininity. We can run the whole damn oil company—but
we're not pumping the gas. If we wait long enough, some
big lug will think that we're helpless girls and will pump the
junk *for* us."

Thus self-service pumping was not only an economic issue but
a social and cultural one. For decades, even centuries, one sex, one
social class, or one kind of person had performed particular jobs
(teenaged-girl babysitters, for example). Powerful social norms
shape work roles. Social expectations had to shift before this new
form of shadow work could displace established customs. The evolution of technology helped. More advanced, cybernetic devices
made gas pumping easier and cleaner, and thus more compatible
with traditional femininity.

Specifically, starting in the 1990s, the pay-at-the-pump option
became the dominant gasoline transaction. Credit- and debit-card
sales captured an increasing share of purchases. A new generation
of computerized gas pumps emerged, complete with interactive
screens. The pump essentially became a robot. To fill the tank,
the most common transaction, a customer simply swiped a credit
card at the pump, which authorized the purchase via a computer
network. The robotic pump recorded the transaction details and
printed out a receipt. A keypad enabled the robot to collect zip
code data for security before authorizing the sale. This also helped
station owners build a useful database, breaking down sales by,
say, time of day and day of the week.

Robotic technology simplified and speeded up the self-serve option—no more trips indoors to prepay. Today, customers rarely get any discount for doing the pumping. Instead, they collect their dividend in the form of *time:* faster and more convenient transactions. They no longer need to wait for an attendant to pump gas or accept payment. In the wake of all this convenience, self-serve pumps have spread to all of America.

Well, not quite all.

Two states—Oregon and New Jersey—ban self-service gas stations by law.

Lobbying by filling station owners led New Jersey to bar self-service in 1949, ostensibly for safety and to protect the jobs of pump attendants. (The Jerseyites saw this coming; recall that Henderson, in Winnipeg, and Urich, in Los Angeles, had introduced self-serve by then.) In 1950, a legal challenge to the New Jersey statute by a small independent service station failed. Decades later, in 2006, New Jersey governor Jon Corzine tried to start a pilot program of self-service pumps on the New Jersey Turnpike, claiming it might save motorists 5 or 6 cents per gallon. He ran into opposition in the state legislature. The chair of the transportation committee, Assemblyman John Wisniewski, said, "Telling a motorist that self-serve will save them money at the pump is like telling someone that they could save money on a new home by building it themselves." The assemblyman apparently overlooked the rather large difference between filling a gas tank and building a house. Nonetheless, Corzine's initiative came to nothing.

The Oregon law of 1951 cited no fewer than seventeen reasons to prohibit self-service, including the flammability of gasoline, its toxic fumes, the risk of crime generated by customers leaving their cars, and preserving jobs for employees, such as the teens who worked after school at service stations. In 1989, the ARCO oil company contested the constitutionality of the Oregon law in court, without success. Full-service gasoline pumps are part of Oregon culture; in 1982 the state's voters defeated a measure, sponsored by gas station owners, to legalize self-service. Dan Lavey, a public relations executive in Portland, told *The New York Times* that "The joke is, when babies are born in Oregon, the doctor slaps their bottom, 'No self-serve and no sales tax.' That about sums it up. It's as much a cultural issue as an economic issue. It's a way of life."

The alleged concerns about safety, toxicity, and crime have not deterred the other forty-eight states from allowing self-serve for decades, without any notable disasters. Publicly advertised rationales like safety and "toxic fumes" are smokescreens raised to conceal the real reason: protection of jobs. Scattered individual towns like Huntington on Long Island forbid self-service gasoline pumping, explicitly to save jobs. That town passed the law during a recession in the early 1970s and never repealed it. Full-serve stations still exist around the country, ordinarily in wealthier areas where the customers simply expect service and are willing to pay for it.

LESSONS FROM THE GAS PUMP

The saga of self-service gas pumping teaches a few lessons about shadow work.

First, new technologies can create new forms of shadow work. Electronic circuits that carried information from the gas pump to a cash register enabled Bill Henderson to offer the self-serve option at Henderson Thriftway. At first, the technologies are rudimentary and cumbersome, like Henderson's pneumatic tube sucking cash up to the register above. But as better devices appear to help consumers handle the task, they smooth the adoption of shadow work.

Second, shadow work *that requires no training* can spread readily. The mechanism needs to be essentially idiot-proof. Recall the spillage and fire concerns in Henderson's early years, before the advent of automatic cutoffs on pump nozzles. The more intelligence, education, or training shadow work entails, the narrower will be its market.

Third, technological advances can also add *benefits* to shadow work. In gasoline retailing, the ability to pay by credit card at the pump, and the screens and keypads that let customers complete all phases of the delivery and sale, have made self-serve transactions generally faster than full-serve. This gives self-serve a competitive advantage. Station owners also benefit by collecting a constant flow of sales data on their customers.

Fourth, traditions and cultural norms can oppose, inhibit, or forestall shadow work. Take the custom that women don't do dirty manual tasks like gasoline pumping. When such norms shift in the wider society, it opens a path for new kinds of shadow work. Feminism may have helped gain acceptance for self-serve pumping by women by reframing the task as one reflecting competence and self-reliance. Meanwhile, new developments like paying at the pump may modify the task to make it acceptable under prevailing norms.

Fifth, entrenched interests may oppose new types of shadow work—sometimes successfully, as in New Jersey and Oregon. However, if shadow work saves customers money or time, it will sooner or later prevail—as it has in the other forty-eight states. Eventually, it can become such an established norm that alternatives—full-serve pumps, for example—disappear or are confined to elite enclaves.

Sixth, shadow work can cost jobs—in retail service, for example, as pump attendants disappear. This resembles job losses due to automation, though here the customer pitches in alongside the robots to displace the employee.

Seventh, shadow work typically decreases human interaction and may even remove it entirely. The self-serve gasoline customer now deals with a robot, not a person. There is no longer an exchange of pleasantries with the pump jockey. Ralph has become part of history. He lost his job to you.

two: shadow work in home and family life

By and large, mothers and housewives are the only workers who do not have regular time off. They are the great vacationless class.

—ANNE MORROW LINDBERGH, *GIFT FROM THE SEA*

HOME AND FAMILY life are the first, most familiar, and most fundamental venue of shadow work. Housework, in different forms, has been around for centuries; the word *housewifery* dates to the 1200s. Let's consider the history of housework for the light it can shed on shadow work today.

In her landmark book *More Work for Mother: The Ironies of Household Technology from the Open Hearth to the Microwave,* sociologist Ruth Schwartz Cowan tells the story of the evolution of housework in America. Up until the Industrial Revolution, *everyone* in the family—men, women, and children—did "housework," which was pretty much the *only* work. Housework embraced all the activities that enabled a family, or a community, to survive: providing food, water, shelter, heat, furnishings, and clothing, for example. Men plowed fields, raised livestock, slaughtered animals, sawed logs, and split wood. (The word *husband* derives from *hus*, an older spelling of *house*, Cowan explains. The husband was "bonded" to his house; hence *hus*-bond.) Women spun and carded wool, sewed clothing, tended the kitchen garden, cooked meals, did laundry, and fetched water from the stream or well—a handful of the items on their to-do lists.

Industrialization created factory jobs and offices located far from home. This redefined work at home dramatically, giving birth to *housework* as we understand it. During the nineteenth century, the United States (and the West) urbanized. American family size dropped from about 7 children per household in 1800 to around 3.6 a century later. Manufactured goods like milled flour replaced the grain that men had pounded into meal at home, or hauled to a local gristmill; cast-iron stoves and coal supplanted hearths and the firewood men had split for cooking and heating. Unlike fireplaces, stoves needed daily cleaning—by housewives. Woolens and, later, cottons from textile mills replaced homespun, though women still sewed the family's clothing until ready-mades appeared later in the century. And when store-bought textiles appeared, people started to own and wear more items of clothing. Hence more sewing—and more laundry.

Whereas men, women, and children all did lots of housework on the farm, the industrial world separated the male and female spheres of work, with *housework* devolving onto the women, especially mothers. "[A]dult males and small children of both sexes were no longer needed to do domestic labor: wood did not have to be chopped, nor water carried, nor grain hauled to the mill," writes Cowan. "Men and children could be spared, to the schools, to the factories, to the offices of the burgeoning industrial economy. Adult women and their grown daughters, on the other hand, could not be spared: meals still had to be cooked; sick children had to be tended; infants to be nursed; clothes to be made, mended, and laundered—and industrialization had done nothing at all to ease the burden of those particular chores." Meanwhile, earning the cash to buy all the new manufactured goods became the job of men, who now worked at a distance from home.

Cowan quotes an 1862 letter that a young Norwegian immigrant, Gro Svendsen, wrote to her parents: "We are told that the women of America have much leisure time but I haven't yet met any woman who thought so! Here the mistress of the house must do all the work that the cook, the maid, and the housekeeper would do in an upper-class family at home. Moreover she must do her work as well as these three together do it in Norway."

Thus women inherited the vast burden of shadow work at home that enabled their families to live in an industrial economy. They did not work directly for schools, in factories or offices, or for the industries that manufactured and sold goods, but neither could these institutions have survived without the shadow work of millions of wives, daughters, and mothers.

To be sure, many households, including those of the middle class, coped with the surfeit of housework by getting help from outside the family. There were indentured servants fresh from Europe and others who helped with chores in exchange for room and board. There were also barter arrangements between families.

In the 1870 U.S. Census, "one woman listed herself as a domestic servant for every 8.4 families in the population," writes Susan Strasser in *Never Done: A History of American Housework*. "Most prevalent in urban areas (where people had more money to spend), in the South (where many black women would work for low wages), and in places with large immigrant populations, domestic service embodied one possible solution—but by no means a universal one—to the cares of nineteenth-century housekeeping. For most of the century, servants cost less than the technological solution; indeed, most of the homes with gas lighting, plumbing, or electricity belonged to the very wealthy, who could afford staffs of servants as well."

Standards of living rose in the nineteenth and twentieth centuries, and this expanded housework. Households consumed more goods and services, and more consumption typically engenders more shadow work. Standards of cleanliness rose and homes got bigger, which meant more furnishings and more things and spaces to clean and maintain more thoroughly. Labor-saving devices did not necessarily save labor. In the nineteenth century, Cowan writes, "There were hand-driven washing machines and taps for indoor cisterns, eggbeaters and pulley-driven butter churns, tinned milk and store-bought flour, porcelainized cookware, airtight heating stoves, and a multitude of additional small gadgets and large utilities, from apple parers to piped coal gas, that were intended to make housework easier." Yet for women of the 1800s, housework did not become "one whit more convenient—or less tiring—during the whole of the century. What a strange paradox that in the face of so many labor-saving devices, little labor appears to have been saved!"

IN THE TWENTY-FIRST century, homes continue to grow in size and fill with furniture and electronic gadgets, spinning off ever more domestic shadow work. Meanwhile, there are fewer stay-at-home moms (and dads) to cope with these chores. (Two-thirds of mothers with school-age kids now work outside the home.) Two-career families leave both parents with less time to look after home and children. Modern fathers do get more involved in child rearing and home care than their fathers did, but the allotment of shadow work at home is still nothing close to 50-50. Various studies confirm that women still handle 70 to 80 percent of housework.

Take, for example, what one might think of as progressive-thinking parents with careers: junior and senior professors at Harvard University, 2,295 of whom were surveyed (72 percent responded) in the 2012–13 academic year. Both men and women logged roughly the same time at their paid jobs—between sixty and seventy hours per week. But among professors with children and a working partner (or no partner), women did ten more weekly hours of housework than men. That gap doubled for junior faculty members. These younger women, living through demanding years when they were striving for tenure, did twenty more hours of housework, childcare, and adult care weekly than their male peers. (Even women with *non*working partners spent seventeen hours more each week on these shadow tasks.)

In a letter published in *Harvard Magazine*, John Gamel, an oph-
thalmologist in Louisville, Kentucky, recalls a story that illustrates
this gender gap. When he served as director of residency training
at the University of Louisville ophthalmology department, "my
unpleasant task," he reports, "was reprimanding those trainees
who did not measure up to our standards. The males who caused
problems did so in a variety of ways: some were late for clinics or
failed to answer emergency calls; others dressed inappropriately or
showed little respect for the technicians or their female colleagues.
In contrast, all the female trainees who got in trouble shared the
same failing: on the annual Ophthalmic Knowledge Assessment
Program they had terrible scores—sometimes below the tenth per-
centile. These women weren't hitting the books.

"When I called them into my office for their quarterly reviews,"
he continues, "each told the same story: they had to spend many
hours every day feeding the family, cleaning the house, bathing the
kids, etc., before collapsing in bed exhausted. When I asked what
their husbands were doing, again came the same complaint: they
were either watching television or studying for their own knowledge assessment program. Some women begged me to dress down
their wayward spouses because of their selfish habits.

"Keep in mind that all these women were the cream of the
crop: only the best students got into medical school, while our
department averaged 100 applicants for each training position,"
Gamel concludes. "So here is the question that has plagued me for
decades: why did those bright, ambitious women put up with such
dreadful treatment? In retrospect, I wish I had bribed my stepson

Arthur—six feet six, 300 pounds, a professional bouncer for ten years—to take those lazy bums aside for an intimate discussion."

In sum, the opening up of careers for women in the late twentieth century has not changed the asymmetry of work at home: Childcare and housework remain chiefly the chores of females. In addition to the full-time demands of a professional career and the round-the-clock work of child rearing, women have been trying to keep up with a sea of domestic jobs that their husbands have not rushed to claim as their own. (One can only marvel at the *Martha Stewart Living* subscribers who also find time to hand-dip candles and dry and press wildflowers in books for floral arrangements.)

In addition to the physical chores, "Moms do all the planning," says Elizabeth, an actress, wife, and mother of two in Albany, New York, who codirects a daycare center. "They have to keep track of everything, like the doctor's appointments for their husbands and children, parent-teacher conferences—everything! Scheduling these calendar things, you never plan things with the dad—he has no idea even when his own doctor's appointments are. The responsibility for making sure stuff actually happens falls on the mother. And we really resent it, it feels like an unfair burden. Women are seething with resentment. If I call up to make a play date and the father answers, he'll say, 'Oh, sure,' but it turns out his wife has something else planned. It's gotten so I just ask to speak to the woman. I don't have time to go through the charade."

The incoming wave of shadow work this book describes, flung at all of us by technology and social changes, may be the last straw. The shadow tasks might fall equally on both sexes, but in the case of women, especially working wives and mothers, they land on shoulders already overburdened with other duties.

LIFE OFF THE GRID, AND VERY MUCH ON IT

Let's consider two extreme examples of lifestyles that reject or minimize shadow work. They are polar opposites: One way of living keeps shadow work at bay with an ethic of self-sufficiency; the other delegates nearly all shadow work to others. Not surprisingly, the two occupy opposite ends of the country's economic spectrum.

The first alternative finds its purest form in those who live "off the grid"—in other words, without connecting to electric utilities and avoiding natural gas and heating oil. Those who leave the power grid behind usually seek to minimize their carbon footprint for environmental reasons. Typically they are young, idealistic people who may also unplug themselves from large commercial systems of food distribution and mainstream commerce. In this way, they can live on very little income while drawing satisfaction from a life that is close to the land, in some ways taking inspiration from Thoreau's *Walden*.

In the green rural landscape outside Amherst, Massachusetts, twenty-seven-year-old Steele, a graduate of nearby Hampshire College, shares a farmhouse with four roommates, including a married couple and another single man and woman. They collaborate on agriculture, selling much of their harvest at local farmers' markets, and Steele plays bass guitar in a successful reggae band.

Solar panels at the house generate enough electricity to satisfy their minimal needs. "You install them, and you're not tied to the power grid," he says. The property includes a large woodlot, which enables the group to heat their well-insulated home with an efficient wood-burning stove; everyone helps saw, split, and stack logs. Water comes from their own well. Hence the group can decouple from all the major utilities. They also grow most all their own food and keep chickens for eggs.

"As much as possible, we try to be producers and not consumers," Steele explains. "We are not buying much from stores. The quality is so much higher when you produce it yourself. And we enjoy using our time to be producers. It's more satisfying mentally, physically, spiritually. You spend less money and you get lots of exercise. It's healthy. Plus, producing our own energy, we don't have to worry about power outages. It's a healthy lifestyle."

This housing group is certainly doing lots of unpaid work. But it is not shadow work because the housemates aren't doing these jobs in the service of an institutional master. Instead, they are approaching a twenty-first-century version of a subsistence economy: creating what they need themselves with minimal expenditure of money.

IN CONTRAST, AT the affluent end of the spectrum, you can throw money at the problem. In Beverly Hills (BH to locals), the wealthy, status-seeking life studiously avoids shadow work. The BH subculture also avoids the do-it-yourself (DIY) mindset: The aspiration instead is to do *nothing* yourself—let's call it DNY. Wealthy Americans, especially those with new money (such as many of those in Beverly Hills), take the DNY ethic to heart. It's easy, as long as you can afford it.

Some years ago, I was walking on a posh Beverly Hills residential street with my friend Alan, a young lawyer and BH native. We were admiring the lush green strip of grass between sidewalk and curb. Alan pointed to its sharp edging and dryly remarked, "The 'nerz did that." By the 'nerz, he meant the garde*ners*.

Delegating homecare tasks like gardening to "the 'nerz," or to the maids and cooks, or childcare to the nannies, is one way to duck the onslaught of shadow work. Hiring domestics reverses the shadow work equation: Instead of taking on jobs that others once did, you pay people to do household chores, turning unpaid tasks into paid ones.

The classic Beverly Hills lifestyle is highly professionalized. Don't plant and cultivate your own garden—let the 'nerz do that. Don't cook: Eat at a restaurant, or if you must eat at home, have take-out delivered. Better yet, hire a personal chef. When hosting a party, don't prepare food for your guests or pour their drinks—bring in high-end caterers, preferably in sexy outfits. (They represent conspicuous consumption, too, as they advertise the fact that you can afford them.) In fact, let party planners handle every detail of your party—flowers, music, invites, entertainment, and, of course, valet parking. You need only show up, greet the guests, and write the checks. Well, you probably need to make up the guest list yourself, unless it's a business party (but aren't they all, really?). The same holds for those de rigueur annual children's birthday parties.

The pool man cleans your swimming pool. The maid vacuums, dusts, mops, and scrubs your house, whose decor was chosen by an interior designer. The nanny minds the young children. By all means hire the riding instructors, the swimming and tennis coaches, plus the kids' violin or piano teachers. The auto detailing men buff your car. The dog walker exercises your dog. Yet all the professionalization eventually backfires: On paper, you have organized the perfect life—the only problem is, *you aren't living it.*

The DNY lifestyle reflects certain values. Its adherents don't find cooking meals, making beds, weeding gardens, walking dogs, or minding children as worthwhile as, say, restaurant lunches, yoga classes, revising one's screenplay, or shopping on Rodeo Drive. It frees you either for watching *Keeping Up with the Kardashians* or actually doing so. "If we can afford to hire domestic help—and we *can*—why wouldn't we?" asks Elaine, a married mother who brokers residential real estate in the pricey precincts of Santa Monica and Bel Air. "The time I'd spend on housework—instead, I can be selling houses and make *much* more than we pay the help. And my job is so much more satisfying than vacuuming."

The underlying assumption is that the food is better, the floral arrangements prettier, the children better coached when "someone who does this for a living" takes charge. Outsourcing those jobs means they will be done to professional standards. Let's face it: You are a mere *amateur* at walking a dog. A professional dog walker will do it better, right?

The rarified set wealthy enough to practice the DNY lifestyle, in Beverly Hills or anywhere else, can turn shadow work inside out. They delegate shadow tasks to their staffs and free their own time for their allegedly higher callings, as Elaine explained. These people exist at the antipode from the DIY pioneers living "off the grid." As the two groups occupy opposite ends of the economic spectrum, in monetary terms, their time has a drastically different value. Yet both have dealt with shadow work, in one case by taking responsibility for everything, in the other by delegating it all to paid help.

THE VALUE OF TIME

Labor economists like Richard Freeman of Harvard University think constantly about the allocation of time. They may take their agenda from Benjamin Franklin's counsel in *Advice to a Young Tradesman* of 1748: "Remember that time is money." Franklin implies that any hour of one's time can be converted into money, and probably should be.

Neoclassical economics agrees with him on equating time and money—hence, as your income rises, the value of your time goes up commensurately. This offers a rationale for DNY. "A rich guy will take the taxi to the airport, because his time is very valuable," Freeman explains. "Somebody else, whose time is worth less per hour, will take the subway. When the airline asks who is willing to be bumped from the flight and take the next plane out, the person with less-valuable time is the one who raises her hand and is willing to wait a couple of hours."

There are two aspects to any purchase: the money it costs to buy it, and the time it takes to complete the transaction, Freeman explains. The *time* expense is an "opportunity cost" because time expended doing A costs you the opportunity to do B. The wealthy consumer can avoid this opportunity cost, which frequently arises from shadow work. She can pay someone to stand in line to buy a ticket to a rock concert, because that outlay is unimportant compared to her opportunity to do something besides stand in line. (Online ticket sales, of course, are phasing out such lines.) Eliminating the transaction time of shadow tasks makes more and more sense with increasing affluence. If you are a billionaire earning, say, $10,000 per day merely on interest, and there are two prices offered for a movie ticket—$10 and $50—the $50 means nothing to you. The only relevant cost is your time.

"The time of the rich is so valuable that they outsource a lot of low-level stuff," Freeman says. "If you are personally in heavy demand, you eventually start to feel that 'My time is so valuable—I want people to be *queued up* for me.'" So others wait to see me, but *I wait for no one.* For example, when former secretary of state Hillary Rodham Clinton agreed to accept a medal from UCLA and deliver a lecture on leadership, she not only charged a $300,000 fee but had a list of other demands. "Clinton seems to always be in a hurry," *The Boston Globe* reported, noting that "she requested 'prestaged' group photos so she wouldn't have to wait 'for these folks to get their act together.' The former first lady 'doesn't like to stand around waiting for people,' UCLA was told."

Then there is the social prestige of conspicuous consumption, identified by sociologist Thorstein Veblen in his 1899 masterpiece *The Theory of the Leisure Class.* The flaunting of wealth and leisure that he defined as conspicuous consumption includes the status symbol of servants, as the wealthy have always known. The DNY lifestyle embraces an ideal that dates to the pharaohs.

In his 1970 book *The Harried Leisure Class,* Swedish economist Staffan Burenstam Linder explains how domestic help can
facilitate increased consumption: "The average person can afford
no more personal services than he could in the Stone Age. For the
income oligarchs, it is easy to spend phenomenal sums on consumption, as maintenance work can be eliminated, and only the
pleasant aspects of consumption remain. Mansions and ski huts
and the things associated with living in them, and away from them,
are more attractive if the owners need not do the washing, sweep-
ing, scraping, polishing, and guarding all by themselves. The ultimate luxury is to be liberated even from the hardships of having to
do one's own buying. The consumer's path is then as smooth as it
can ever be."

Ironically, though, supervising your army of helpers can itself
become a major job, spinning off its own form of managerial
shadow work. To avoid this, you need a personal assistant to ride
herd on them. "The ultimate thing is having a personal assistant,"
says Freeman. "They make all the decisions. You trust them."
And you'd better; otherwise, your job becomes supervising the
assistant.

Imagine the monthly expense that this army of helpers amasses,
and the effect on home life of a phalanx of servants traipsing in
and out of one's rooms. The chores are not optional. Someone has
to do housework. Otherwise family life, or even the life of a single
person, falls apart: Neglect housework, and you will soon be living
in starvation, disorder, and filth. But though the jobs are the same,
amateur and professional work aren't always interchangeable.

There is a place for amateur work. Those domestic chores ground you in daily realities that sometimes go by the name of *life*. They connect you with your home, those rooms and furnishings that serve you without complaint. They bond you to your family, because the shadow work of housekeeping can be a tangible form of love. The fact that my mom cooked our meals, washed our clothes, and hung them on a clothesline to dry—even in winter—and kept our home clean and orderly, meant so much to my father, sister, brother, and me. Mom wanted us to have the conditions for a healthy and happy life. Keeping house remains the most meaningful form of shadow work. When a paid cook, laundress, nanny, or maid does household tasks, the jobs may be executed very well, but they're done for a salary, not from love of family. Inevitably, the work of servants has a different feeling.

THE CONVERGENCE OF career, childcare, housework, and shadow work attained its apotheosis in the myth of the superwoman. In the 1970s, feminism bashed open the door for women to have full-time careers. Most also wanted families, and some tried, at least, to become the "superwomen" who could do both. A noble aspiration, but one thwarted by the stubborn clock, which held firm at twenty-four hours per day. Even with smaller families, very few, if any, women could successfully play the roles of wife, mother, and ambitious careerist without making compromises. Something had to give.

In fact, many things did give. Society changed. Home-cooked family dinners, for example, gave way to prepared foods, entrée bars, microwavable meals, and take-out deliveries. "There is no way I can get home at 6:30 and start cooking something from scratch for dinner," says Celeste, a stock analyst and mother of two in Manhattan. "Brad [her husband] is in the same boat. It is take-out on weeknights. On weekends we can cook. Maybe." Nannies and daycare centers stepped up to take care of very young children. Housecleaning services got keys to the home and weekly appointments. Sleep deprivation kicked in.

The entry of women into the workplace paid off in both gender equity and professional fulfillment. Inevitably, it also reduced time women spent on the shadow work of homecare and childcare. This generated more *paid* work for restaurateurs, nannies, daycare providers, and housecleaners. This scenario might look like a middle-class version of DNY, although these two-career spouses are hardly "doing nothing." Instead, they are ultra-busy with their jobs, their kids, each other, and all the home tasks they haven't outsourced.

Yes, there is always time for the kids, though not enough of it, as many report. "It just kills me," says Margot, a litigator in Chicago married to an intellectual-property attorney. "Andy and I have such demanding jobs that it feels a lot of the time as if Andrea [their six-year-old daughter] gets pushed to the margins. I really, really want more time with her, but where does it come from? We do our best to make it up to her."

Indeed, time spent with children is, for many parents, the most rewarding thing in life. Many feel it's something they *should* do for the offspring; Baby Boomer parents, for example, fondly recall childhoods with their stay-at-home, noncareerist moms, and play-ing with dads who had genuine leisure, untethered by laptops, mobile devices, and texts. Today's two-career parents haven't got that kind of free time to spend with their kids (hence the invention of "quality time" as a substitute for *quantity* time), and the fallout is guilt. That guilt has fueled the middle-class epidemic of hyper-parenting, another rich vein of shadow work.

HYPER-PARENTS IN OVERDRIVE

In the 2006 movie *The Devil Wears Prada,* fashion doyenne Miranda Priestly (Meryl Streep) thinks nothing of officiously assigning purely personal chores to her assistant Andrea Sachs (Anne Hathaway). The imperious Priestly even involves Sachs in building a science project for her twin girls to take to school.

The film dramatizes the way Priestly expands Sachs's job descrip-tion to the point of abuse, but also makes a sociological point on how norms of childrearing have changed. Schoolchildren once did their own homework. Parents neither did it for them nor "helped" with the assignment, figuring it was something between the pupil and her teacher, and that correcting flaws in a student's work was part of the learning process. Students also did their own special projects, like science-fair entries. Teachers received the work of the unassisted pupil, rather than that of a team of parents and other mentors assembling constructions far beyond the student's ability to create or perhaps even to understand. The schoolteacher who gets such ghostwritten submissions cannot meaningfully evaluate his student's progress. *The Devil Wears Prada* merely takes the charade one step further: It's not even the mother who "helps" with the homework, but one of her executive assistants.

The extreme case in *Prada* illustrates the modern norm of parents doing their kids' schoolwork. No doubt this has always happened, but beginning with the Baby Boom generation, parents have escalated it drastically. Some school systems even require parents to sign off on homework, attesting that their kid got it done. "I thought the *teacher* was the one who checked on whether the kid did his homework," says Elizabeth, the Albany actress. "Why are they asking me, the mother, to do this?" Reporting honestly to a teacher about the completion of homework reinforces the habit of integrity. This is actually one of the more important life lessons of early school years. Making parents responsible for this undoes a powerful character-building exercise.

Understandably, Mom and Dad want their children to succeed in a competitive environment. The father who knows that other students in his son's classroom get parental "help" on homework feels that this legitimizes the practice: "Everybody does it." And if everybody does it, why put his son at a disadvantage by insisting he do his own work? That would almost be cheating the boy of his chances to receive (if not earn) high grades and prosper in this world where academic success means so much—eventually, admission to college and graduate school and a secure upper-middle-class career. It all starts here in grade school, where the youngster needs every possible advantage, and needs it now.

Parents who actually *do* the homework or build the science project convey the message that they don't trust their child's innate abilities, that cheating is OK, and that one good way to succeed is to take credit for someone else's work. (Perhaps they are preparing the kid for a political career.) More often, parents operate in the gray area of "helping" with assignments. They might act as in-house tutors, working with the child to learn and master the material, doing the job of the teacher: shadow work, plain and simple.

The complication is that, as with all amateur work, people bring a wide range of skills to the table. Some parents may actually be gifted teachers (or even trained teachers themselves) who genuinely understand how to foster the learning process. Others are ham-handed instructors working at cross purposes to the schoolteacher and actually interfering with the child's progress, either with intellectual and pedagogical goofs or by creating an anxious atmosphere around schoolwork that paralyzes the young student. Shadow work can cut both ways.

Interestingly, it turns out that parental participation in children's education, from homework to Parent Teacher Association meetings, does not help kids' academic performance, and may even hinder it. *The Broken Compass: Parental Involvement with Children's Education* (2014), by sociologists Keith Robinson of the University of Texas and Angel L. Harris of Duke University, analyzed numerous studies done from the 1980s to the early 2000s. They coded sixty-three different types of parental involvement and collected demographic information as well as academic results for children of all grade levels. "We found that most forms of parental involvement yielded no benefit to children's test scores or grades," the authors wrote in *The New York Times*. In fact, there were more instances of higher academic achievement when parents were *less* involved than more involved. When involvement did matter, its outcome was more likely negative than positive. "Consistent homework help almost never improved test scores or grades," the authors write. "Most parents appear to be ineffective at helping their kids with homework. . . . Even more surprising to us was that when parents regularly helped with homework, kids usually performed worse." The authors found only one type of parental engagement that seemed to matter: when parents consistently communicated the value of schooling to their offspring.

TWO SOCIAL CHANGES underlie parents' increased engagement with schooling. First, the unsatisfactory quality of public education in the United States has led families to try to compensate for what they find lacking in schools. This trend reaches its logical conclusion in homeschooling, in which parents completely take over the jobs of schoolteachers and administrators. (Many homeschoolers also reject the secular public education that the U.S. Constitution requires and choose to instill their preferred religious precepts at home.)

Secondly, social norms have evolved to sanction, even encourage, increased parental involvement in children's lives. To be sure, parental overinvolvement in schooling crops up mostly among the privileged. Upper-middle-class mothers and fathers were the first "helicopter parents" to hover ceaselessly over all their offspring's activities. The even more aggressive "snowplow parents," who are determined to plow a clear path before their kids, have now joined them. A new trend has parents of boarding-school students moving to towns near the prep schools to hover close to their offspring, who are living in dorms. "As the students get to be juniors, we hear more people saying, 'I have to be there as a support system as they are getting through that college push,'" Elyse Harney Morris, a Realtor in Salisbury, Connecticut, told *The New York Times*. Sadly, at the low end of the social-class spectrum, millions of unfortunate youngsters grow up with parents who are *under*involved in their schooling. A shortage of parental time or attention puts these schoolchildren on their own in the classroom at tender ages.

Hyper-parenting kicks off long before the school day starts. Millions now drive their kids to school, logging shadow work as unpaid school-bus drivers. This was hardly the childhood norm for the Baby Boom generation. As a friend from that era told me, "I don't think my old man even knew where my school *was*." Round-trips to school can mean hours of shadow work each week, but they do have advantages. "It lets us set our own schedule," says Eric, an industrial designer in Albany. "And driving to school gives me some extra time with Samantha, which is precious."

On the other hand, this form of shadow work is a fossil-fuel disaster. Instead of a single school bus, a flotilla of sedans, SUVs, and minivans now converges on the schoolhouse each morning. Chauffeuring parents represent the antithesis of high-occupancy vehicle (HOV) lanes that discourage solo driving. Yes, there are at least two people in those "parental school buses," but compared with *real* school buses, private cars are low-occupancy vehicles indeed. Mom and pop chauffeurs, as a group, might offset the energy savings of all the HOV lanes in America. They waste millions of gallons of fuel and spew pollution, idling their engines in long lines of cars waiting to discharge their kids. (Some states, including Virginia, Hawaii, and Vermont, and many municipalities, discourage this habit with anti-idling laws.) Certainly, these shadow-working parents don't *intend* to amp up CO_2 emissions and accelerate global warming. If asked, they might well favor reducing fossil-fuel consumption—just as long as it doesn't mean their kid having to ride a school bus.

In addition to homework, parents also get heavily involved in the educational process, not only with Parent Teacher Association meetings and consultations with teachers but by making a plethora of unsolicited phone calls and sending email messages to administrators, teachers, guidance counselors, and coaches. "The larger parenting trend is that parents are trying to become increasingly involved in the education of their children," University of Toronto professor Rubén Gaztambide-Fernández, author of *The Best of the Best: Becoming Elite at an American Boarding School*, told *The New York Times*. "There is increased anxiety around school success to ensure economic success later. Parents are highly invested in individualized attention on their kids, and they don't trust the schools to do that."

Parents weigh in on the kids' extracurricular activities as well as academic ones. After school and on weekends, parents take control of leisure time, arranging "play dates" for their offspring and sometimes sitting in on them as well. Initiatives for violin, piano, or other music lessons are at least as likely to come from parents as children, and likewise with dance lessons, chess clubs, or organized, coached sports. (See "Shadow Work Saga" at the end of this chapter.)

The bumptious moms and dads sustain their overinvolvement even through the college years, calling professors and coaches with advice on how to mentor their (adult) kids. "I asked one mother how many years of varsity eligibility she had," recalls Bill Cleary, former director of athletics at Harvard. "Because if she couldn't play for Harvard, I didn't understand why I was talking with her." It's not unusual for undergraduates to pull out their mobile phones and call or text parents several times a week—even several times a *day*—to discuss which courses to take, the status of relationships with roommates and friends, or extracurricular activities. The parents text right back. Yet, if achieving adulthood means learning to make decisions and take responsibility for them, one has to wonder if such parental shadow work—trespassing on the jobs of deans, proctors, professors, and academic advisers—actually helps students or infantilizes them in ways that retard maturation.

ON THE MAKE

Housework qualifies as a DIY activity—as does shadow work in general. In the United States, though, DIY usually refers to something related to hobbies. Even so, DIY now covers a wide range of pursuits, which also include forms of shadow work.

The do-it-yourself ethic has long been popular in America. As noted earlier, before the Industrial Revolution, households did pretty much *everything* for themselves, producing all the basics of survival at home. Perhaps DIY taps into the national values of individualism and self-sufficiency; recall Emerson's most famous essay, "Self-Reliance."

In any case, citizens usually welcome shadow work when it lets them *customize* the result—to get precisely what they want. Technology can move shadow-working customers into early phases of the production process. The trend toward *personalization*—perhaps a reaction against the sameness of mass-produced goods—turns them into industrial designers. For many years, shoppers have been able to customize the cut and style of their jeans. Now, a New Balance kiosk lets them design their shoes. In 2013, Foot Locker presented an interactive touchscreen kiosk that lets shoppers choose everything from colors, laces, and logos to fabric and heel phrases on the New Balance 574 sneaker. The kiosk offers forty-eight quadrillion combinations of elements, enough to guarantee a unique shoe for whoever wants one, barring a *real* population explosion. True, your design might be hideous—after all, shadow-working shoppers aren't shoe designers—but it is indisputably *yours*. No one else will be wearing the shoe on your foot, even if, quite possibly, they wouldn't want to.

Social changes frequently line up with new social norms to create a different way of doing things—and spin off a new form of shadow work.

When I was in college, for example, there was a unique retailer in Harvard Square called the Door Store, or Furniture-in-Parts. Staffed by lissome Scandinavian salesgirls, it attracted droves of students to its pleasant, studio-like sales floor. The Door Store sold unassembled furniture. You could buy wooden tabletops of various sizes and legs of various lengths, and put them together at home to make a dining table, a coffee table, or an end table. The store sold lots of doors (hence the name) that students laid atop filing cabinets for an instant desk. This gave the customer good-looking, affordable furniture, flexible designs, and a dose of shadow work. Perfect for a college town. The Door Store still does business, now at a different Harvard Square location and, alas, minus the Scandinavians.

The Door Store offered a taste of what Ikea, the Swedish furniture and housewares company, now rolls out in forty-three countries. Founded in 1943 by Ingvar Kamprad, then a seventeen-year-old, Ikea sells clean, inexpensive Nordic designs. One way it keeps prices down on larger pieces is by selling them unassembled. (In the 1980s it also curbed prices via forced labor from political and criminal prisoners in East Germany.) Customers schlep their Ikea boxes home and tackle the shadow work of building the furniture, something that salaried workers do in furniture manufacturing plants. The process isn't always a cakewalk; couples who've assembled Ikea items together may come to appreciate the sardonic joke that *Ikea* is actually a Swedish word for *argument*.

Yet for most, this shadow work pays off both financially and psychologically. In 2011, Michael Norton of Harvard Business School, in collaboration with Daniel Mochon and Dan Ariely, published a series of experiments in a paper called "The Ikea Effect: When Labor Leads to Love." Their subjects assembled furniture from Ikea kits, folded paper in the style of Japanese origami, and constructed objects from sets of Legos. "Participants saw their amateurish creations, of both utilitarian and hedonic products, as similar in value to the creations of experts," the authors wrote, "and expected others to share their opinions." Making things boosts the user's feeling of pride and competence. It also creates a showpiece that advertises your expertise. The Ikea effect comes packed with rewards.

SUCH EMOTIONAL PAYOFFS have always made DIY endeavors attractive, at least to a certain audience. The magazines *Popular Science* (founded 1872) and *Popular Mechanics* (1902) and have long celebrated the joys of home craftsmanship. Home winemaking and beer brewing tap into a related trend. Today, *Make* magazine offers guidance into all manner of DIY fabrication, including high-tech options like robotics, drones, and 3-D printing. Many DIY jobs, like building your own robot just for the hell of it, provide their own satisfactions and thus are hobbies, not shadow work. On the other hand, when we brew beer to save money, or reduce fuel costs by converting a car to electric power (a $12,000 to $18,000 project *Make* ranks as "very difficult"—you'll break even by 2032, easy), we are taking on shadow work.

The "making movement" takes the home workshop into the electronic age. Makers build devices that will not only water the lawn but signal your smartphone when the grass *needs* watering. Equally superfluous, but amusing to its creator, is an alarm clock that automatically fills a dish of water for your cat. Or try a unicycle whose spokes light up with LEDs. These diversions, again, are hobbies, not shadow work.

In contrast, the technology of 3-D printing is opening tracts of shadow work that will grow exponentially. A 3-D printer is a type of industrial robot that has become affordable to consumers, with some priced well under $1,000. Such printers can manufacture three-dimensional objects of nearly any shape by "printing out" a design from a digital file. Websites like Thingiverse.com offer thousands of such designs. The 3-D printer builds up the object by an additive process, laying down successive layers of a material (typically plastic, though ceramics and even steel are available at the high end) under computer control. Manufacturing one object at a time allows the user to customize it—very useful for, say, printing out a replacement tooth, as some dentists now do with ceramic 3-D printing.

Such technology essentially enables home manufacturing—and so begins the shadow work. Suppose the door handle on your GE refrigerator breaks. Normally, this would mean contacting GE for a replacement part that you, or a repairman, would install. Instead, with 3-D printing, you could download the handle's design from a GE website and print out the replacement part. Similarly, customers could print out spare parts for vertical window blinds, dishwashers, or furnaces. Appliance manufacturers like GE enthusiastically welcome this development, which will ultimately free them from storing thousands of spare parts in inventory. Instead of warehousing real parts, they will warehouse virtual ones in the form of digital designs—*much* cheaper. The shadow-working customer then inherits the job of manufacturing the actual part on a 3-D printer.

As this process becomes established for appliance maintenance and repair, companies will reverse-engineer it, designing more user-serviceable products. Industrial designers should welcome this development, which makes the design the *only* product sold after-market, so their commissions might rise markedly. More sophisticated designs, or materials like steel, may attract consumers to a storefront 3-D printing business, where higher technology can do more things. Such businesses will establish themselves in communities, much like the copying/printing centers that handle photocopying jobs too large or complex for the home office or small business. This trend is already under way. During the 2014 holiday season, Piecemaker Technologies rolled out a kiosk 3-D printer for retail sites like toy stores. Customers can print out customized jewelry, pendants, rings, plastic toys, or guitar picks from templates, at a price typically in the $5 to $15 range.

Currently, laws require manufacturers to make spare parts available for a certain number of years after release of a product. As 3-D printing shifts the job of producing those parts to the consumer, corporations will lobby, probably successfully, to repeal such laws, releasing them from this onerous duty as their shadow-working customers take over the job.

WASH YOUR GARBAGE

Though many of us think of our homes as independent social units, in truth every home connects to the surrounding community and even the world environment. Some of the shadow work we do at home reflects our civic and political commitments. Recycling, for example, manifests social responsibility and enhances community life while protecting our natural surroundings.

Fifty years ago, we Americans threw away everything we didn't eat or use. "Buy soft drinks/In throwaway cans," sang a TV jingle of the 1960s, celebrating those disposable aluminum soda cans that had just come on the market. Now, glass, metal, plastic, paper, textiles, and electronics are all reusable materials, and most of us willingly perform the shadow work of recycling them, diverting tons of trash away from landfills.

Recycling has always been with us: Plato was an early advocate. Scrap metal like brass has long been collected, melted down, and reused. World War II promoted recycling as a path to victory on the domestic front: Civilians salvaged metals like copper for the war effort, reusing other materials to conserve resources. In the 1970s, the environmental movement advocated recycling to preserve natural resources and reduce stress on landfills. Surging energy costs offered another incentive: Recycled aluminum consumes only 5 percent of the energy needed to make aluminum from bauxite, and other recycled materials produce smaller, yet meaningful, energy savings.

Recycling has spawned industries. The European Union claims about 50 percent of the world's waste and recycling industries, with 60,000 companies employing 500,000 workers and producing revenue of €24 billion. Recycling not only reduces the need for raw materials and landfills but can also save energy, reduce air pollution from incinerating trash, lessen water pollution from garbage-packed landfills, and diminish the greenhouse gas production of plastic factories. Many governments throughout the world now mandate recycling and distribute special containers for recyclable items from households and businesses.

Societies harvest these advantages from untold hours of shadow work. Rather than simply chucking everything into the trash can, 1950s-style, citizens now sort out recyclable paper, plastic, glass, and metal and store them separately until they get dumped into the recycling cart. In the 1950s, people were little inclined to wash their trash before heaving it; cleanliness standards at garbage dumps were, after all, quite relaxed. Recycling kicked off the "wash your garbage" movement, as organic matter isn't welcome in the recycling stream. Citizens undertook the shadow work of rinsing their bottles and cans, and fastidious ones even use soap and water.

Historically, recyclers separated metal, glass, plastic, and paper from each other before collection, and still do in many places. But beginning in California in the 1990s, communities started to offer single-stream recycling that allows users to toss all recyclables into one cart. The municipality then transports them to a materials recovery facility (MRF) that, with mechanical and manual methods, divides the single stream into its varied components. (In 2012 there were 248 MRFs in the United States.)

CONSIDER THE SHADOW work created by beverages. The United States guzzles an ocean of soft drinks, beer, bottled water, iced teas, juices, and "sports drinks" every day. Many come in single-serving containers, which pile up as mountains of waste. Beverage containers may represent as much as 58 percent of all litter.

Beginning with the Oregon Bottle Bill of 1971, eleven of the fifty American states enacted laws that make beverage industries and those who drink their products responsible for the containers they put into use. Customers pay deposits of 5 or 10 cents on each bottle or can, reviving the traditional practice of refundable deposits and refillable bottles that prevailed in America until the 1930s, when disposable steel cans began to replace glass bottles. (In England, Schweppes initiated bottle deposits as early as 1800.) Consumers can redeem empty bottles or cans for their deposits at stores or designated centers. Those who cash in the empties have simply rented the container; those who don't have bought it. Similar laws exist in Canada, Australia, and New Zealand, throughout Scandinavia, and in Switzerland, Germany, the Netherlands, Croatia, Israel, and elsewhere.

The simple insight is that people throw away garbage but not money. Bottle bills are not exactly philosopher's stones that turn lead into gold, but they do turn garbage into money: That empty Coke bottle is *cash*, not trash. And thus is born the shadow work of managing empty bottles. We store them separately and carry them back to redeem. Some people, like myself, place them on the sidewalk on Sunday for whoever who wants them. They disappear quickly.

Bottle bills now have long track records: more than twenty-five years in California, thirty years in New York and Massachusetts, thirty-five years in Michigan, and more than forty years in Oregon, whose law took inspiration from British Columbia, which enacted its bottle bill in 1970. The overall U.S. recycling rate for beverage containers is 33 percent; states with bottle bills average 70 percent. Michigan sets the highest deposit of any state at 10 cents per container, and its 97 percent recycling rate from 1990 to 2008 also leads the nation. States with bottle bills have seen roadside litter decrease by 30 to 64 percent—folks just don't heave cash out of their car windows. It does mean plenty of shadow work, but bottle bills also mean more efficient use of resources and a cleaner landscape for all.

SHADOW WORK SAGA: Herd of Zebras Drives Kids off Sandlots

Shadow-working adults have barged in on children's play. Believe it or not, kids once played without adult supervision. Doing so was, in fact, one of the joys of childhood. With no coaching at all, we played sandlot baseball, basketball, and football, as well as tag, hide-and-seek, jump rope, Mother, May I?, hopscotch, and legions of other games. Spontaneous play by kids has given way to "play dates"—sessions of play that parents arrange and often oversee—either directly, or indirectly by their looming presence.

As a boy, I played every single day after school and on weekends with neighborhood friends. The idea of our parents setting up a play date would have been as alien as a Martian showing up in our New Jersey town. Why would anyone's *parents* stick their noses into our *playtime?* Frankly, one of the great things about free time with friends was the chance to get away from Mom and Dad for a few hours and play by our own rules.

The lack of adult supervision is a core element of what makes it *play*. Playing meant that we got to live in a children's world, created by kids. Making our own rules helped us feel free and capable. For a couple of hours, we did not even *think* about what agenda our parents might have for us. Adult intrusions have now ruined much of that children's world.

Sandlot games were my scene as a boy. That word is now going out of style. For the historical record, a sandlot was any vacant lot where kids could gather to play whatever game they wished, including ones we made up ourselves. Another term for this is a *pickup game*—suggesting, accurately, that the players made up their teams on the spot.

We didn't need foul lines, pitching mounds, backstops, or goalposts. We made our own fields: "That rock is your goal line—ours is this big tree over here." A "sandlot" could actually be anywhere: Often it was somebody's backyard. It might also be a quiet city street or sidewalk. Kids invented "stoop ball" in Brooklyn after World War II. You play this game by throwing a pink rubber ball against the stoop (the stairs in front of a building) and adapting certain baseball rules for nine-inning games. Sandy Koufax, a Brooklyn native, began his Hall of Fame pitching career with the Brooklyn and Los Angeles Dodgers playing stoop ball on the sidewalks of New York.

You can even play sandlot games on an unused high school football field, complete with goalposts and sidelines. The physical setting isn't the important part: What defines sandlot play is that kids (or even older players) create the game. There is no organization—and no higher authority than the players themselves. Starting with the known rules of a sport, we'd improvise our own variations, like counting off a two-second delay after the snap in touch football before rushing the passer, to give the offensive play a chance to develop. In street basketball, guidelines like "no blood, no foul" can apply: harsh, perhaps, but totally sandlot.

Boundaries like boulders and oak trees are pretty inexact. Like many facets of competitive sports, this naturally leads to disputes. We'd have to settle those disagreements among ourselves, since no adult "zebras" were running back and forth in black-and-white striped shirts, blowing whistles. We, the children, learned to resolve our conflicts. Frequently, that might mean playing a do-over: cancel the disputed play, start from scratch, and resume playing. Do-overs teach kids some basics of sportsmanship: respect each other's opinions, set aside the rhubarb, and keep playing. Today, shadow-working referees have erased such lessons from childhood. "Kids today have no idea of a do-over," says Rick Wolff, a longtime sports-parenting advocate who hosts a weekly radio show on the subject for WFAN in New York City. "They have grownups to tell them what is fair or foul. Things like do-overs are being lost in the dust."

In a pickup football game, two boys might be the captains, who choose their teams. Perhaps the sides turn out to be mismatched, and after fifteen minutes, one team is already leading by four touchdowns. Sandlot players would stop the game and reorganize the teams to equalize talent. It's more fun to play in a competitive game, and a rout is neither sporting nor enjoyable, even for the winning side. But parent-organized leagues like Pop Warner football do nothing of this kind: Teams continue the blowout to its bitter end, and another sportsmanship lesson vanishes.

Sandlot games are being sidelined by organized competition: Little League baseball, Pop Warner football, youth soccer, and a raft of other juvenile leagues with uniforms, sponsors, umpires, adult coaches, practices, playoffs, tournaments, and national championships. These organized contests emulate college and professional sports, and like them, demand serious infusions of money. The only expenses my parents had for my extensive athletic pursuits were for a baseball bat, a couple of mitts, and a baseball, football, and basketball. There was also a bowling ball, as I bowled in an organized kids' league for several years, though for years, I used balls from the racks at the lanes. They fit my hand and were very round; believe it or not, that was all I needed to become one of the top scorers. Today, outfitting a single youth ice-hockey player might cost ten times as much as all the sports equipment I owned as a child.

THE ADULT TAKEOVER of children's sports churns out tons of shadow work. Mothers and fathers now put in endless hours organizing and administering sports leagues, keeping their books, and lining up local businesses as sponsors. (Young athletes also pitch in on soliciting sponsors, adding another job to their days. Sponsorship is something that never enters a sandlot player's

mind.) The parents also perform shadow work as coaches, sometimes struggling to mentor a sport they have never played and may
barely understand. Well, good for them—somebody's got to do it.

Yet this has its downsides. In Vancouver, British Columbia,
I once watched a soccer match played by girls around ten years
of age. One particular play drove home how profoundly ignorant
some parental spectators are—though their cluelessness doesn't
deter them even slightly from bellowing out advice. At one juncture, a speedy girl won the ball from an opponent at midfield and
dribbled it down the side of the pitch toward the opponents' end
line. Unfortunately, none of her teammates had made it downfield
with her; meanwhile, the other side fell back to clog the penalty
box in front of the goal. Nonetheless, near where I stood, one
father yelled, "Cross it! Cross it!" He was urging her to make a
standard soccer move: passing the ball across the field to a teammate near the goal, who might get off a shot. There was only one
problem: *No teammate was anywhere in the vicinity.* Exhorting
her to "cross it" at that moment amounted to telling her to give the
ball back to the other team.

One hopes that these benighted adults aren't coaching the kids,
though no doubt some are. The main point is that having grownups oversee young athletes isn't always the best way to develop
their skills in a sport—and never mind the kids' *enjoyment* of the
game, once thought to be the main reason to play. Parental mentors may not be older and wiser. They may just be older.

In addition, even if a parent—or coach—has good advice to
offer during a contest, he should zip his lip on the sideline. During

practices, coaches can provide all the guidance they want. These are hours for teaching and training. But in a game, that young girl deserves the right to decide what to do with the soccer ball. She should make her own decision and learn from the outcome, for good or ill. Competitive athletics require all the concentration you can muster. Voices of parents and coaches intruding from the sidelines can distract or confuse the youngster, actually hindering her.

The simple fact is that athletic talent can develop very well without adult coaching. Like helping on homework, it may even interfere with the learning process. Ted Williams became the greatest hitter in baseball history just by hitting for endless hours throughout his childhood and teen years on the playgrounds of San Diego. In his superb biography *The Kid: The Immortal Life of Ted Williams*, Ben Bradlee Jr. narrates how one of Ted's childhood friends first saw "this big, tall string bean hitting the ball a mile, and all the other kids were chasing after it. . . . This was his life. Ted never shagged for anybody. Nobody wanted him to. Everybody loved to see him hit." Soon thereafter, another friend describes how their friend Rod "would take and throw balls to Ted, and he'd hit them over the fence, and we'd chase them for him. We did that for hours every day." Williams probably hit tens of thousands of pitches as a boy.

Imagine the result of giving this much batting practice to an exceptionally talented boy like Ted Williams. Actually, there is no need to imagine it: He became one of only three hitters in major league history to reach the career milestones of .300/.400/.500/.600 (batting average/on-base percentage/home runs/slugging percentage).

The others are Babe Ruth and Jimmy Foxx, who both struck out more (72 and 75 percent more per at-bat, respectively) than Williams.

Contrast Ted's sandlot play with what a Little League hitter would experience today. That youngster might get three or four at-bats in his sponsored, uniformed, six-inning game with adult coaches and umpires running the show. Yes, there'll be practices and maybe even batting cages, but he'll see many fewer pitches than he would have in an hour or two of sandlot play. Furthermore, having a coach analyzing your swing and barking corrections while baseballs zip in could actually rattle you, making it *harder* to learn hitting. There's a lot to be said for just seeing a few thousand pitches and figuring out how to hit them by trial and error. Worked for, well, *Ted Williams*.

To be sure, mentors have their place. Concert pianists or violinists do not develop their dazzling virtuosity by just sitting down and teaching themselves to play. Mastering something like the classical piano repertoire is an almost unfathomable task without an experienced teacher. Today's great scientists are certainly not autodidacts. In most every sport, coaches play a profoundly important role in nurturing athletic skill. Yet in a sense, everything we learn is ultimately self-taught. There's wisdom in the epigraph of my 1973 edition of *The Joy of Cooking,* a quote from Goethe's *Faust:* "That which thy fathers have bequeathed to thee, earn it anew if thou wouldst possess it."

WHEN ADULTS HORN in on children's sports, they import elements that turn games into shadow work. For example, it may well dawn on Mom and Dad that their young athletes' skills could win them admission to college (or prep school) and perhaps an athletic scholarship. Suddenly the stakes rise steeply: Sports are now a path to career and financial success. Money changes everything. Instead of a way to have fun, sports become a tool to build one's future. This transforms play into shadow work. (Remember: Play is something we do *for its own sake*.) When stakes increase, so does the pressure to perform. Parents no longer settle into their grandstand seats just to see a good game. Money and prospects are on the line. Such spectators can become obnoxious, injecting a sour note into what was once a kids' game, played to have fun, not as a staging area for college admissions.

"It's finals season in sport," wrote columnist Sarah Macdonald in 2013 in "Abusive on the Football Field" for the Australian newspaper *Daily Life*. "There's increased evidence of bad behaviour, abuse, screaming, and rule breaking. And that's just the parents." She takes note of a brawl started by a parent at an under-eleven rugby game; parents swearing at and harassing referees; a mother horrified to hear nearby spectators exhorting their kids to kill hers. Nor is it just the Aussies, she says that 60 percent of parents in India have also seen abuse at youth sports contests.

In the United States, parents have stormed the field, knocked referees unconscious, and caused such a ruckus at one Little League game that the police were called. Rude crowds at American youth soccer matches have led referees to declare "silent games," during which they eject any spectator who says *anything*. Junior tennis is famous for insufferable parents who ride both their kids' opponents and umpires mercilessly, and teach their offspring to cheat on line calls. In the late 1980s, I interviewed a varsity women's squash player at Harvard who had switched from tennis to squash just to avoid the toxic ambience of tennis parents.

Research by Sam Elliott of Flinders University in South Australia suggests that "ugly parent syndrome"—"parents providing excessive instruction, putting down their child in view of others, coaching from the boundary and verbally jousting with their child"—is demotivating kids, actually turning them off to sports.

In the United States, research by the Institute for the Study of Youth Sports at Michigan State University and elsewhere has found 35 percent of participants dropping out of organized sport programs each year, 50 percent ending their participation by age twelve, and 70 to 80 percent of youths aged thirteen to fifteen having left organized sports programs entirely. When asked why they quit, the kids' answers mostly boiled down to this: It just wasn't fun anymore.

Youth sports touch an enormous number of children. Thirty to forty million kids play organized sports each year in the United States. Two to four million coaches work with them, though 80 percent of these coaches are untrained. The vast majority (85 percent) of these are shadow-working fathers coaching their own children. Four-fifths of the young athletes are in nonschool programs like Little League, CYO basketball, and the ubiquitous travel teams we are about to discuss. Participation in travel teams has increased while that in school programs has been declining.

IF A CHILD shows aptitude, some parents turn into athletic versions of *My Fair Lady*'s Henry Higgins, intently grooming their offspring for greatness. This opens up vast tracts of shadow work. There's the time spent coaching the child oneself, then finding and paying for the best professional coaches available. This can include bundling the youngster off to commercial child-athlete complexes like the renowned Nick Bollettieri Tennis Camps, now part of an academy run by the worldwide sports marketing firm IMG. This academy also offers programs in baseball, basketball, football, golf, lacrosse, soccer, track and field, and cross-country.

If the child plays a team sport, the budding superstar's shadow-working parents immerse themselves in the complex politics of organized team play. This can mean officiously calling the coach to ask why young Noah isn't in the starting lineup, why Rory hasn't been stroking the eight-oared boat—and can't Hannah have some extra help with her lacrosse shot? At private schools or on travel teams, parents write big checks; many feel this entitles them to advise the coaches—quite strenuously. Even at a major college football program, the University of Southern California, former head coach Pete Carroll routinely got calls from parents, lobbying him on behalf of their sons.

During their middle and high school years, talented, ambitious athletes often play on travel teams in addition to, or instead of, their high school squads. In different regions, these may be called club, elite, or premier teams. Though there are many exceptions, high school teams and leagues frequently are not strong enough to test the skills of top young athletes. They join regional travel teams that collect top players from several high schools (or middle schools) to form elite teenaged units that compete against similar squads. Families, of course, pay handsomely for this privilege and for the professional mentoring it includes, just as they do for Bollettieri or for specialized programs like the Kohl camps for football placekickers.

Rick Wolff outlines a typical career in the travel-team world. Parents might put their small girl on a soccer or basketball team, or start her playing tennis at age five or six. "The children are never asked if it's something they want to do," Wolff explains. "It's just expected of them. Organized sports with a time clock are what sports *are* for kids today—they don't even realize they can play sandlot games." (Sandlot games, let's remember, are ones the *children* choose to play.)

Nearly every part of America now has travel teams in several sports. Most of these didn't exist twenty years ago. What happens is that "some gung-ho dad decides that his son or daughter is a very gifted athlete, and wants to accelerate their development," Wolff explains, "so he joins up with another father or two to start a travel team." They announce "tryouts," and parents assume that those will be as fairly judged as tryouts for any local recreational program. (Of course they are no such thing. The founders' kids have made the team before tryouts begin, and the goal isn't recreation but honing athletic skill and winning games.) The tryouts typically involve seven- or eight-year-old kids, and they are a watershed moment. "If you don't make the travel team," says Wolff, "that's the end of your athletic career."

Such teams hire professional coaches, schedule practices, and set up matches with other travel teams in the region. Parents pay hundreds or thousands of dollars for their child to take part, and pitch in with hours of shadow work. This includes countless hours at the wheel, driving children to practices and matches. It can mean a three-hour auto trip, each way, to see your daughter sit on the bench for most of a soccer game.

Taking sports this seriously squeezes spontaneity, creativity, and playfulness out of the game. Imagine a boy piping up to ask his Little League coach, "Can I play shortstop tonight instead of outfield? That looks like fun!" The coach's dismissal of this request would likely include some version of "We're in a *game* here, son— we're here to *win*." (And we certainly have no desire to experiment with new things, let alone have *fun*.)

National federations of travel teams now seek to dominate their sports so completely as to take them out of the public schools. The U.S. Soccer Development Academy oversees seventy-nine travel teams organized into seven divisions under its East, Central, and West conferences. The presenting sponsor is Chevrolet, an appropriate choice in view of the vast amounts of auto mileage the organization manufactures for parents. In 2012, the academy announced that it was extending its season from seven to ten months for the 3,000 boys on its teams. The added three months overlapped with the fall high school soccer season, so this meant that none of the boys could play for their high schools. "This is heartbreaking," says Wolff. "They're making a high-school junior tell his varsity coach that he can't play for the team anymore." It's a severe loss for the athlete as well as his school, because it is so much more fun to play on a high school team, with the pals you go to classes with every day—and to compete with your friends rooting you on. It began with one or two gung-ho, shadow-working dads deciding that their kids needed to get on the fast track.

IT CAN TURN out well. Take Joey Yenne, a soccer forward who grew up in Texas, Michigan, and Florida before completing high school in the small town of St. Cloud, Minnesota. At age nine, she was already playing on a select travel team of girls from several Florida towns. "She's probably the most competitive person I've ever met," Peter Stephens, her coach in Pensacola, Florida, told the website Ivy League Sports. During her last two years of high school in Minnesota, Yenne's shadow-working mother, Susan, drove her three nights a week to the Twin Cities—seventy miles away—to practice with a travel team there in sessions that sometimes ran from 11 PM until 12:30 AM. Joey did her homework in the car.

She finished first in her class and got recruiting letters from soccer powerhouses like North Carolina. Instead, Yenne turned down the free rides to enroll at Harvard, where as a sophomore she led the Ivy League in goals scored with eleven. She graduated in 2003; in Harvard's career record book, she ranked fifth in points (eighty-two) and assists (twenty-six) and sixth in goals scored (twenty-eight), as of 2014. Without question, Joey is a talented, hardworking athlete who gave her all to the game. But she couldn't have accomplished so much without her shadow-working parents, John and Susan Yenne.

Joey is a success story. After a few years in management consulting, she earned an MBA from Stanford and married a

Dartmouth graduate with his own Stanford MBA She settled in Connecticut and started a family while working for a hotel chain; her job includes responsibility for global sports and entertainment sponsorship.

But few accomplish anything like what she did. Of 209,000 girls playing soccer in high school, only 3.3 percent, or 7,000, will go on to play at Division I or II colleges. Less than half of those will win full scholarships. About one million boys play high school football each year; 41,000, or 3.8 percent, will make Division I or II college squads. The odds against making it to the National Football League are 6,000 to 1—and the other 5,999 boys were all high-school athletes. In pro basketball, the odds are 10,000 to 1.

The great majority of parents who dream of athletic scholarships or pro careers for their offspring have no idea how vanishingly small their chances are. Few of these parents have ever played a varsity sport. They should make a point of viewing a practice session—not a game, but a *practice*—of a college team in their child's sport. That can provide a reality check on the size, strength, and skill level of intercollegiate varsity athletes. Unfortunately, for most of these families, the payoff for untold hours of shadow work on youth sports will be disappointed hopes and a lost opportunity for their kids to savor one of the joys of childhood—not *working* at sports but *playing* them.

LESSONS FROM THE PLAYING FIELDS

First, the "beneficiaries" of shadow work do not necessarily seek or want the benefits they allegedly receive. The very young children who begin playing organized sports often have no particular interest in doing so. Their parents push them onto teams and into leagues, or stick a tennis racquet or golf club into their hands. Parents do these things for their own reasons and with their own motives. Dropping this type of shadow work could simplify parental schedules while also giving kids the freedom to find out what sort of recreation they actually want to pursue.

Second, launching a new, nonprofit activity or organization generally opens up acres of shadow work. Youth start-up teams and leagues normally have little funding, so they depend on large inputs of shadow work from both adults and children, including, for example, selling sponsorships to local businesses. You may call this shadow work or call it volunteer work by categorizing it as a gift. It all depends on whether you see the activities as chores or as a donation of time. Either classification can apply.

Social pressure plays a role here. It's easy to imagine that some mothers drafted as, say, bookkeepers for the Little League don't embrace this job as their first choice for their free time. They feel they have to do it. Situations like this recommend the *shadow work* interpretation over the *volunteer work* option.

Third, shadow work taints realms of play with a work mentality. Grafting external goals like college admission and scholarships onto a youth baseball game, for example, makes recreation into a task. By conscripting young athletes into work mode, shadow work by adults begets more shadow work by their kids.

Fourth, shadow workers may push themselves and their agendas forward to encroach on spheres of real, professional work.

When parents call college football coaches to lobby for more playing time for their sons or daughters, they are grasping for the prerogatives of the full-time professionals hired to make such decisions.

Fifth, never overlook the enormous amount of shadow work involved with transportation. Parents—archetypally, "soccer moms"—spend much of their middle-adult years driving children, their own and others, to practices and games. Just as with commuting, getting there is *not* half the fun.

three: shadow work at the office

[Author and columnist Glenn] Greenwald's only problem with the idea of a journalist's privilege is that some people don't recognize that he's a journalist. He is right that he is just as entitled to this honor as Bob Woodward. But so is everyone else. Especially in the age of blogs, it is impossible to distinguish between a professional journalist and anyone else who wants to publish his or her thoughts. And that's a good thing.

—MICHAEL KINSLEY, *THE NEW YORK TIMES*, MAY 22, 2014

FOR DECADES, KRYPTONITE bicycle locks were the gold standard of bicycle security. Developed in 1971, the U-shaped locks became a staple for urban cyclists. Based in Canton, Massachusetts, Kryptonite named itself for the one substance that could disable Superman. The locks' names, such as the New York Chain, implied that they would stymie even the hard-case bicycle thieves of New York City. Kryptonite was so confident in its products that it offered "insurance" payments of up to $3,500 to any customer who lost a locked bicycle to thieves. Decades of cyclists' experience confirmed that Kryptonites were indeed impregnable.

If there *was* any way to compromise them, doing so took so much time and trouble that thieves preferred to move on to easier prey. Which was hard to find, as Kryptonite dominated the upscale bike-lock market.

This all changed in September 2004, when Chris Brennan, a twenty-five-year-old San Francisco cyclist and computer security consultant, successfully opened a Kryptonite lock with a Bic plastic pen instead of a key. Brennan simply removed the plug from the nonwriting end of the pen, pushed it into the lock, and turned clockwise. The lock fell open, along with Brennan's jaw. He posted an urgent alert on the bulletin board bikeforums.net. Soon thereafter, a twenty-eight-year-old graphic designer in Brooklyn, Benjamin Running, similarly cracked his $90 Kryptonite in thirty seconds. "I was in awe," he told *The New York Times*. His short video showing how he'd done it quickly attracted 125,000 views on his website. Meanwhile, 170,000 cyclists had read Brennan's post, triggering a full-fledged panic.

The story made a splash in the *Times* and other national media. The locks' vulnerability didn't affect all Kryptonites, only certain models manufactured after 2002. But the flaw did compromise other tubular-cylinder locks, such as those on vending machines, other coin-operated machines, and some security devices. Kryptonite, owned since 2001 by industry giant Ingersoll-Rand, quickly responded to protect not only its customers' bicycles but also the company's bulletproof reputation. It created a voluntary lock-exchange program that replaced 400,000 locks in twenty-one countries at no charge. Doing this, Kryptonite says, involved redesigning the equivalent of nine years' worth of new products in ten months. Ten years later, the company remains the gold standard of the bicycle-lock world.

For our purposes, the most interesting thing isn't the thousands of hours of shadow work those 400,000 cyclists put in to get their vulnerable locks replaced with ones that worked. Rather, it's that a handful of *amateurs* triggered this international brouhaha. They were just garden-variety bicyclists. Chris Brennan worked in computer security; Benjamin Running was a graphic designer. They were not *experts*—not journalists, not radio or TV reporters; they didn't own bicycle shops or write for cycling magazines. They were not even locksmiths. A few average citizens had just stumbled onto something surprising and risky and put the word out.

These young men got their extraordinary leverage from the Internet and its marvelously democratic accessibility. Had Chris Brennan picked his lock a decade earlier, before the web had attained its wide reach, the Kryptonite story might have died in its tracks—and thieves might have taken home thousands of bicycles.

THE KRYPTONITE STORY has many implications for the American, and global, workplace. It hints at the power that untrained amateurs can wield, using the leverage of the Internet. So much of professional work depends on the knowledge and expertise that employees bring with them to the office each morning. But today's open information environment is undercutting their proprietary grip on knowledge. Shadow-working amateurs now carve inroads

into once-exclusive domains. This underlying dynamic, deeply disruptive to the workplace, is *the democratization of expertise.*

FLATTENING THE PYRAMID OF EXPERTISE

The web has democratized knowledge in two ways—roughly parallel to downloads and uploads. First consider downloads, one
form of the web's *output.* Google, Wikipedia, YouTube, and millions of freely accessible websites have revolutionized access to
information. Some large fraction of the world's knowledge—at
least knowledge captured in words, images, and audio or video
recordings—is now available, free of charge, to anyone with an
Internet connection. The web has cracked open the safe that stores
the human species' archive of information. Virtually anyone can
now learn things once restricted to special groups.

Second, consider uploads, or the web's *input.* It's so easy (and
cheap) to buy a web domain, post blogs or videos, or comment
on news articles. The global audience is sitting there—literally—for
anyone, like those Kryptonite whistle-blowers, to reach. Cultural
traffic cops—such as newspaper, magazine, and book editors, television and radio producers, even motion picture executives—who
once monitored access to the information highway no longer control
the on-ramps. Today, we can all barrel onto the highway unchecked
and broadcast our opinions, poems, books, songs, or videos.

To be sure, *posting* creations does not guarantee them an audience. Far from it. Take the songs that anyone can now publish online
and sell as downloads. In 2011, eight million different songs sold
at least one copy. "But people don't realize that about one-third of

these songs sold *exactly* one copy," says Harvard Business School professor Anita Elberse, author of the 2013 book *Blockbusters: Hit-making, Risk-taking, and the Big Business of Entertainment.* "There is an enormous amount of content that gets no demand at all." With some noteworthy exceptions, the global audience is just not queuing up for homemade movies, self-published e-books, and garage recordings.

Nonetheless, the fading power of professional gatekeepers leaves Internet users unprotected by their screening. If you read *The New Yorker* or watch CBS, you have their editors and producers working as your filtering agents, separating wheat from chaff. But on Google outlets like YouTube or Blogger.com, you're on your own. Sifting through the haystacks of web material for silver needles worthy of attention creates more shadow work in the barn lofts of the Internet.

This democratization of knowledge arrives with all the virtues and drawbacks of any democracy. Now we can all tap "professional" knowledge. Open access tears down the walls between "experts" and everyone else. Ordinary citizens may invade restricted domains—even those of doctors and lawyers. Amateurs, however, usually don't perform as well as professionals. Regardless, the average citizen is getting more options—including many more chances for shadow work.

THE CURRENCY OF expertise has been devalued. Its gold standard is the know-how of specialists—doctors, lawyers, dentists, CPAs, and engineers, as well as plumbers, electricians, and carpenters.

We ask them to handle problems that fall in their bailiwicks. Make no mistake—the experts remain with us. Cities don't build suspension bridges across rivers without structural engineers; the law requires licensed plumbers and electricians to install the pipes and wires of a new house; and most everyone who needs an operation leans toward a board-certified surgeon.

Traditionally, the distribution of expertise in society takes the shape of a pyramid. At its broad base live large numbers of people with minimal skill. Rising up the pyramid, each level includes fewer people, but they have progressively greater knowledge and ability. At the very top are the world-class experts—a few standouts with a rare level of talent. These are people like Michael Jordan in basketball, Warren Buffett in investing, Meryl Streep in film acting. (Of course, every field has its own pyramid. Warren Buffett's poetry? Don't ask. Ask Michael Jordan to sing, and you'll be sorry—he wasn't even that good at baseball. And don't even *think* about Meryl Streep at quarterback.)

Yet the populism of the information economy is leveling this classic pyramid. The Internet has melted the pyramid of expertise down to horizontal form—it is now more like a lake. That lake spreads out much wider than the pyramid ever did, opening reservoirs of knowledge to the masses.

Consider lawyers. Laypeople have long viewed attorneys as professionals with trained expertise—and of course there are specialties within law, like torts, taxes, intellectual property, criminal law, and so on. Lawyers have college and law degrees, belong to the bar, and hold a state's license to practice. Diplomas and documents hang on their walls.

Yet shadow-working consumers now do their own legal research online, saving attorneys' (usually large) fees. We can all become jailhouse lawyers, without even going to prison. Just log onto the web and download generic forms like leases and wills, plus legal documents for probate, bankruptcy, divorce, contracts, incorporation, real estate, trademarks, and patents. You can fill out and file such forms yourself, perhaps adding a "lite" version of lawyering by consulting an attorney to ensure that the details are correct. "We wanted to incorporate," says Eric, an MIT graduate who, with two partners, launched a tech start-up outside Boston. "So I asked a law firm what it would take. At their rate of $400 an hour it was going to cost us thousands of dollars. Instead we downloaded the legal documents online. My partners and I tackled it one weekend and got it done. It cost $49, plus the state filing fees."

The Internet also increases the transparency of professional work. This is disruptive because the lucrative status of many professions depends on the opacity of work. The client doesn't know exactly what the expert is doing, and so pays willingly for . . . well, whatever it is. From plumbers to brain surgeons, anyone who speaks in baffling jargon makes customers feel they must be getting their money's worth. Lawyers and doctors deal in Latin-based terms like *nolo contendere* and *ulnar neuropathy* not only to communicate precisely with each other but also to exclude and mystify clients and patients. Shadow-working customers who crack this code demythologize those who use it, as they find out what goes on behind the scenes.

It is hard to quantify, but shadow work may be eroding the demand for legal services. About 15,000 attorney and legal-staff jobs at large firms vanished over five years beginning in 2008, according to a Northwestern Law school study. In 2013, law school applications reached a thirty-year low at 54,000, a decline of nearly 50 percent from the 100,000 applications of 2004. There are many factors in play, including the economic slowdown that caused big clients to balk at paying robust legal fees at white-shoe law firms, the heavy student debt that saddles many law school graduates, and alternative employers that promise quicker payoffs, like high-tech start-ups. But the contraction of the legal market also reflects the fact that attorneys now compete for work with the people who were once their clients.

THE DISAPPEARANCE OF SUPPORT STAFF

The democratization of expertise also means that those atop the pyramid do routine jobs once reserved for ordinary proles. The workplace hierarchy has flattened. To be sure, this makes for a more egalitarian office, as everyone pitches in on the mundane tasks. We've come a long way from the days when legions of under-paid women did gofer jobs like fetching coffee for their male bosses.

The *Mad Men* television series nostalgically recalls antiquarian aspects of business life like support staff and even secretaries. Support staff is becoming a quaint concept, a fossilized curiosity like typewriters, stenography, and executive washrooms. Today, few if any workers have jobs making photocopies or stamping and mailing envelopes—much less taking dictation or typing letters. We all have our own computers and we type and print our own letters, copy our own reports, and send our own mail. Senior management handles these humdrum jobs, and let their six-figure salaries be damned.

Smartphones by themselves have taken over much of the work of executive assistants. They can do almost everything a secretary used to do: keep your appointment calendar, handle incoming and outgoing telephone calls, maintain a file of contacts, send and receive email and texts, research information. You support staff is there in the palm of your hand—no wonder executive assistants have disappeared! One consequence, though, is that "there is never any downtime with these 'conveniences,'" says Phyllis Barajas, a Boston-based executive and social entrepreneur. "It used to be that there was an answering machine, and that was it. Now, the phone is always with you."

In magazine publishing, interns—usually college students or young people earning minimal wages—have for years performed tasks like mailing out complimentary issues, known as comps. (Comps go to subjects of articles and to freelance contributors.) With the publication of each new issue, interns placed the right number of magazines in envelopes; sealed, addressed, and weighed them; ran them through the postage meter; affixed postage; and mailed them. In recent years that routine has been phased out. At many publications, mailing comps has become an editor's job, a new piece of shadow work.

The evaporation of such support is hardly unique to magazines. For example, the international technology consulting firm Forrester Research, Inc., has 1,300 employees—and just five executive assistants. Another consulting firm, SelecTel Communications, notes that "in order to stay profitable, [telecommunications] carriers have cut costs by decreasing support staff and moving the burden of service onto their customers." This means that, among other burdens, customers wait longer on hold when they call customer service. In this and many other ways, shadow work by the consumer compensates for the laid-off support staff.

Similar trends ripple through many industries. In healthcare, electronic health records (EHRs), used by nearly 70 percent of hospitals and outpatient practices as of 2014, are time hogs. "A doctor's cost runs up to $4 a minute or $240 an hour," said Asfer Shariff, M.D., in a report on the Medscape/Business of Medicine website. "Would you pay $240 an hour to have someone type and click information into an electronic medical record? Would you take your most expensive employees and make them data entry staff? That's what has been happening." Some doctors now hire "medical scribes" to enter notes, lab results, and other data into EHRs. Shariff, of Toledo, Ohio, started a firm that supplies doctors with such scribes. He saw the need because catching up on charts was adding two hours of shadow work to his day. With scribes, "I got my family back," he says.

Medical scribes are a countertrend toward *adding* support staff, but the problem they address—a new information technology spinning off shadow work—characterizes today's office. In

general, office workers are experiencing "job-description creep"—
and unlike doctors, most of us cannot hire assistants to field the
new duties. It goes far beyond offices. "I was doing prep work in
the kitchen—chopping things, filling the coffeemaker, unpacking
rolls and stuff," says Chuck, a young man working at a fast-food
outlet in Dayton. "Then one day they laid off our janitor. Guess
who got his mop?"

The disappearance of support staff also touches home life. "A
minor irony of the suburban dream," wrote Philip Slater in *The
Pursuit of Loneliness,* "is that, for many Americans, reaching the
pinnacle of their social ambitions (owning a house in the suburbs)
forces them to perform all kinds of menial tasks (carrying garbage
cans, mowing lawns, shoveling snow, and so on) that were performed for them when they occupied a less exalted status."

Websites have unleashed a torrent of office shadow work.
Again, consider magazine publishing. Before the web, a monthly
periodical printed and mailed twelve issues per year, period. A
print magazine's fixed number of pages limits the space available
for articles and advertisements. In contrast, websites offer infinite
space for, theoretically, an infinite number of articles, pictures, and
ads—produced by an infinite amount of work.

Every established magazine now maintains a voracious website
alongside its print edition. These sites have grown prodigiously to
include more and more online postings, including breaking news
written on deadline, audio clips and extra photos, originally produced videos, and, for each of these, a riot of unseen metadata—
page titles, article descriptions, lists of keywords, captions, Internet

links to track down and add, and much more. The job of creating all this new content has simply plopped onto the desks of "print editors" as shadow work, typically with no new staff hired to cope with the raft of web chores. Similar stories play out wherever there are websites—in other words, almost everywhere.

Shadow tasks can slip into the workday so smoothly as to go unnoticed. For example, not long ago, it was standard practice for human relations departments to record employees' vacation, personal, and illness days. Technology is now pushing that job back onto each worker. Software packages for "absence management" require employees to enter all relevant data. "I am not sure why it has become my responsibility to do data entry for any time away from the office," says Henry, a software developer in Cranston, Rhode Island. "Frankly, I have enough to do writing code. Why am I doing HR's job?"

Job descriptions are also expanding with "emotional labor," a phrase Berkeley sociologist Arlie Hochschild coined in her 1983 book *The Managed Heart*. Emotional labor involves getting staff to fabricate states of feeling that put customers and coworkers in a positive mood. The worker must "induce or suppress feeling," wrote Hochschild, to realize the sought-after effect in others. Pret A Manger, a London-based fast-food chain, has nearly made emotional labor into an aspect of management science, as Timothy Noah explained in *The New Republic* in 2013. The chain spelled out a list of "Pret Behaviors" recommended for anyone who wants to become "a really successful Pret Person." The list includes "is charming to people," "creates a sense of fun," and "has presence."

Pret enforces its exhortations with policies "vaguely reminiscent of the old East German Stasi," according to Noah. Each week, a plainclothes "mystery shopper" visits every Pret restaurant. If the cashier displays enough bouncy enthusiasm, everyone in the place gets a bonus; if not, no one does. This system "turns peers into enthusiasm cops," Noah writes, "further constricting any space for a reserved and private self."

In 1983, Hochschild estimated that one-third of jobs entailed substantial emotional labor; thirty years later, she pegged it at about one-half. The attitudinal shadow work isn't limited to fast food but extends throughout the service economy to nail salons, healthcare, dry cleaners, and auto rental. This could help women in the job market, as females learn early in life how to please others; it may also help explain why men often fail to prosper in the service economy.

DOWNSIZING SUPPORT STAFF doesn't eliminate the *jobs* that need doing; they simply get reassigned to others. The new chores never show up on one's job description, let alone justify a salary increase. Shadow work just gets grafted onto people's duties without their consent or sometimes even their awareness.

The unpaid aspect of shadow work may seem absent here, as we do draw salaries while taking on these extra jobs. But when your paycheck remains fixed while your workload does not, that extra toil is essentially unremunerated—it is shadow work on the job. "Terri, who worked with us here, got married and moved to Atlanta," says Dan, an insurance claims adjustor in Charlotte, North Carolina. "They didn't bother to hire anyone to take her place. So the rest of us adjustors had to divvy up Terri's work and do it. It's not like we work on commission here. It just makes for a longer day, and less money per hour of work."

In 2013, David A. Banks, a PhD candidate at Rensselaer Polytechnic Institute in Troy, New York, blogged on thesocietypages .com about the shadow work of graduate-school study. A vaguely defined role like "graduate student" leaves plenty of room for shadow tasks. Banks listed seventeen skills he had been expected to acquire, with no training whatsoever, if he hoped to remain competitive in the job market after graduation. These included public relations writing, typesetting, sound engineering, videography, web design, institutional procurement, event catering, and conference planning and management. Banks writes:

> First, there's the simple fact that all of this informal learning takes time. Lots of time. In between reading Foucault or waiting for spores to bloom in petri dishes, a grad student might learn WordPress or Maya. They might spend an hour in a campus computer lab . . . learning the entire Adobe Creative Suite. Once you develop a passing fluency in InDesign or Logic, you have to decide if you want to keep that skill a secret within your department, lest you become known as the go-to person that knows how to make posters, film a speaker, or speak in the arcane language of the Business Office. It's a fine line between establishing your worth in the department—showing off the fruits of your new skill—and becoming the grad student that fills the

gaping hole left from the last round of your department's staff lay-offs. "Oh, can you order the food for next week's department brownbag? Great! Barbara used to do that before they consolidated the offices."

Secretaries still exist. But only high-level executives now have underlings to help them through the daily routine. Receiving live human service has become a mark of the elite. Indeed, service from an actual person, whether in a fine-dining restaurant or on a customer-service phone call, is a twenty-first-century luxury.

NONETHELESS, IF THE work is interesting, some organizations can attract support from unpaid shadow-working assistants. The burgeoning field of citizen science is a prime example. The Galaxy Zoo project is a joint venture of astronomers at Johns Hopkins University in the United States and Portsmouth and Oxford universities in England. It enlists lay astronomers in classifying galaxies from telescope images based on shape. In its first year, more than 150,000 participants contributed more than fifty million classifications, at times sending in 60,000 per hour.

David Baker, a biochemistry professor at the University of Washington, developed an online game called FoldIt that welcomes citizen participants to contribute hypothetical ways of folding protein molecules; these shadow workers have resolved some problems that have baffled supercomputers. Launched in 2008, the Great Sunflower Project lets citizen field-workers log and share data points about pollinators such as bees and wasps, according to a report by Katherine Xue in *Harvard Magazine*. And the Cornell Lab of Ornithology maintains a platform called eBird, where amateur bird-watchers can help ornithologists track bird populations and migration patterns around the world. Thousands of shadow-working field assistants are grabbing their binoculars and heading out.

INTERN FEVER

Nineteenth-century textile mills often hired both parents and children to work in factories. Around 1900, an abolition movement directed at child labor gathered steam, and in 1916, the U.S. Congress passed the first federal law regulating child labor, though the Supreme Court struck it down two years later. Not until 1938 did President Franklin Roosevelt sign the Fair Labor Standards Act, which today bans employment of children under twelve (other than in agriculture) and limits work by those aged twelve to eighteen.

In addition to the agricultural exception, which allows families of migrant workers, such as Mexican *braceros*, to pick crops for American agribusinesses, there's another exception to the child labor statutes: internships. Very few interns are literally children—precocious shadow workers, they—but many high school students, college students, and young adults intern as they try to launch careers. Some are even over fifty. Typically they do not collect salaries, so interns are not legally *employees* and thus are exempt from employment law. (As they work voluntarily, they are also exempt from the Thirteenth Amendment, which abolished slavery.) The upshot is an army of young people doing full-time shadow work for months or even years, trying to break into the job market as unpaid trainees. The internship juggernaut represents a massive, widespread, institutionalized form of shadow work.

The 2011 exposé *Intern Nation: How to Earn Nothing and Learn Little in the Brave New Economy*, by Ross Perlin, offers a biting critique of the internship explosion. Many college students now see internships as a requirement for a white-collar career: They dismiss traditional student jobs like camp counselor, waitress, or mailroom clerk as irrelevant to their ambitions (though the mailroom is exactly where many interns land). "Restaurant jobs are nice to have but you need something bigger," says Isabel, a secondary-school teacher in Philadelphia who worked as a waitress one summer and the next summer interned for a Texas congresswoman in Washington, D.C. "It's supposed to demonstrate your ability to handle this kind of work." If internships really *are* the only path into professional careers, then the current system perpetuates inequality, as low-income people can't afford to invest years on all this shadow work. Only the affluent can spend a year or two, or even a summer, working without pay.

"Business internships are much more likely to pay than nonprofits or government," Isabel says. "You intern the summer before your senior year and hope the company will hire you after you graduate. If you don't get a job offer at the end of the summer, that's a really bad sign."

There are 9.5 million students attending four-year colleges in the United States, Perlin reports, with a large majority of them, perhaps as many as 75 percent, pursuing at least one internship before graduating. Universities and colleges collaborate with employers in nurturing the intern boom, often designating an internship as a degree requirement. (One school in Leeuwarden in the Netherlands required that students perform a "social internship," so in 2010, two girls, aged fourteen and fifteen, decided to intern as prostitutes in a red-light district. They never actually reached the street, but they did have sex with a thirty-five-year-old pimp who was later arrested. In retrospect, the girls described their decision as "stupid.")

As late as 1980, internships were relatively rare, but they have mushroomed since then. Each year, somewhere between one and two million people work as interns in the United States, with many millions more around the world. (The exact number is difficult to pin down because internships, which inhabit a hazy area between employment and volunteer work, have no legal definition.) Though employers frequently flout minimum wage and overtime laws, these violations rarely get enforced—and the interns themselves obviously are in no position to complain.

Disney World in Orlando, Florida, runs one of the world's largest internship programs, with 7,000 to 8,000 college students and new graduates doing full-time, minimum-wage, menial internships. Most stints last four to five months. The interns "are subject to a raft of draconian policies," Perlin reports, "without sick days or time off, without grievance procedures, without guarantees of workers' compensation or protection against harassment or unfair treatment. Twelve-hour shifts are typical, many of them beginning at 6 AM or stretching past midnight."

The advantage of internships for employers is obvious: free, or very cheap, labor. They recruit a throng of healthy, energetic, young shadow workers who collect very little in either salaries or benefits. The world economic recession that began in 2008 strengthened the intern trend. Managers economized by replacing full-time jobs with internships, solidifying unemployment in some areas. They also cut expenses by substituting unpaid internships for paid ones.

Internships can become little more than a way for employers to sidestep labor laws. For their part, the interns supposedly learn something meaningful about the field they are trying out, and in the best case they jump-start a career. Sadly, it rarely turns out quite that way. "Focused training and mentoring are vanishingly rare, as interns soon discover," Perlin writes. "[M]ost ultimately learn the ropes on their own if at all, on the sly if necessary." Isabel says that "some interns get coffee and answer the phone all day; some are very hands-on. Lots of interns did nothing but run the tunnels [the underground passageways in Washington that connect major legislative sites like the Capitol and Senate Office Building]. I got to write some statements that the congresswoman made on the floor of the House—*that* was cool. But I never got any direct mentoring."

Worse, interning can demoralize young people and undermine belief in their value in the marketplace. "Once you're told that your work isn't worth anything, you stop taking pride in it, you stop giving it your best," Perlin writes. "A tacit mutual agreement sets in between supervisor and intern: I'll write the letter of reference, you make the coffee."

THE FUTURE OF EXPERTISE

In a sense, the Internet has externalized the collective memory of humanity: Just about everything we know as a species is recorded somewhere on a server. Memory exists as a trace of information, whether on a silicon chip or a neuron. Traditionally, experts were those who could draw on a vast repository of information stored in their brains. Now that information resides on disk drives or in the cloud.

This fact is triggering upheavals throughout the economy, from home repair to tourism to accounting to higher education. The skill set that humans bring to projects now depends less on memorized data—less on facts, or pure information. In the twenty-first century, we need human brains to do things that computers and the Internet *cannot* do. In particular, people are good at discovering *relationships* between facts. The modern expert's skill is recognizing patterns. For this, artificial intelligence cannot equal the human kind.

Digital technology is just not particularly good at solving analog problems—that is, perceiving similarities. There have been many attempts at computer-generated poetry, for example, but the results are uniformly awful. There are many reasons for this, including the sound of poetry, but a critical factor is that computers lack a gift for metaphor. Silicon chips are poor at comparisons. Asking a computer to write a poem is like asking a home entertainment system to compose music.

Furthermore, for pattern recognition, a long memory can come in handy. The legendary broadcaster Daniel Schorr, senior news analyst for National Public Radio for more than two decades until his death in 2010, consistently demonstrated how long experience (he was nearly seventy when he joined NPR in 1985) could illuminate current events. In one of his on-air commentaries, Schorr discussed a news report that the U.S. Congress was planning to tackle the subject of sex and violence on television. Schorr began his analysis with the words, "I can save them a lot of time." He went on to narrate how Congress had grappled with this same issue—never with any success—every few years since the 1950s. The repeated pattern of failure made it clear that the legislative apparatus is simply ill equipped to regulate the content of television and that it was a waste of time even to attempt—again.

A younger reporter could not have connected the historical dots as Schorr's long memory did. Neither could a computer have done so, running the best search engine: Even well-chosen keywords would retrieve too many web pages. The essential problem is that digital searches tap *literal,* not *metaphorical,* data. You can search for keywords but not patterns. Try valiantly to sketch a pattern with multiple tags or even a four-word phrase in Google Advanced Search, but the unique *relationship* among the keywords still goes missing. In contrast, Daniel Schorr did very well in the realm of analogy. Humans uncover structures embedded in experience that remain invisible to data sets—even Big Data sets.

From now on, human intelligence will operate alongside the digital fortress of the Internet. Machines and people excel at two complementary modes of expertise: one for recording and retrieving data, another for finding *meaning*—in other words, patterns—in this data archive. Such meanings could take the form of a design for a Sufi temple, a diagnosis of a rare viral infection, a judicial finding in a patent-infringement case, or a documentary film on a restaurant start-up.

In the future, people will find it increasingly difficult to compete with computers on their digital playing field. The growth of cybernetic power threatens any career that depends solely on command of information. This can include even highly educated, trained specialists.

Consider pharmacists, who are college graduates with additional years of professional training. The pharmaceutical and healthcare industries are huge, growing, and highly profitable. Pharmacists would seem to have a secure future. But if kiosks with secure ID controls now dispense medical marijuana, what is to stop the kiosk army from marching into drugstores to distribute *any* prescription drug? The answer is, essentially nothing. About 75 percent of prescriptions refill existing orders, which streamlines the robotic task.

Take Berkshire Health Systems, a comprehensive hospital and healthcare organization based in Pittsfield, Massachusetts, which introduced a pilot system for its 3,500 employees. Its employee pharmacy opened in 2010 and fills 70 percent of prescriptions for staff and their dependents. The hospital recognized that it needed a convenient, cost-effective way to serve second- and third-shift employees, whose work schedules didn't match those of the registered pharmacists. It installed an automated kiosk called ScriptCenter that enables second- and third-shift workers to pick up prescriptions filled by pharmacists during the day: a kind of time-shifting. Berkshire Health Systems says the kiosk program has saved the hospital money, increased co-pay revenues, and improved employee satisfaction. ScriptCenter does not create shadow work for the employees, but it does automate one function of pharmacists and so could pave the way for future shadow work as the technology evolves.

SHADOW WORKERS CAN also pool their expertise to reach shared goals. Take higher education. University professors are highly educated employees with impressive reservoirs of expertise. Yet they have begun to share their teaching responsibilities with untrained shadow-working clients, otherwise known as students.

Physics professor Eric Mazur of Harvard pioneered a peer-instruction method that gets students teaching each other. Here's how it works. Mazur will pose a physics problem to the class and ask students to solve it individually. Next, the professor displays several possible answers. Using wireless clickers or smartphones, the students vote for the answer that matches their own. Mazur seeks "controversial" problems for which 30 to 70 percent of the class gets the correct response. Without announcing the right answer, he asks students to pair off, matching someone who got it right with someone who didn't. ("If you chose D, find somebody who had A or C," he might announce.) Each pair then discusses how they reached their solutions.

Naturally, those with correct responses nearly always convince their partners, as "it's hard to talk someone into the wrong answer when they have the right one," Mazur says. "More important, a fellow student is *more likely* to reach them than Professor Mazur—and this is the crux of the method. You're a student and you've only recently learned this, so you still know where you got hung up, because it's not that long ago that *you* were hung up on that very same thing. Whereas Professor Mazur got hung up on this point when he was seventeen, and he no longer remembers how difficult it was back then. He has lost the ability to understand what a beginning learner faces."

Students profit from teaching each other, Mazur says, because "the person who learns the most in any classroom is the teacher." His charges are involved in "active learning." This means emphasizing what students *do* in class—their engagement with ideas, not just the information absorbed. Instead of giving lectures to transmit information, Mazur assigns students to read his lecture notes *before* class. Then, in the classroom, he poses physics puzzles for students to solve with help from peers. The result has been to triple the knowledge they absorb as measured by conceptual tests, to strengthen retention of knowledge, and to produce more science, technology, engineering, and mathematics majors. Active learning and peer instruction are gaining ground in education at all levels, from kindergarten up. Students are learning more via shadow work.

THE DEMOCRATIZATION OF expertise also raises the question of which jobs the ordinary citizen *cannot* do, even with access to the relevant information. Surprisingly, in an information era, jobs that require a physical skill rank among the most secure. No amount of online data will make you into a skillful hairstylist or surgeon. Such skills grow by repeating something until you get good at it, rather than by simply knowing information. If you want a torn rotator cuff repaired, it is reassuring to learn that your surgeon has done this operation hundreds of times.

In the kitchens of fast-food and casual-dining eateries, automation may eliminate human expertise, or even humans. But chefs in fine-dining restaurants will likely remain people with educated taste buds who understand ingredients and culinary techniques. Pro athletes, dancers, musicians, and actors will stay in business; their unique physical presence is irreplaceable.

Landscapers who build retaining walls, remove trees, and dig ponds will keep doing so, but landscape *designers* may find shadow-working clients replacing them with software packages with names like Realtime Landscaping Plus. Similarly, entrepreneurs can build their own websites with Squarespace instead of hiring a web designer. (Many start-ups, after all, do not need an elaborate website choreographed by a professional.) TurboTax likewise enables taxpayers to cope with the huge shadow task of income tax preparation without an accountant or H&R Block.

Vulnerable careers, therefore, include those for which a software *template* can replicate a professional's function. A good template lays out the fundamentals, the basic decisions involved in a task, at least generically. It distills expertise into an algorithm that becomes the engine of a software package. The product will probably not be as good as what a professional would produce, but it is good enough for many customers, and far less expensive. The shadow-working consumer simply customizes the template for her needs and goes ahead with it—planting the garden or going live with the new website.

Such templates are examples of "disruptive innovation," a term Harvard Business School professor Clayton Christensen coined in his landmark 1992 book *The Innovator's Dilemma.* Disruptive innovation happens when a new company introduces a product that is cheaper, simpler, and/or faster than those on the market. Toyota and Honda, for example, disrupted Detroit's Big Three automakers by bringing out cheaper, smaller, no-frills cars like the Corolla and Civic. The Japanese imports were not as good as Detroit's models—not as powerful, safe, comfortable, or loaded with features—but they were *good enough* for many drivers at the low end of the market and far less expensive to buy and operate. In much the same way, a $79.95 software package from Realtime Landscaping Plus may not produce as good a design as what a landscape architect will draw up for $10,000—but it will suffice for many homeowners, at a fraction of the cost.

This disruptive dynamic applies widely and is now overthrowing the reign of authorities. Online legal forms, home pregnancy tests, and TurboTax demonstrate how technological innovation can undercut specialists. The Internet has pried open their toolboxes, and consumers are now grasping the tools. Shadow-working amateurs don't wield those instruments with expert skill, but the results they produce may yet displace the experts.

SHADOW WORK SAGA: Docs Populi

Some years ago, I attended a conference on mind-body medicine sponsored by the Ema Yaffe Foundation of Providence, Rhode Island. Keynote speaker Deepak Chopra, M.D., described some psychoneuroimmunological research on medical students. The study suggested that their mental states could essentially immunize them from colds during exam periods. Epidemiological data showed that the students came down with significantly more colds immediately after exams (though not before). Apparently they knew they couldn't afford to get sick until exams were over—so they didn't. The session ended with a panel discussion including Chopra and a few other doctors, one of whom offered a tongue-in-cheek caveat. "On that study of medical students, Deepak," he said, "don't forget: That research hasn't been replicated on, umm . . . human beings."

The witty physician was alluding to something every doctor understands: The demands of medical school leave little time for a "normal" human life. Indeed, with the possible exception of the military, no profession requires more arduous training than medicine: college, medical school, internship, residency, and continuing education throughout one's career. Few, if any, experts are more steeped in knowledge than doctors. Yet the social trend of shadow work is diluting even their power. The pyramid of expertise has collapsed in healthcare, as it has in so many fields. In sickness and in health, patients are now performing many jobs once restricted to doctors and medical professionals.

ANDERS, A FIFTY-FIVE-YEAR-OLD man, received a serious diagnosis: stage II (nonmetastatic) colon cancer. He sat down for a
lengthy conversation with an oncologist. The doctor explained
three major treatment options, involving surgery, chemotherapy,
and/or radiation, along with their risks, chances of success, side
effects, and tradeoffs. One chemotherapy drug had a better chance
of killing malignant cells but ran the risk of causing neuropathy
and permanent loss of feeling in the feet. The protocols were complex. There were even political factors like experimental drugs that
might or might not receive FDA approval. After this nearly overwhelming narrative, the doctor asked Anders a simple question:
"So, which protocol do you want?"

The oncologist was framing a reasonable and very modern
question. He was empowering his patient—putting the treatment
decision in his hands. A few decades ago, a physician might simply have told Anders what he was going to do about the cancer.
Now, doctors and patients share responsibility. Yet the question
befuddled Anders. *"You're asking me?"* he thought. "Aren't *you*
the expert here? I thought *you* were going to sort through all these
factors and tell me which treatment was best."

The oncologist was giving Anders shadow work. The doctor could have added, "Yes, I have the knowledge, but only you
know how it fits you and your life." Physicians still have the academic credentials, the board certifications, and the legal power to
write prescriptions or perform surgery. But many patients now
choose to participate actively in their healthcare. Furthermore,
they can go online and investigate even fairly arcane medical

topics—at times becoming better informed on a specific subject than their doctor.

The melodramatic story of the middle-aged executive shocked in the prime of life by a cancer diagnosis who begins researching the disease obsessively and becomes an overnight "expert" has nearly become a cliché. Shadow-working patients are nothing if not motivated. No one minds the hours of research when life and health are at stake. (Such patients confirm the riddle about the difference between major surgery and minor surgery: Minor surgery is surgery on someone *else*.)

Doctors once enjoyed a near-divine aura of omniscience and beneficence. But so did presidents and pro athletes. The public remained unaware of Franklin Roosevelt's paralysis, John F. Kennedy's philandering, and Mickey Mantle's alcoholism due to a conspiracy of silence by the news media. In that era, journalists gave the public a similarly whitewashed picture of medicine. Now, medical writers unblinkingly cover the foibles and failures of doctors and the sprawling medical-industrial complex. Citizens increasingly grasp medicine's profit-driven aspects, as well as the pharmaceutical industry's predatory pricing, all-out lobbying, and political power plays. Such revelations undermine the *ex cathedra* authority of doctors. In the age of "Question Authority" bumper stickers, patients may respect their physicians but no longer revere them.

This humanizes doctors and to some extent relieves them of the burden of having to seem flawless and omniscient. Doctors are people, too. Yet the deconsecration of the medical office also places physician and patient on a more equal footing. It sets the stage for medical shadow work: patients taking on prerogatives, actions, and responsibilities once restricted to physicians. A doctor friend has on his wall a framed cartoon of a patient telling his physician, "I've already got my diagnosis from the Internet. I'm just coming to you for a second opinion."

THE HEALTH AND medical information available to the public has undeniably increased in both quantity and quality—even if it is often inaccurate, contradictory, and confusing. The Pew Research Center reports that one in three Americans have used the Internet to diagnose a condition, either for themselves or others. Furthermore, 72 percent of Internet users sought online health information in 2013.

Wikipedia, the sixth-largest website in the world, channels much of this medical data. It is, in fact, the top source of health information for both doctors and patients, according to a report from the IMS Institute for Healthcare Informatics that Julie Beck cited in *The Atlantic* in 2014. Fifty percent of physicians consult Wikipedia for information, particularly on specific diseases. Tuberculosis, Crohn's disease, pneumonia, multiple sclerosis, and diabetes were the top five conditions for which Internet users tapped Wikipedia in 2013.

Wikipedia's crowdsourced medical entries tend to be lengthy and comprehensive. Its 6,000-word article on coronary heart disease, for example, cites scores of references and covers signs and symptoms, risk factors, diagnosis, prevention, treatment, epidemiology, and research. Wiki's throng of lay editors constantly tweaks it. The IMS examined five popular Wikipedia entries (diabetes, multiple sclerosis, rheumatoid arthritis, breast and prostate cancer) and found them perpetually in flux: On average, editors changed the pages from sixteen to forty-six times monthly. In itself, this is healthy: All scientific knowledge is emergent, as new research constantly revises earlier understandings.

The problem is that doctors and shadow-working patients are leaning on an unreliable source. In 2014, *The Journal of the American Osteopathic Association* published a study of Wikipedia entries for the ten most costly medical conditions by Robert Hasty, M.D., of Campbell University in North Carolina and his colleagues. The research found that nine of the ten Wikipedia entries contained statistically significant discrepancies from peer-reviewed medical literature. Sometimes these deviations reflect Wikipedia editors' lack of expertise, producing a distorted picture for users.

At the same time, even the peer-reviewed consensus is not sacrosanct. Some deviations may simply be dissents from medical orthodoxy. After all, the professional consensus can be, and often is, upended. For example, for decades, doctors believed that stress and spicy foods caused peptic ulcers, and they prescribed relaxation and bland diets as treatment. Then, in the early 1980s, Australian scientists Barry Marshall and Robin Warren published findings that the bacterium *Heliobacter pylori* could act as an infectious agent in the stomach and was a likely cause of up to 90 percent of ulcers. (They received the Nobel Prize for this work in 2005.) Pharmaceutical companies (antacids like Tagamet were then the top-selling drugs), gastroenterologists who had been performing surgery on ulcer patients, and psychotherapists who'd treated ulcer sufferers for stress all fiercely resisted the bacterial hypothesis. But study after study showed that giving patients antibiotics that eradicated *H. pylori* quickly knocked out their ulcers. It took until 1997 for the Centers for Disease Control in the United States to launch a physician education campaign that advocated antibiotic treatment.

In other words, you not only can't believe everything you read in the newspaper, but you can't believe everything you read in *The New England Journal of Medicine*. Unfortunately, the untrained, shadow-working patient is rarely well equipped to weigh the balance of evidence and assess the scientific validity of studies she may turn up on the web.

Some experts are now trying to strengthen Wikipedia's scientific accuracy. Wikiproject Medicine, a collaborative project among physicians, other medical professionals, and Wikipedia editors interested in health issues, aims to raise the quality of medical entries on the site. This effort indicates that at least some doctors recognize the shadow work patients do on Wikipedia. In 2014, the University of California, San Francisco, even began offering academic credit to fourth-year medical students for editing Wiki's medical pages.

YOUTUBE, THE THIRD-MOST-POPULAR site on the Internet, posts thousands of health-related videos that many patients view and believe. Videos may affect viewers even more than Wikipedia's text entries, due to the vividness of image and sound. Furthermore, while legions of volunteer editors monitor Wikipedia's content, YouTube is essentially unmoderated—anyone can barrel onto its lane of the information freeway. Nilay Kumar, M.D., a physician at Cambridge Health Alliance in Cambridge, Massachusetts, searched YouTube for videos related to high blood pressure and found 400,000 results. His team asked independent experts on hypertension to rate 209 of the most relevant videos (as ranked by YouTube) for accuracy and usefulness. They found 63 percent to be useful but flagged about one-third of the videos for inaccurate information—for example, stating that hypertension is unrelated to strokes, that treating it can *cause* strokes, or that salt consumption is unrelated to the condition. Ironically, the misleading videos generally attracted a larger number of views and "likes" than more accurate ones.

Accuracy, of course, can be a subjective call. "Common among the misleading videos was promotion of holistic health and natural cures," reported a Reuters article on Kumar's research. "More than half of them included ads for alternative treatments not recommended by the American Heart Association." Well, the American Heart Association is a major mainstream player in the cardiovascular disease field, but its recommendations are hardly sacred; nor are lavishly funded Big Pharma lobbyists strangers to the Heart Association's offices. Here as elsewhere, the democratization of expertise reflects the political and business pathways that shape consensus and define "accuracy" in the public realm.

The well of data that shadow-working patients draw from contains both errors and contaminants. Pharmaceutical companies and nutrition chains that market dietary supplements can manipulate the Internet to enhance sales. There are faux web pages, reviews, and blogs, and planted comments on established consumer-review sites. Those misleading YouTube videos frequently touted some proprietary treatment like nutritional supplements. Again, the average citizen is not especially qualified to extract genuine knowledge from the barrage of web noise.

Furthermore, *too much* information can spook patients. Many of them can't readily put unfamiliar facts in context. In a blog titled "The T.M.I. [Too Much Information] Pregnancy" in *The New York Times*, Patricia Volk wrote of accompanying her six-months-pregnant daughter to a prenatal scan and learning from a technician that the fetus had a "short long bone" (femur). "Home after lunch, I perform the new masochistic ritual," Volk wrote. "I Google 'short long bone' and find: 'Short FL [femur length] may be a part of a malformation such as a skeletal dysplasia.' I decide nothing good can come from researching the long list of conditions associated with short FL, including aneuploidies, pyelectasis and enlarged nuchal translucency." Of course her grandchild was born completely normal.

THE UNITED STATES is one of only two countries in the world (the other is New Zealand) whose governments allow television advertising of prescription drugs. In 1997, the Food and Drug Administration relaxed its guidelines to permit such commercials, opening the floodgates. Over the next decade, the pharmaceutical industry's spending on direct-to-consumer ads soared to $4.9

billion per year. A deluge of prescription drug commercials, estimated at sixteen hours per person annually, now washes over American TV viewers—plus radio, print, and Internet ads.

The pharmaceutical industry, often called the world's most profitable business, focuses its advertising on a few brand-name drugs. Typically, these treat chronic conditions with wide and durable potential markets, such as high cholesterol (Crestor), insomnia (Ambien, Lunesta), and osteoporosis (Evista). The introduction of Viagra in 1998 helped push erectile dysfunction treatments to the top of the TV-ad category.

At first glance, these huge outlays seem puzzling. These are *prescription*, not over-the-counter, drugs. Only doctors can order them. (And to be sure, Big Pharma spends lavishly on advertising to doctors and provides them with endless blandishments, like junkets and golf outings. The companies also use physicians as shills to write medical journal articles that are little more than advertisements ghostwritten by the drug producers.) Consumers cannot prescribe drugs. The FDA's 1997 liberalization of rules did not alter this. So why the surge of direct-to-consumer advertising?

The answer is the power of the shadow-working patient. Drug advertising is part of the "education" that patients absorb on their ailments. A television ad touting an antiallergy prescription like Claritin convinces the patient to mention the brand on his next visit to the doctor. She, too, knows of Claritin and, all else being equal, wants to keep her patient/customer happy, so she gladly writes the script. Everyone is happy, including the local pharmacy and especially Schering-Plough, manufacturer of Claritin.

EVEN WITHOUT THREATENING illnesses, people are doing jobs doctors, nurses, and their staffs once did. Diabetics prick their fingers and test blood glucose levels, sometimes several times daily. Using consumer equipment, individuals monitor their own blood pressure. Patients can obtain genetic testing by mail order or test urine in their own bathrooms. In 2012 a home test for HIV went on the market for $40.

Shadow-working patients who do home self-care in collaboration with medical professionals can undertake some fairly sophisticated procedures. Neil Wassner (a pseudonym), a sixty-seven-year-old lawyer with the federal government in Washington, D.C., developed a prostate infection, resulting in fever, increased frequency and urgency of urination, and irritation while urinating. Three courses of oral antibiotics failed to knock it out. Unfortunately, the treatment only ensured that the remaining pathogens were highly drug-resistant strains. "I was developing a superbug," he says.

His doctor next recommended a six-week course of home infusion therapy with a different antibiotic, Ertapenem, which could reach the site of Wassner's infection when infused each day directly into his bloodstream. "In terms of bookkeeping, it's a pharmaceutical service," Wassner says. In practice it involved quite a bit more than swallowing pills. A nurse installed a PICC (a peripherally inserted central venous catheter) in a vein in Wassner's arm. A national home healthcare company and licensed pharmacy assisted Wassner with the self-administered treatments.

Each evening at about 6 PM, Wassner connected the plastic bag of medication dissolved in water. "The connection has to be antiseptic and it takes two hands to put together, so my wife had to help me," he explains. Next, the infusion would flow from the bag into Wassner's arm for one hour. He finished the ninety-minute process by disconnecting the bag, flushing the area, and screwing a saline syringe onto the IV portal to take a dose of the anticoagulant heparin.

"At first it's hair-raising," Wassner says. "At each juncture you have the opportunity to do something wrong, like air bubbles getting into the line. The infusion is a gravity feed; once, I dropped the bag below the level of my arm and blood rushed into it immediately. It's pretty radical. In so much of medicine, a doctor is in control, particularly with this kind of procedure."

The therapy ended Wassner's infection, though "it was definitely a gigantic pain in the neck," he reports. Even so, he got off easier than some patients, whose infusion courses can last a year.

HOME PREGNANCY TESTING may be the simplest example of medical shadow work. In 1968, while working at the pharmaceutical company Organon in West Orange, New Jersey, Margaret Crane invented a test for human chorionic gonadotropin (hCG), a hormone that fertilized, implanted ova produce. Discovered in 1930, it is a marker for pregnancy. In the 1970s, Crane's patented test went on the market in Europe and the United States. Most modern home pregnancy tests check for hCG using a urine sample on a plastic stick. They are inexpensive and convenient, and women today nearly always use them before seeing a doctor.

Since egg implantation occurs six to twelve days after fertilization, and during that interval hCG has not yet been secreted, testing urine sooner than this can produce a false negative test result. A 1998 *Archives of Family Medicine* review of home test kits found home testing nearly as accurate (97.4 percent) as medical lab results when experienced technicians conducted the test—but the rate dropped to 75 percent when unassisted consumers tested themselves. The researchers suggested that consumers obtained false results because they either misunderstood test directions or failed to follow them. In other words, shadow work is still amateur work, and it doesn't necessarily mirror the results of professionals. (Similarly, in 2014 the Food and Drug Administration warned that consumers using blood-pressure kiosks may receive inaccurate readings, due to factors like variations in cuff size. Reliable readings also depend on adopting a seated posture with back supported, feet on the ground, legs uncrossed, and arm extended at heart level. Kiosk users may not sit this way consistently.)

In any case, home pregnancy tests remove the doctor's office and medical lab from the process. In days of yore, the pregnant woman was *not* the first to learn of her status; her doctor's office called with the joyous (or confounding) news. Now, only the woman herself needs know she is with child. This grants her more privacy and more control. It also transforms what can be a memorable shared event into a solitary encounter with a plastic stick. The epiphany occurs in a silo.

LESSONS FROM HEALTHCARE

First, shadow-working amateurs now infiltrate even highly trained professions like medicine. This shapes a new type of doctor–patient relationship that is more egalitarian, as it includes shared responsibility for medical decisions. (In the long run, this shift could diminish the number of malpractice lawsuits, as doctors shoulder less of the overall responsibility for treatment.)

Second, taking responsibility for treatment decisions engenders shadow work for patients. The newly empowered patients who want to negotiate with their doctors about whether to take statins for cholesterol tend to bone up on the topic by searching the Internet, especially sites like Wikipedia and WebMD. Doctors, too, consult Wikipedia, which to some extent gives them a base of information they share with their patients.

Third, Wikipedia and other online medical sources have now reached a fairly impressive level of sophistication in the data they provide. Yet all such sites suffer from inaccuracy and distortions introduced by commercial interests. The untrained medical patient is less equipped than the professional to separate valid information from canards. Furthermore, the lay user may be overly impressed by splashy presentations like YouTube videos, which physicians might more readily put in perspective.

Fourth, shadow-working patients now also perform a wide range of diagnostic and treatment procedures on themselves, outside any healthcare facility. These include even quite complex protocols like daily intravenous infusions. Various businesses have appeared to support such patients with professional help, usually with employees trained at the paramedic level rather than licensed doctors and nurses. The rational move is hiring people with *enough* training (but no more) to administer the prescribed medical intervention. Quite often, that level of training is none at all—and the people in question are shadow-working patients.

four: shadow work in restaurants, travel, and shopping

Each evening I found a pleasant auto court [motel] to rest in, beautiful new places that have sprung up in recent years. Now I began to experience a tendency in the West that perhaps I am too old to accept. It is the principle of do it yourself. At breakfast a toaster is on your table. You make your own toast. When I drew into one of these gems of comfort and convenience, registered, and was shown to my comfortable room after paying in advance, of course, that was the end of any contact with the management. There were no waiters, no bell boys. The chambermaids crept in and out invisibly. If I wanted ice, there was a machine near the office. I got my own ice, my own papers. Everything was convenient, centrally located, and lonesome.

—John Steinbeck, *Travels with Charlie*

T HE DRAMA CLUB at my high school in Dover, New Jersey, took an annual field trip to New York City. A few dozen of us would be bused in to see a matinee performance of a Broadway show like *How to Succeed in Business without Really Trying*.

Many of us had slight interest in theater, but the trip was a day off from school and a chance to taste the excitement of Manhattan, only forty miles away but a world apart from our small-town life.

We arrived early enough to have lunch before the show, and so on one of these trips I first ate at a Horn & Hardart Automat. Horn & Hardart was an old restaurant chain, founded in Philadelphia in 1888, which had branches all over New York City. Their Automats were unlike any restaurant I have seen before or since. There were no waiters, waitresses, or menus. Instead, the walls gleamed with chrome and glass: columns of boxes, each with its own door that displayed some item of food through a small glass window.

Inside the compartments you could see ham-and-cheese or tuna fish sandwiches on rye; bowls of green salad; bagels with cream cheese; cups of fresh fruit; slices of apple pie. Beside each was a coin slot. Cashiers ("nickel throwers") made change, dispensing the nickels needed for your purchase. You'd insert the requisite number of coins. You'd turn the chrome-plated knob with its porcelain center, and the little door unlocked, letting you slide out a small plate with your desired food. Once the door closed, a lazy Susan revolved, bringing a new sandwich or other item into view. Restaurant-as-vending-machine.

Delightful. The food was normal diner fare, but the prices were good and the Automat experience priceless. In the Automat *you*, the customer, directed the show. It was quite unlike being seated by a hostess, ordering from a menu, then having a waiter bring your meal. Instead, you picked your table and could choose exactly *which* slice of pie you wanted. You paid before you got the food and carried your own dish to the table. No server controlled your pace. There was less waiting, plus the added satisfaction of eliminating needless steps.

As Horn & Hardart customers, we were doing jobs that the staff did in other restaurants. We *were* the staff. I was my own hostess and my own waiter: taking my own order, retrieving my own food, and transporting it to the table I had chosen with my friends. With a handful of nickels, I was also the cashier, settling my own bill by inserting coins in the slot. No change needed to be made, and there was no tipping. Though I didn't know it at the time, I was performing shadow work.

THE KIOSK ARMY

Shadow work often comes into play when a technological innovation enables a business, like a restaurant, to remove one or more employees from transactions. It's a form of *disintermediation*, a long piece of business jargon that means removing an intermediary—taking out the middleman. Customers can deal directly with the technology instead of an employee. This produces payroll savings for the business, and shadow work for the consumer.

The Horn & Hardart Automats used mechanical technology to remove hostesses, waitresses, and cashiers from restaurant dining. Ingenious as they were, the Automats came into being long before the advent of computers and the information revolution. Today's digital technologies have opened a far wider range of opportunities for this kind of disintermediation, with a consequent explosion of shadow work. Venues and activities that provide some of our more enjoyable hours—restaurants, travel, and, for many, shopping—are evolving in ways that foster shadow work. Robotics are shaping the service industries, displacing human exchanges with kiosk touchscreens.

Indeed, an army of kiosks is marching out to take up stations across the country. And it's an army of occupation: once those kiosks settle in place, they aren't going anywhere. They occupy malls, street corners, airports, schools, medical centers, drugstores, supermarkets, banks, casinos, and turnpike rest areas. A few colorful examples suggest the diversity of jobs that kiosks are taking on:

- In 2008, three drugstores in Los Angeles installed machines that dispense medical marijuana. Qualified patients provide documentation and fingerprints to the dispensary, which issues a card to insert into the machines. After the 2012 elections in which Colorado and Washington legalized recreational marijuana, MedBox, a company that makes vending machines for medical applications, saw its stock price skyrocket from $4 to $125 per share in five days. In 2014 the first age- and identity-verifying marijuana vending machine appeared in Eagle-Vail, Colorado. It uses radio-frequency identification technology to check customers' driver's licenses.

- The Australian government announced in 2012 that it would install kiosks with face-recognition technology to process ePassports of Australians returning from abroad. The kiosks perform customs and immigration checks that airport customs staff previously handled, allowing the government to reduce staffing and purportedly save $11.9 million over four years. The Dallas–Fort Worth International Airport claims that deployment of kiosks for customs clearance has shortened wait times by 40 percent, as 70 percent of its international travelers go through automatically, waiting an average of less than fourteen minutes.

- PaleoExpress, a California-based company, rolled out its paleo diet vending machines in 2014. They offer grass-fed meats, organic, grain-free, nut-based granolas and bars; sweet potato and apple purées; and recovery drinks. Meanwhile, in Hollywood, tourists can pay up to $1,000 for a tin of caviar dispensed by a kiosk.

- The IntoxBox, "the world's first smart blood alcohol testing kiosk for bars," appeared at a Las Vegas trade show in 2012. It guides users through a Breathalyzer test and at the end offers the option of calling a taxi by touching a screen icon. The IntoxBox challenges users to guess their blood alcohol content; a correct answer leads to a text that allows a free future test.

- A new Pepsi machine's videogame-like screen has an animated avatar that, in a series of skill challenges, mimics the customer's soccer moves before dispensing the soft drink. Pepsi timed its release for the 2014 World Cup.

- The Portuguese postal service opened a never-closing post office in Lisbon in 2012. Staffed entirely by kiosks, the twenty-four-hour facility offers virtually all the services that previously required a visit to the counter and a postal worker.

- In Manhattan, Stack's Rare Coins opened a gold-dispensing ATM kiosk that sells gold bars and silver coins, with prices updated every sixty seconds.

- In 2011, Bonn, Germany, required street prostitutes to pay a nightly tax at kiosks by feeding €6 to the machines. They then receive tickets entitling them to work the streets from 8:15 PM until 6 AM. "This is an act of tax fairness," said Monika Frombgen, a spokeswoman for the Bonn city council. "Prostitutes in fixed establishments such as brothels and sauna clubs already pay tax."

- The town of Gothenburg, Nebraska, where 3,600 people reside, approved a $10,000 appropriation in 2012 to install a touchscreen information kiosk at the local cemetery that will print out maps of graveside locations. Families of decedents can post pictures or obituaries on the kiosk for a fee, generating revenue for the town.

Clearly, kiosks have entered the social landscape and now stand in for people in a wide variety of venues. Let's explore some of the ways the kiosk army generates shadow work for the humans it serves.

RESTAURANTS MINUS SERVICE

Restaurant dining was once a highly social occasion. It might begin with a warm welcome from the hostess, who seated you and your companions. Then a waitress would come by, make some friendly chitchat, and take your order, even if you were sitting at a diner counter. The server would deliver your drinks, carry your food out from the kitchen, ask "Is everything OK?" and make needed adjustments, and finally bring the check. You'd have exchanges with her at every stage of the meal. A busboy cleared away the dishes afterward.

Upscale fine-dining restaurants still do things this way, with staff guiding their customers all the way through the experience. But fine-dining establishments account for only about 10 percent of restaurant sales. In recent decades, fast food (McDonald's, Taco Bell), fast casual (Panera Bread, Chipotle Mexican Grill), and casual dining (Olive Garden, Applebee's, or Harvester in the United Kingdom) have come to dominate the industry. As you move downscale, with fine dining at the top and fast food (in industry lingo, quick-service restaurants, or QSRs) at the bottom, the dining experience gets progressively streamlined.

Customers not only pay less at QSRs but eat their food and guzzle their beverages in less time. Fewer staff serve them—and shadow work by customers expands. Since downscale eateries control so much of the market, there's been an overall upsurge in shadow work for those who eat meals out. In addition, diners now tend to eat in a silo—that is, with minimal or no contact with staff. Restaurants are pruning back food service toward an endpoint where there will be nothing but customers and machines: taking meals inside a giant vending machine with tables.

Casual- and fine-dining restaurants still offer hostesses and table service, but in less-expensive places, customers look for an empty table and seat themselves. Fast-food and fast-casual eateries employ no waitstaff; transporting food becomes a diner's shadow job. The ultimate version of minimal service is the drive-through with its squawk box: The customer never even enters the building. (The SunSet & Hill Café on the South Korean island of Jeju offers an extreme form of minimalism. Customers brew their own coffee or tea, make their own snacks, wash their utensils, and, on the honor system, leave money to settle the bill. Beverage prices are only about two to three U.S. dollars.)

In QSRs, customers step up and order from counter help; in fast casual, they generally walk down a cafeteria-style line, ordering from servers, who fill their requests directly. The kitchen only replenishes the serving line. Beverages mean shadow work: The cashier simply provides a paper cup, and the customer fills it with ice and a drink. (The new Coke Freestyle and Pepsi Spire touchscreen dispensers even give customers the job of creating the soda; such kiosks let them mix carbonated water and flavor shots to produce up to 1,000 different soft drinks. Similarly, SodaStream mixer/dispensers bring the soda-manufacturing process home, giving consumers the job of making their own soft drinks in their own kitchens.)

Fast-casual customers carry their own food to the table, having paid the cashier *before*, not after, the meal. The bakery/café chain Panera Bread, and many other eateries, hands the customer a vibrating and flashing "electronic table locator" that either helps waitstaff identify whom to serve or summons the shadow-working diner to retrieve her order and schlep it back to the table.

In fine-dining establishments, waiters bring plated salads to the table. A few decades ago, this was the norm everywhere. Salad bars changed that norm, inventing another species of shadow work. Some accounts trace the origin of salad bars to as early as 1950. *Merriam-Webster's Collegiate Dictionary* dates the term to 1973. In any case, by the 1970s, many casual-dining restaurants offered salad bars, and still do, as a complement to their table service. (They have also sprung up in supermarket chains like Whole Foods.)

Salad bars delegate the task of making salads to customers, who take over that job from kitchen staff, who do only the prep work. This gives diners more to do but also lets them select ingredients and add dressing exactly as they prefer. (Similarly, coffee drinkers sweeten and cream their coffee at side stations rather than having employees guess at their preferred ratios.) "Sure, I'm making the salad, but they're doing the hard part—the prep work," says Andrea, a nurse in Portland, Maine. "Plus, I don't like raw onions, broccoli, or carrots, so I just leave those out. And I don't have to ask for dressing on the side to keep them from drowning it."

Fast-food restaurants also turn their customers into busboys. You may recall those entry-level employees who clear restaurant tables of dishes, cups, glassware, napkins, trays, and utensils, along with uneaten food and unquaffed drinks. Yes, busboys and busgirls still do this at fine-dining restaurants, where diners eat from china plates with real silverware and drink from glasses made of, well, glass. The restaurant *owns* all these table settings—the diner only borrows them for a meal. The house washes and reuses them over and over.

Contrast this with the scene at Wendy's, Starbucks, or Dunkin' Donuts, where customers drink from paper or Styrofoam cups and eat from paper plates with plastic utensils. At McDonald's, there won't even be a paper plate, just an onionskin wrapper festooned with McDonald's logos enfolding your burger. (The avalanche of fast-food debris is, of course, an environmental disaster that channels enormous tonnage of waste into landfills.) When the QSR provides these disposables, it hands over their ownership to *you*. Whether you know it or not, you just *bought* them along with your meal. Hence, disposing of these things becomes your job, not that of the busboy—if there is one.

After you slurp the last of your iced caramel macchiato at Starbucks, don't neglect the shadow work of clearing the table. Leave your detritus behind and fellow diners might view you as a lazy litterbug. Norms have changed enough to make busboy work routine for QSR customers, and disposable tableware underlies this shift. The table-busing ethic has even spilled over to eateries that use plates and bowls made of melamine, and sometimes even china.

THE KIOSK ARMY is marching into restaurants. For years, customers at chain eateries have seen waitstaff enter their food orders on computer touchscreens that send the information to the kitchen. Now comes the self-order kiosk, which eliminates the waitress from the equation entirely by turning the touchscreen over to a shadow-working diner. In a poll by the National Restaurant Association, chefs ranked computerized menus as the top tech trend of 2014. And in 2011, McDonald's announced that it would replace human cashiers with touchscreens at more than 7,000 European venues.

It works this way: a fast-food outlet installs a few freestanding kiosks in *front* of the counter. They display menus and let customers enter their choices on a touchscreen. One cashier might move out from behind the counter to "host" the kiosks, tutoring diners in the new technology, much the way a Safeway cashier can oversee a few self-serve checkouts in a supermarket. In drive-through locations, touchscreens may also displace the scratchy dialog of the squawk box. One marketing survey determined that 63 percent of QSR customers were willing to use a kiosk to order and pay for food, and 96 percent of younger (eighteen- to thirty-four-year-old) customers view a kiosk in a restaurant as a benefit.

Kiosks also help downsize the payroll, producing a 20 to 25 percent drop in the number of waitstaff needed to run a restaurant. They offer fast, accurate ordering and can provide audible talking menus for the visually impaired or bilingual ones for Spanish speakers. Some have animated displays, making the meal-ordering process a form of cartoon viewing, with its corresponding air of unreality. (Avoiding reality might even help increase check size by 15 to 25 percent, as kiosk vendors claim.)

Like other forms of shadow work, taking over the waiter's job gives customers greater control, and many welcome this. Kiosk ordering can shorten wait times by reducing menu options at peak hours to funnel diners into fewer choices, just as movie theaters minimize options for food and drink. "We're in a fast, fast, fast, me, me, me, now, now, now world," says Don Turner, CEO of kiosk supplier ProTech Solutions, "and to be successful, the self-service industry has to feed and ride that trend." Speed now rules eating. *Fast, fast, me, me, now, now* mean less human contact. He dines fastest who dines in a silo.

Ronald Shaich, CEO of Panera Bread, stopped by one of the chain's outlets to pick up school lunches for his children, which he had ordered ahead. "It suddenly occurred to me that this was a wonderful system for the CEO, but what about the other eight million people who order from Panera?" he told *The New York Times* in 2014. "Everyone else got in line to get to the register, then got in another line where they had to play a game called Go Find Your Food. For drinks, they had to go to another line, and if they wanted any kind of espresso drink, we sent them to a fourth line." All this shuttling of customers among lines and waiting to pick up one's food order could have been Shaich's summary of the shadow work his customers were logging. He decided to invest $42 million to streamline Panera. "The goal is to eliminate friction points," he explained, "so that customers have a better experience."

UPMARKET ICE-CREAM PARLORS have been selling super-premium ice creams and frozen yogurts to the public for years. Local companies like SoCo Creamery in Great Barrington, Massachusetts, employ youthful employees to dish out a couple dozen flavors. They stack scoopfuls onto cones and sprinkle on custom toppings like Heath Bar pieces. They'll gladly hand you a sample of an unfamiliar flavor like Chai Spice, Earl Grey Supreme, or Lavender Honey on a taster spoon.

Robots are closing in on these young people's jobs. Automated frozen yogurt parlors get shadow-working customers to perform most of these tasks for themselves. In the New Jersey shore town of Avalon, for example, Toppings of Avalon offers "self surf" non-fat frozen yogurt. Nozzles embedded in a wall offer six flavors of frogurt, which customers dispense themselves into plastic dishes. (Dishes only—no cones, please, as the price is pegged to weight.) The consumer may add one or more of twenty toppings offered at the counter. A cashier weighs the dish and charges by the ounce; she is the only employee on duty. No free tastes, though that hardly matters as the six nozzles offer only mainstream flavors. Toppings of Avalon provides the product; the customer provides the service. (In Chicago, U-Vend has installed six ice-cream-selling kiosks that even eliminate the cashier, with forty more planned for 2015.)

Banter with bartenders provides much of the fun in taverns, but they, too, face competition from robots. A new self-serve beverage system called IPourIt turns customers into bartenders: They dispense their own beer, wine, or other drinks from taps and pay, as with frogurt, by the ounce. After checking in with a state-issued ID, a customer receives a radio-frequency-encoded wristband that records the volume of any drink she drafts from a line of taps on the wall. The system lets the bar set controls on consumption based on the customer's height and weight, as well as the alcohol content of beverages.

Billing by the ounce encourages IPourIt drinkers to sample craft beers before tapping a larger serving, and with no need for a bartender it can speed up service at busy venues like casinos, cruise ships, and stadiums. At the 2014 Major League Baseball All-Star Game in Minneapolis, DraftServ sold time-limited cards to those with appropriate IDs that let fans draft their own beer and pay by the ounce. One astonishing beverage industry statistic says that bars lose 27 percent of every keg due to rushed bartenders overpouring the foam. With shadow-working drinkers, that loss goes onto the customer's tab instead of the bar's.

For take-out food like pizza, online ordering can eliminate human dialog; customers order from a menu on their computer screen and then either accept delivery (90 percent of orders) or pick up the pizza themselves. In the 1995 cyber-thriller *The Net,* Sandra Bullock plays a computer jock who orders a pizza online, the first instance of cyber-chowing on film.

The high-tech industry naturally led the way in Internet food gathering. In 1994, a Pizza Hut franchise in Santa Cruz, California, tested the possibility, and nearby Silicon Valley got it established as techies ordered their pizzas delivered for dinner without budging from their screens. (In Sydney, Australia, Pompei's Pizza has rolled out a Pizza Gio kiosk at a shopping center. It cooks an eleven-inch pizza in three minutes, and its touchscreen accepts cashless payments. Pizza Gio holds eighty-four refrigerated pizzas that are about halfway cooked. The customer completes the baking process.)

With web ordering, "I can do it at my own pace, and stare at the menu as long as I like," says Melanie, a marketing specialist in

St. Paul, Minnesota. "And I never get put on hold." Furthermore, seeing the entire menu on a web page seems to increase orders by as much as 40 percent, as hungry customers add on salads, drinks, and side dishes. The web page can prompt regulars with a reminder of their most recent order, further accelerating the process, as most of us habitually order the same thing time and again. And online transactions result in fewer "abandoned orders" for the pizzeria.

GrubHub, "an online and mobile food ordering company," connects customers with take-out restaurants in more than 800 U.S. cities and London via the Internet. Its slogan could hardly be more bluntly antisocial: "Everything great about eating combined with everything great about not talking to people."

FAST-CASUAL AND CASUAL-DINING chains like Chili's, California Pizza Kitchen, and Legal Sea Foods have begun installing tabletop devices resembling iPads that allow diners to order from their seats via touchscreens and then receive delivery of food at their tables. Touchscreen ordering is ascending the restaurant hierarchy, penetrating sectors well beyond fast food. It remains unacceptable in fine dining, where customers insist on the "luxury" of service by a human being. Tablet ordering has long been available in Europe; the United States is running several years behind in adopting this technology.

Shadow-working diners who order from menu tablets need not wait for a waiter, as there is none. The tablets can display a running total during ordering and offer a tip guide—though customers doing the waiter's job might be tempted to tip themselves.

Restaurateurs can add revenue by selling advertising space on the tablets. Customers pay at the table with a credit or debit card, eliminating the wait to get a check and process it; this expedites business lunches, say, that need to wrap up within an hour. "I like it that the credit card never leaves my hands," says Allen, an actuary in Dallas who has used the tablet system. "That feels safer, because you never know what is happening to your account number when you hand your card to a stranger." For retailers, faster service can mean quicker turnover of tables and consequently increased volume at peak hours. It's a marvelously efficient model.

The only thing missing is humanity.

SERVANTS, TIPPING, AND WAITING

In the United States, we feel a profound ambivalence about receiving personal service. In this respect, America differs from the Old World, where monarchs ruled for centuries. Europeans are accustomed to royalty, nobility, and aristocracies, settled in their palaces and great mansions with domestic servants. Indeed, hereditary monarchs still sit on thrones in Britain, Spain, Luxembourg, Belgium, the Netherlands, Norway, and Sweden. Europe has long lived with an entrenched class structure that included a servant class waiting on their "betters." Consequently, Old World cultures feel a degree of comfort with personal service.

But it provokes unease in the United States, where the Declaration of Independence famously announced that "all men are created equal," royalty and hereditary aristocracies are illegal, and social mobility is the ideal, if not necessarily the reality. Receiving care from servants clashes with our national ideal of equality. The cognitive dissonance might also reflect our collective memory of America's history of slavery in the South and indentured servitude. (Landowners in the colonies would pay the transatlantic passage of immigrants from Europe in exchange for a period of unpaid labor, during which the indentured servant worked off his or her debt. In the seventeenth and eighteenth centuries, more than half of immigrants to America worked an average of three years of indentured servitude.) Throughout the nineteenth century, new immigrants and even the next generation often took on domestic duties in other people's households, often in some kind of barter arrangement between families. There was simply too much housework for families to handle without outside help.

We resolve our guilt by *tipping* employees—waiters, hotel maids, barbers, taxi drivers—who provide the personal comforts that domestic servants like cooks, butlers, maids, and chauffeurs once gave in private homes. Such services often involve care of the body—eating, sleeping, grooming. In a restaurant, by giving cash to the waitress directly, rather than via the owner, the customer can assuage some of the guilt for having received personal service from a stranger. Though they aren't domestic servants, many such employees earn less than minimum wages, with the expectation that tips will compensate for the shortfall. Tipping has bloomed as a form of shadow work in which consumers take over a core task of employers: paying the staff.

European countries, too, now enjoy long histories of democracy and may share, to a lesser degree, Americans' ambivalence about personal service. But tipping on the Continent is neither as automatic nor as generous as in the States. It can be involuntary (the 15 percent "service charge" added to a French restaurant check) or minimal (5 or 10 percent, and often 0 percent) when compared with American norms. In the United States, 15 or 20 percent tips have become routine, and Americans grant them for a far wider range of services—valet parking, for example—than do residents of Europe, where waitstaff are also better paid. The European style of adding a service charge to the check depersonalizes tipping, as it removes the decision about the size and even the fact of the tip from the customer's hands. It becomes a straight business transaction, with guilt factored out.

Tipping seems to be growing in America, perhaps in response to the stagnation of wages. In recent years, tip containers have sprouted beside cash registers at places like donut shops and convenience stores. They're attempting to pioneer a new norm: tip the cashier for taking your money.

Tipping and personal service relate directly to social status, which in turn correlates with waiting. Who waits for (or on) whom? The answer is simple: Those of *lower* status wait for those of *higher* status. Royalty and movie stars may arrive as late as they please—we will wait for them. Patients wait for doctors, who relieve suffering just by appearing. Litigants wait for judges. Waitresses pace their work to their customers' eating rhythms—they *wait on* tables. We devalue those who wait; that hard-charging Type A overachiever is "a man who will not be kept waiting."

In this sense, shadow work can temporarily demolish distinctions of social class. When the customer provides the service, that edits the "servant" out of the scene. At the filling station, a wealthier driver might pay a few cents more per gallon to get "full serve" attention from a live person. Yet a nearby shadow-working customer who pays the lower self-serve rate and pumps his own gas may wind up with a shorter wait by filling up and paying the bill at his own pace, not that of the pump jockey. Less waiting usually means higher status. Shadow workers can level status distinctions—for a few minutes, anyway—by minimizing waits.

ROBOTIC TRAVEL

Contemporary travel, whether for business or vacation, involves robotic transactions. Kiosks and shadow work now replace many of the people who formerly worked in the travel and hospitality industries. When journeying, people naturally use services they don't need at home (transportation, lodging, restaurant meals, and tourist attractions, for example), and kiosks help dispense them. Before long, it may be possible to wend one's way through an airport without a single human interaction.

The shadow work begins well before arriving at the train station or airport. Airline travelers can check in on their mobile devices or home computers and print out boarding passes on their printers. This shifts the printing process from the airline to the shadow-working traveler. On arrival at the airport, you show the boarding pass not to a human agent but to a member of the kiosk army. Seventy-seven percent of global travelers now check in for flights at kiosks. Airline ticket agents, who once handled the entire check-in process and even sold flight tickets, may now do little more than check in baggage—and even that is disappearing. In 2012, Alaska Airlines enabled customers to print out their own luggage tags from a kiosk and attach them to their bags, which they could then drop off with an airline staffer for security screening and loading. In 2014, Finnair in Helsinki, United Airlines in Boston, and China's Tianjin Airport installed baggage kiosks; 90 percent of European airports either have or plan to deploy bag-tag kiosks by 2016.

Yet turning shadow-working travelers into baggage handlers doesn't always end well. At the Schiphol Airport in Amsterdam, KLM Airlines installed a self-service kiosk for luggage check-in. Freke Vuijst, a Dutch American journalist, was about to fly home to the United States when she first encountered this new species of shadow work. The KLM kiosks were asking passengers not only to print their own luggage tags but to weigh the bag, affix the baggage tag, and hoist the luggage onto a conveyor belt that would take it to security screening and then the tarmac. Unfortunately, this new task befuddled many passengers, resulting in a long, very slow-moving line of fuming travelers. Vuijst had a bright idea: She left the kiosk line and walked a few feet to an unoccupied KLM agent, who gladly checked her luggage with a smile. Vuijst suspected that her suitcase might have been slightly above the free weight limit, but the agent waived any overage charges. "She used her human discretion," Vuijst says. "The kiosk would simply have automatically charged me for excess weight. I was relieved that KLM had not done away with human beings altogether."

Hotel arrival is a far cry from the days of the innkeeper who welcomed you with a handshake and a key to your room. Robots from the kiosk army may instead greet you. For years now, chains like Hilton, Hyatt, and Sheraton have installed check-in kiosks at some locations. Customers with reservations can select or change a room, request upgrades, encode their room-key cards, and eventually check out of the hotel with the robot for company. Kiosks also offer concierge functions like directions and wayfinding. Aloft Hotels has replaced concierge stations with tablets. None of these things necessarily means shadow work for the traveler, but they do remove contact with staff from the hotel experience. In this respect, they resemble the radio-frequency transponders on windshields that speed motorists through "fast lanes" on toll highways: Payment gets easier and faster by deleting those time-consuming exchanges with error-prone humanity.

Throughout Europe, you can find railway stations that are 100 percent automated, lacking any human staff to assist travelers or answer questions. Such places abandon travelers to the kiosk army. In the Netherlands, outside of major cities, you cannot buy a train ticket from a human being at the station. And your Visa card won't work: The machines accept only Dutch debit cards or euro coins. In Holland's big cities, if you buy from a human agent, the national NS train company imposes a .50-eurocent surcharge per ticket. (In Dutch, this fee is called *ontmoedigingsbeleid*, "policy to discourage." What's discouraged is human contact.)

For tourists, automated train stations extinguish some of the serendipitous pleasures of travel. "I used to enjoy trying out my French on a friendly railroad agent," says Laurette, a mother and personal trainer in Brookline, Massachusetts. "They are getting harder to find." More importantly, robotics can shut out the elderly and others who lack the physical or cognitive skills to deal with kiosks. These unfortunates will probably have to ask another customer for help—which does start a live conversation, meanwhile spinning off some shadow work for the fellow traveler as she takes over the job of the missing railway employee.

Robotic check-in and checkout also shrink the jobs of rental-car agents. Shadow work comes clearly into play with Zipcar, the worldwide car-sharing company that parks its autos in designated spaces in cities, neighborhoods, and airports. For a monthly fee, members can rent cars by the hour or day. A membership card unlocks the vehicle, and after use, the driver returns it to the same parking space. It's an economical alternative to auto ownership. Part of its efficiency, relative to a car rental company like Hertz, is that Zipcar has no staff on-site. Shadow-working Zipcar customers and digital technology perform the tasks that rental agents do elsewhere.

Something similar takes place with Uber, a company that has been competing successfully with the taxi industry since 2009 and now operates internationally in more than 200 cities. Uber eliminates taxi dispatchers and garages by connecting ride-seeking customers directly with drivers via an app. It's a type of disintermediation that makes consumers their own taxi dispatchers.

U-BOOK-IT JOURNEYS

In America, as rugged individualists, we shop ruggedly on our own, without assistants. We need no agent to help us buy bananas at the supermarket, tennis rackets at the sporting goods store, or tree-pruning services from a landscaper. New cars, with their complicated warrantees, financing agreements, or lease provisions, may be the largest purchase most of us make on our own. Beyond that, transactions become costly and complex enough to make an agent advisable. Real estate is a familiar example. Paying a 5 percent Realtor's commission seems to many a worthwhile investment when buying or selling a house.

Travel is an anomaly. Though travel expenses can be high, most trips cost only a couple thousand dollars, or even a few hundred. Yet historically, many travelers have used agents to buy their airline tickets, reserve hotel rooms, rent cars, and book tours. The intricacies of the transactions argue for the agent's expertise. Airlines, for example, price their tickets in an unfathomable way that even travel agents have not quite figured out. As a traveler, it's reassuring to have agents at least do the navigating. The agent can protect you from being mugged on the airfare.

For much of the twentieth century, travel agencies prospered as the world population grew, transportation (especially by air) improved dramatically, and global tourism mushroomed. Yet throughout their history, travel agencies have depended on relationships with transportation and tourism businesses, making them vulnerable to disintermediation by both their suppliers and their clients. In the 1990s, the Internet began to undermine travel agents' informational niche. Since then, travel agencies have been disappearing. Several factors are in play, including the rise of travelers' shadow work.

THE ROOTS OF travel agencies were, in a way, spiritual. In 1841, Thomas Cook (1808–92), a former Baptist minister in England, organized an eleven-mile railroad trip to take 540 people to a temperance meeting. They paid one shilling apiece (lunch included) and became the first customers of a travel agent, though Cook's motives at the time were for doing good rather than making money. Soon he started booking pleasure excursions, raking in a percentage of the rail ticket fees, and had a breakthrough when (as he claimed, anyway) he brought 165,000 visitors to the Great Exhibition of 1851 in London. Cook branched out into international travel; by 1888, Thomas Cook & Son had offices worldwide, including three in Australia. In 1919, Cook pioneered pleasure trips by air and in 1927 ran the first group air tour, a New York-to-Chicago trip to see the Jack Dempsey–Gene Tunney heavyweight title fight. The Thomas Cook Group remains one of the word's biggest travel agencies.

In 1850, American Express started in New York as a delivery business (hence the name) that took freight and parcels to the West. AmEx introduced travelers' checks in 1891 and entered the travel agency business in 1915, eventually becoming the world's largest travel retailer. Another large American agency, Ask Mr. Foster Travel, was born in St. Augustine, Florida, in 1888; it evolved into Carson Wagonlit Travel, the second-largest American agency after AmEx. Early agencies also included many "Mabel at the table" operations. These tour operators included empty-nest mothers with enough time to run an interesting and profitable small business that allowed them to see the world.

Travel agencies made money on commissions from airlines, steamship companies, and railroads, as well as hotel and auto rental commissions. Their commissions ranged from 5 to 10 percent, and the agents often had little identity apart from the transportation and hospitality companies they represented. They were essentially an outsourced sales staff.

Air travel boomed after World War II, and by 1950 travel agents handled 70 percent of overseas air reservations. Jet aircraft boosted passenger volume, which ran into the millions. Agents advised customers on passport and visa requirements, currency exchange rates, shopping, sightseeing, weather, and recreation. In 1978, airline deregulation stimulated another surge in business, as airlines and airfares suddenly proliferated to both woo and confuse travelers. Corporate travel expanded, fueling growth.

The first global distribution systems (GDS) appeared in 1976. Travel agents use these automated systems to arrange air travel, lodgings, and auto rentals. A GDS does not own an inventory of reservations but gives agents a real-time link to vendors' databases and so enables them, say, to instantly reserve a seat on any participating airline via direct access to its computer reservation system. (Four national airlines survive in the United States: American, United, Delta, and Jet Blue, with smaller brethren like Southwest.) Currently, the main GDS firms are Travelport, Amadeus, and Sabre.

In the go-go period of the 1980s, travel agencies flourished. The number of agencies in the United States more than doubled between 1977 and 1985, to 27,000. Customers regarded their agents as experts who could call up specialized information unavailable to the public. And indeed they were. Using a GDS, agents booked trips that minimized clients' costs or travel time and could map out complex itineraries that might have overwhelmed the uninformed traveler. Tickets that agencies wrote came to represent about 75 percent of airline revenues.

Of course, airlines would happily sell tickets directly to passengers, but they did not offer ancillary services or advice. And naturally, they would never do comparison-shopping on their competitors' rates. Buying a ticket directly from an airline was a no-frills transaction, and you just had to hope you were getting a good price. The ticket itself then held a kind of special status as a document. "There was a paper ticket printed on official stock," says Carol Pine, a travel agent at The Travel Collaborative in Cambridge, Massachusetts. "There was so much ritual and ceremony in having your ticket with you. You had something substantial."

In 1995, the party ended when airlines imposed commission caps on agents. Instead of paying agents a straight percentage commission, the carriers capped their fees at $50 for domestic tickets and $100 for international ones. Later they cut these further to $25 and $50, and then ended commissions entirely. What had happened was that by the mid 1990s, the Internet had attained a significant public presence and the airlines "felt they could sell their product directly to customers via the Internet," says Thom

Mulhern, another agent at The Travel Collaborative. "We were shocked when Al Italia ran an ad that did not have 'call your travel agent' at the bottom. We thought it was Armageddon." With airline revenue drying up, agencies tried imposing ticket surcharges on consumers. But clients who had never paid extra charges for their tickets resisted. "Why should I suddenly have to pay a fee for your expertise?" they asked.

The Internet spawned travel websites like Expedia, Orbitz, and Kayak.com. Customers could visit these sites, plug in their travel destination and dates, and comparison-shop for fares. They could see an array of available carriers, itineraries, and prices. With lodging sites like hotels.com they could do the same for accommodations. Customers thought this was the same information their travel agents had (although it was not, as agents use GDS services). In 2012, a study by eMarketer found that thirty-six million people researched their travel options on a mobile device and sixteen million booked reservations with one. That September, Hertz announced an app that lets users search for, book, and modify car rental reservations on a handheld device.

The ascent of Internet travel sites had two results: the democratization of the exclusive expertise that once gave travel agents their credibility, and an ocean of shadow work for travelers. It was a clear case of disintermediation: In a pincer movement, airlines and websites squeezed travel agents out of the transaction. The number of travel agencies in the United States shrank from 33,715 in 1996 to less than half that number, 15,564, in 2010 (in part due to mergers). Even by 1997, agencies' share of domestic airline business had plummeted to 52 percent. Shadow-working customers had appointed themselves their own travel agents.

Nonetheless, the outcome for the traveler is not always as rosy as she believes. "You see ads for Orbitz or Kayak, and you'd think you are getting the best information available," says Mulhern. "Well, they've done an admirable job of marketing themselves." Professional agents, he explains, never consult Orbitz or Kayak. "It's not a point-and-click task," he says. "The consumer is actually in an information-scarce environment." With a GDS facility, "I can see the inventory, the time frame, and have a good idea of what flights are more expensive," he says. "We can see how many seats are left in a given 'bucket' [price point]."

Though airfare pricing is irrational, the law of supply and demand generally applies; Carol Pine says that when a flight has many unsold seats, fares will drop. "Expedia and Orbitz are showing you what they want you to see," she adds. "I can pull up a display of Boston-to-Chicago flights and advise my client that if he flies out forty-five minutes earlier and comes back thirty minutes later, he can save $125." Or an agent might advise a client that the difference between the rental rates for an intermediate and a full-size car is only $1.

International flights magnify the advantages of a travel agent's knowledge. Sometimes clients who have already booked their overseas travel consult Pine, who asks questions like, "Do you realize you have an eighteen-hour layover here?" Even when customers engage with a travel website, they "don't always take in everything on the display," she explains. They might miss anomalies like cases when two one-way tickets are cheaper than a round-trip. "You wouldn't find that on Kayak," she observes.

Furthermore, when plans get derailed, an experienced agent can come in handy. "In Chicago, it's snowing, your flight has been canceled, and there are fifty-two people standing in line ahead of you to see the customer service agent," Mulhern says. "That's when you call your travel agent and say, 'Get me on the next flight to Miami so I can be on my way to Rio'—and it's done in twenty seconds. *That* is fun."

SHOPPING: THE HUNT FOR A HUMAN

Retail merchandising and its handmaiden, customer service, are witnessing the extinction of human workers. In this age of big-box stores, try going into a Wal-Mart, Target, or Staples and finding someone to help you purchase, say, a printer. Good luck. You're on your own, left to wander the aisles in search of an unoccupied staff person. Tracking down sales staff in a big-box store is like trekking the wilds of the Yukon Territory looking for a human settlement. Furthermore, should you be lucky enough to find someone, he or she will likely know next to nothing about the merchandise. "Without doubt, the most annoying aspect of shopping is the dumbing-down of the retail workforce," says Edward, a media-company executive in Washington, D.C. "They don't even try to learn a few things about their inventory to appear at least vaguely knowledgeable."

In retail, there was once a job called floorwalker. Floorwalkers flourished during the heyday of department stores, through the middle of the twentieth century. Typically, the floorwalker was a man in a suit and tie who, as the title suggests, walked the floor of a retail establishment. They roamed freely, supervising sales staff and helping customers find what they wanted. Floorwalkers thrived in a bygone era when retailers hired people to help their customers shop, not only to take their money.

In today's big-box store, the customer has become the floorwalker, minus the supervisory role and the paycheck. This means shadow work. Consumers must educate themselves about the product, including its features, limitations, requirements, competitive advantages and disadvantages, and warrantees. Some do this via online research at home. But a large number (84 percent) of mobile shoppers accomplish it on smartphones right in the store. A 2012 survey of 1,507 smartphone owners by the Google Shopper Council determined that one-third would rather consult their phones than ask a store employee for information. The biggest task for smartphones in stores was finding information about products, which 82 percent of respondents cited.

Fifty-three percent of subjects used phones to check prices at competing vendors, a practice known as showrooming. Smartphone-wielding shoppers treat the bricks-and-mortar store like a showroom that displays items for sale. Then they check competitive prices on their handhelds and if they see a lower one, they order online, leaving the physical store empty-handed. A 2013 survey of 750 consumers in the United States found that nearly three-quarters of respondents had showroomed in the prior six months. Yet once they are inside the store, the easiest choice is to purchase it there. Smartphones expand the retail playing field. "Winning the key decision moments at the physical shelves," said Adam Grunewald of Google, "means owning the digital shelves, too."

While the paucity of sales staff minimizes service for customers, it also prolongs the time they spend meandering around the vast emporium. "Whenever I go to Staples, I know I'm going to come out with two or three things I hadn't planned on buying," says Brent, a psychotherapist in Northampton, Massachusetts. "You are drifting around the aisles trying to find something and you notice stuff. Last time it was a box of erasable pens—great for crosswords. And a package of blank DVDs." Some supermarkets seem to constantly change the shelving locations of items, making customers wander the aisles trying to track down their quarry, and so prolonging their time in the store.

CLASSICALLY, RETAIL MEANT a three-stage flow of products, from manufacturer to wholesaler to retailer. In the 1980s, huge "club stores" such as Costco, Sam's Club (owned by Wal-Mart), and BJ's chopped one step out of this chain by selling in a warehouse environment at prices deeply discounted from retail. To join the club, customers pay an annual fee, typically around $50, which allows them to buy merchandise, often in large, almost wholesale-level quantities. (Those with small cars need not apply.) These are no-frills outlets, stripped of niceties like convenient supermarket shelves, unusual products, music, free samples, or sales staff. Forklifts, not teenagers, stock the aisles.

The secret of warehouse clubs is, again, disintermediation. Removing the retailer (who traditionally sells for twice the wholesale price, that is, "keystoning") lets the club slash its prices. The lack of amenities keeps overhead low. Warehouse stores are one answer to online merchants, whose minimal overhead helps prune prices.

For customers, warehouse clubs mean bargains and shadow work. Other than shopping carts and cashiers, the warehouse offers no help. Bring your own bags, please. The largest piece of shadow work, however, comes when the customer pulls into the driveway with his outsize purchases. He must find the space to store twelve-roll packages of paper towels and restaurant-sized containers of ketchup, plum tomatoes, and pickles. The customer's home, in other words, becomes the aftermarket warehouse. Instead of leasing space somewhere to stock inventory, Costco stores it, free of charge, in the customer's basement, *after* the sale instead of before it.

HUNTING DOWN A human for customer service takes us back to the Yukon Territory. If you have any problem with your purchase, you will be flying solo. For online vendors like Amazon or eBay, clicking their Help or Contact Us buttons (if you can find them) will not pull up a telephone number. Such websites are designed to keep customers at a distance rather than to connect with them. Email has become the preferred corporate mode of dealing with consumers.

Should you somehow find a telephone number, calling it typically entails punching your way through a sequence of menus, entering data like your account number, and answering multiple-choice questions. Next comes a lengthy wait on hold, as Muzak plays or recorded advertisements repeat in cycles. "When I finally get a representative," says Gwendolyn, a golf-shop salesperson in California, "she always asks for my account number. The same one I punched in at the start of the call."

This is all shadow work, and a far cry from the predigital era. "The way it used to be, you'd ring the number up and a person would pick it up and ask you, 'What can we do for you?'" Dorothy Meyer, an eighty-two-year-old resident of Escondido, California, told *The New York Times* in 2004 for a piece on customer service. Writer Katie Hafner said that Meyer voiced this recollection "as if describing life on Mars."

For a few years now, I have used a credit card from Chase Sapphire. I especially like their customer service. When I have a question, I phone a readily accessible number and quickly reach a live human being who speaks intelligible English. This is so rare that I feel like I have joined the aristocracy.

"Live chat" is often the best one can do for online customer service. This means a real-time typed interchange with an allegedly live customer-service representative. I say "allegedly" because live chats inevitably call to mind the Turing test, a test of a computer's ability to "think" that British mathematician and computer scientist Alan Turing outlined in a 1950 paper.

The common understanding of the Turing test is this: Using a text-only channel like a keyboard and screen, after five minutes of questioning, can someone tell whether a computer or a human is on the other end? If a robot passes as human, it has passed the Turing test. (Conversely, if there is no discernible difference and if it actually *is* a human, that person has apparently flunked the Human test.) Bona fide successes at the Turing test have been vanishingly rare. In my own live chats, I have not encountered any robots that have passed it—at least none to my knowledge. The live chats I've had *are* with real people. They can be very helpful, even if lacking certain personal elements, like a voice. And, unlike a real conversation, there's typically a lag time of thirty to sixty seconds of waiting for the representative to respond.

A television ad for Verizon offered this blandishment: "You can even talk to a real person." The ad then cut to a clip of an online live-chat dialogue between a customer and a Verizon representative. Note to Verizon: A typed keyboard-to-keyboard exchange is not "talking to a real person." Corporations are trying to blur certain distinctions and redefine words in order to upgrade consumer perceptions of services delivered.

In general, businesses seek to steer customers away from actually speaking with their people. Best of all are website lists of FAQs (frequently asked questions), which make shadow-working consumers scroll down to locate their own question—if they're lucky—and its boilerplate answer, rather than asking a person. Some companies have imposed surcharges on customers who want to do business with their employees rather than their robots. In 2000, First Chicago Bank & Trust announced $3 teller fees for customers who visited a teller rather than an ATM. Three years later, Northwest Airlines began levying a $50 fee for changing a frequent-flier ticket via an airline agent—double the sum charged when doing so via website or kiosk.

WHEN PERSONAL COMPUTERS entered the marketplace in the late 1970s and 1980s, manufacturers faced the formidable job of educating their customers on how to use the new technology. Most users were not computer literate and had loads of questions. IBM, Apple, Microsoft, and their fellow hardware and software vendors offered technical support at toll-free phone numbers, where tech-savvy representatives fielded user questions, often talking with customers at length. For years, vendors provided this service at no charge, but it was a labor-intensive, costly venture.

After a few years, companies phased out such painstaking support. They unplugged the telephone lines and instead directed customers to websites. There, users could consult lists of FAQs and email queries. The basic idea was to get the company's staff off the hook and put the technical problem back in the customer's lap.

In the next phase, manufacturers began to delegate the job of solving user problems to fellow users: in essence, crowdsourcing tech support. Apple online "communities" at discussions.apple. com, for example, include forums for users of most kinds of Apple software, like iTunes and Apple Pay, as well as Apple hardware like iPhones, iPads, and Macintosh desktop computers. Users may join such forums and pose their questions about Apple products. Fellow users will step up and try to provide an answer online, of course at no charge. Even the forum moderators are often simply advanced users. These users are performing serious shadow work—a bonanza for Apple to have shadow-working customers taking over the job of technical support. The corporation is harvesting a dividend of having built a global community of enthusiastic Apple customers.

Similar forums exist for Microsoft, Hewlett-Packard, Quicken, and other vendors, tapping the expertise of customers who are often highly sophisticated technically. Nor are support forums limited to high-tech products. A year ago, I posed a question on the BMW user forum bimmerfest.com about how disconnecting the battery on my BMW 528 had seemingly disabled the car's radio. Responses, some of them very helpful and even including photos of the BMW fuse panels with diagrams, poured in from as far away as New Zealand. This peer support eventually led me to a missing fuse that a mechanic had apparently removed and forgotten to replace, and my radio came on again.

Such BMW drivers are real enthusiasts, comparable to passionate hobbyists who are eager to share their accumulated knowledge with fellow travelers. Other car manufacturers have similar forums for their vehicles and those who drive them. They are certainly a helpful, free resource for consumers, as well as a source of shadow work for those who so generously address the problems of strangers.

It is easy to see why corporations want customers to do shadow work instead of consulting a staff member. In 2004, Forrester Research indicated that a customer-service phone call with a live agent could cost a company as much as $35, compared with only 75 cents for an online query. That's a savings of 98 percent per transaction. This mounts up rather quickly; consider that in 2003, Hewlett Packard got more than a million phone calls monthly from customers seeking help, while five to six million used HP's e-support website. No need for an HP calculator to add up the corporate savings.

Minimizing the investment of "people time" can motivate consumers as well as corporations. Consider gift certificates, aka gift cards, which greatly simplify the gift-giving process. Instead of choosing an object to give someone, you send a printed card (or a digital file—it can all be done online) that awards the recipient, say, $50 to spend at Macy's, Victoria's Secret, Dunkin' Donuts, or wherever you bought the card. It is almost like cash, except that you can spend cash anywhere; a gift card limits you to a specific vendor.

Nearly every commercial entity of any size offers gift cards, and it is easy to see why. Unlike most purchases, the payment for gift cards arrives well before delivery of the merchandise. It is immediate cash in the bank for the vendor, who has no expense until the card gets redeemed. *But many gift cards never get redeemed.* In late 2007, *Consumer Reports* announced that recipients had not used 27 percent of gift cards issued a year beforehand—usually because they hadn't had time, they forgot about the cards, the cards expired, or the cards were lost. In 2011, TowerGroup business advisers reported that in the previous six years, no less than $41 billion in gift card merchandise had gone unclaimed. Gift cards, in other words, can turn into free ATMs for merchants, who collect their fees in exchange for . . . well, nothing. Vendors, of course, love them. The card arrives, but not the gift, because the recipient never takes on the shadow work that comes with it.

Socially, gift cards represent a radical redefinition of gifting. There was a time when selecting a gift for a beloved relative or friend took a great deal of attention, thought, and caring. The best gifts show how well the giver knows the recipient. They reflect a deep knowledge of what that person wants or needs. Such gifts are very touching for those lucky enough to get them: they demonstrate how much time someone has spent on finding just the right present for you and you alone.

At the opposite extreme we find gift cards, a device arranged more for the convenience of the giver and merchant than the pleasure of the receiver. Gift cards express little, if any, consideration of the recipient, beyond knowing where he or she shops. A Dunkin' Donuts card, for example, is a generic present appropriate for just about anyone who drinks coffee.

Furthermore, gift cards award the unintended present of shadow work. Instead of the *giver* taking the time to shop and purchase a gift, the cards hand those tasks to the *recipient*. An executive I know received a Christmas present of a gift card accompanied by a Williams Sonoma catalog. Picking out an item might be fun, but even so, it feels closer to mail-order shopping than getting a present. As with other forms of shadow work, gift cards mean you will get exactly what you want—because you took over the job of gift shopping. Meanwhile, an important human interchange drops out of the picture.

THE CEASELESS MARKETPLACE

In 1961, City Bank of New York (now Citibank) introduced an experimental Bankograph, an early automated teller machine (ATM). It could accept cash and check deposits but did not dispense cash; the bank removed it after six months due to lack of consumer acceptance. But by the early 1970s, ATMs were dispensing cash and getting a workout. (At the time, some bank executives worried that customers might be hesitant to have machines handle their money.)

Since then, ATMs have grown into a major regiment of the kiosk army. They have even commandeered small storefronts that contain nothing but ATMs. (Welcome to the "bank" without employees.) Automated tellers are making live ones obsolete. Shadow-working customers handle all the details themselves.

In 1984, when my dad retired as CEO of our small-town bank in New Jersey, ATMs were still a fairly new technology. In my speech at his retirement dinner, I mentioned that Dad had once asked me, "Why would anyone use an ATM when the bank is open?" Having spent years at the teller window, he understood that the machines made sense at night and on weekends. But why would customers choose to deal with a *machine* when right inside the door were human beings, happy to serve them?

In a way, the entire history of human commerce lay behind his question. People in towns and villages have always done daily business with each other, getting to know their neighbors through transactions that might be brief but that happened often enough to build up friendly relations. (The word *commerce* can mean either buying and selling or social relations—or both.) Such everyday contacts matter. They knit a community together. In our small town of Dover, banking had a human face, not a robotic one, and for many who lived there, that face belonged to my dad.

Today, in contrast, it's quite possible to do one's banking without seeing a human being, let alone a smile. Banking no longer requires even an ATM. Sitting at your home computer, or on your smartphone, you can deposit money, write checks, make mortgage and bill payments, and download statements. It's banking in a silo. Just about the only transactions you can't handle from a screen are those involving that ancient medium, cash. For that, there's the ATM.

Robots alter our relationship with banks. "Bankers' hours" are becoming irrelevant, since kiosks and the Internet run twenty-four hours per day, regardless of when bank offices open or close. Though kiosks are called interactive, algorithms actually control their interactions. Kiosks don't relate to us as humans do. People *improvise*. They have feelings, and they pay attention to more than the task at hand. We don't form cordial relationships with ATMs. The kiosk army and the penetration of robotics into relationships are reshaping our habits, instilling patterns of behavior that are foreign to human nature. The robots are coaxing us to act more like them.

Acting in robotic style includes having no emotions and never making errors. Because ATMs dispense real cash, they are built to operate in a 100 percent error-free mode. If an ATM were to dispense $200 cash to a customer whose receipt recorded only $100, that money is simply lost to the bank. There is no recourse. Hence, these kiosks are engineered to operate at a standard as close to perfect as any machine in my experience. In thirty years of ATM use, I can't recall a single error.

Yet flawless performance may spoil us in a bad way. It establishes a new standard, and in our minds, we raise the bar. We start to expect similarly perfect performance from humans—why can't they do as well as these mere robots, which don't even have brains? There's a subtle, unconscious recalibration. Much digital technology performs with very low error rates. (In fact, people probably get so upset by computer goof-ups precisely because they *are* so rare.) Recorded music, for example, reaches the consumer in a highly produced, fault-free state; it can also resound with engineered effects that musicians cannot repeat in live performance.

The kiosk army may make us impatient with human mistakes, adding a peevish edge to our interactions. Unlike robots, people *do* have brains, which take in far more information than the immediate task. Having a brain also bestows a natural tendency to slip up at times—as well as a capacity to self-correct. Unfortunately (or perhaps luckily), to err is human.

In some ways, the power of the Internet as a communications medium is also raising performance standards. Shortly after founding Amazon.com, CEO Jeff Bezos declared that in online retailing, impeccable service is crucial. The reason, he explained, is that the customer who gets poor service at the corner store tells five or ten friends, but the one who gets poor service on the Internet tells a million friends.

The equation changes when there is a human connection rather than just a cybernetic one. The owner of a burger-and-brew restaurant in Boston once explained to me that it costs a lot of money in advertising and publicity to get a new customer into a restaurant.

However, if he enjoys himself and has a good meal, he is likely to return. But what if something goes wrong? Then, the way the waitstaff handles the unhappy diner is crucial. If a waitress fails to resolve his complaint, that diner will never be seen again. But if she promptly corrects the problem, or even adds a bonus like deleting a charge or offering a free dessert, the result, the restaurateur explained, "is even better than if there had been no problem. Fixing something the right way really builds customer loyalty."

ROBOTS AND PEOPLE differ in essential ways. One is that humans need rest. Yes, it is good to power down your computer and let the chips and circuits cool off when you can. But robots do not sleep, and their electronic circuits can work twenty-four hours a day. People cannot. The Internet never hits the hay: Amazon, eBay, and every other online seller of goods and services have their doors open at all hours. Add the globalization of commerce, and we find ourselves perpetually in the marketplace.

The New York Stock Exchange rings its opening bell at 9:30 AM and clangs the closing gong at 4 PM, Monday through Friday. That's 32.5 hours of trading weekly. But your computer gives you 168 hours per week (seven days of twenty-four hours) to buy, sell, or option stocks, bonds, mutual funds, commodities, derivatives— any publicly traded investment. Those orders may not be *executed* until the exchange opens, but otherwise they resemble any other trade. If it is 2 AM and you are in a hurry, you only need a broker with a seat on the Tokyo Stock Exchange or the Deutsche Börse in Frankfurt.

Twenty-four-hour commerce affects both staff and customers. Most employees still work traditional eight-hour days. *But customers are always available to work.* This fact sows seeds of shadow work, since consumers are, by definition, awake and available to deal whenever they feel the need. You can't get a salesperson at Ann Taylor or Brooks Brothers to help you buy a jacket at midnight, but online, you are welcome to perform that job yourself: view pictures of the garment from different angles, check fabrics and sizes, compare prices. Without leaving home, at 3 AM, you can order a box of teabags from Barry's Tea in Cork, Ireland, and have it shipped to the States at no charge; it arrives a few days later.

It just seems there isn't enough time or energy anymore to do all the tasks that want doing. You wonder why you feel exhausted. Well, for one thing, you are working around the clock. If you aren't doing your paid job, you are doing shadow work. Or might as well be. The endless marketplace means that people aren't sleeping so much these days, thereby creating a sleep-deprived nation.

Most Americans now sleep less than people did a century ago, or even fifty years ago. The National Sleep Foundation, in a 2005 poll, showed adult Americans averaging 6.8 hours of sleep on weeknights—more than an hour less than they need, according to Charles Czeisler, who chairs Harvard Medical School's Division of Sleep Medicine. "We are living in the middle of history's greatest experiment in sleep deprivation, and we are all a part of that experiment," says his colleague Robert Stickgold, a Harvard professor of psychiatry and sleep researcher. "It's not inconceivable to me that we will discover that there are major social, economic, and health consequences to that experiment. Sleep deprivation doesn't have any good side effects."

Shadow tasks, too, may be tiring us out. A 2007 telephone survey of the U.S. workforce published in the *Journal of Occupational and Environmental Medicine* found fatigue prevalent in 38 percent of workers; the tired employees cost employers $136.4 billion in lost productive time annually. It is difficult to quantify how much of that fatigue comes from performing extra jobs that were once done by someone else, but it is no doubt a contributing factor.

The ceaseless marketplace also puts a certain psychological dynamic in play. When there is a *chance* to buy, sell, trade, research, review, or otherwise connect with the marketplace, that possibility preys on your mind. Maybe you are not transacting, but part of your brain knows that you *could* be. This knowledge siphons attention away from the present. It divides your awareness between the book you are reading now and the stock trade you could be making online—with the price changing every second. The Internet user unceasingly asks: *What am I missing? What else could I, or should I, be doing?*

Infinite options lure people into the trap of multitasking. We try to keep up and not miss out by attempting to do several things at once. Yet multitasking and divided attention may tire us out even more than focused activity. Hours and hours sitting in front of a computer screen, clicking through multiple windows, fatigue us. Much of this exhaustion comes from the steady accumulation of shadow work in modern life.

SHADOW WORK SAGA: The History of Supermarkets

Shopping for food is a modern invention. There was once little need for it. In Benjamin Franklin's time, the vast majority of Americans farmed. They grew their own apples, peas, and carrots, preserved food when possible, raised and killed their own livestock, milked their own cows. They bartered with neighbors for what they didn't raise at home.

Some farmers raised a surplus, and soon public markets arose in small cities. Governor John Winthrop established a marketplace in Boston as early as 1634. (It still exists in the form of Boston's Faneuil Hall marketplace; the nearby Haymarket deals exclusively in foodstuffs.) These large, central marketplaces brought farmers, dairymen, butchers, and other vendors together with customers on market day. Walking from farm stand to farm stand, vendor to vendor, shoppers would bring their baskets to carry their edibles home. It resembled today's farmers' markets, except there was only one per city.

General stores, which sold "everything you need," appeared in the seventeenth century; by 1690, Philadelphia had twenty-nine storekeepers. In country towns, general stores served their surrounding areas. As the 1700s wore on, some city merchants began to specialize in groceries. The storekeeper's family often lived above the storefront, making for a short commute. A customer would hand his shopping list to the merchant, who would fetch the desired items from shelves or scoop them out of barrels of bulk items like nuts or grains.

Townspeople met and socialized at the store—a "third place" that was neither work nor home. Stores played this role for centuries. Edith Wharton's 1917 novel *Summer*, set in the late 1800s, describes Mr. Royall, a small-town lawyer in western Massachusetts, going "over to the store on the opposite corner, where Carrick Fry, the storekeeper, always kept a chair for him, and where he was sure to find one or two selectmen leaning on the long counter, in an atmosphere of rope, leather, tar, and coffee-beans." It wasn't unusual for the congregants even to prevail on the owner for refreshments. In 1825, a Missouri storekeeper told a newspaper:

> I am a storekeeper, and am excessively annoyed by a set of troublesome animals called loungers, who are in the daily habit of calling at my store, and there sitting hour after hour, poking into my books whenever they happen to lie exposed to their view, making impertinent inquiries about business which does not concern them, and ever and anon giving a polite hint that a little grog would be acceptable.

At times, such self-invited guests also helped themselves to the store's cracker barrel. This kind of imposition, along with the sociability and community-building aspects of lollygagging around the store's wood-burning stove, disappeared with the rise of chain stores, whose architecture and management discouraged the lounger lifestyle. Chain stores banned credit sales and limited home delivery, helping to distance local merchants from their customers.

The Great Atlantic & Pacific Tea Company, which at first specialized in tea, was a New York City start-up in 1859. Its business plan was to buy large quantities of tea off the New York docks and then retail it widely. It eventually diversified into other groceries and became the A&P Company, the country's first large food-store chain. The mechanical cash register, invented in 1879 and soon sold widely by National Cash Register, became the reigning technology for cash transactions in stores.

In the 1880s, Bernard Kroger launched his own chain in Cincinnati. He, too, leveraged mass purchasing to cut prices. Grocery stores became high-volume, low-margin businesses for which low prices were the main axis of competition. They remain very much that way today. Many items are brand-name or generic products sold everywhere, and profit margins as low as 1 to 2 percent are the rule in grocery stores.

Early grocery stores typically had a counter-and-wall design, with customers congregating in a vacant space in the middle of the store and viewing goods for sale on high tiers of shelving along the side walls. Shoppers weren't allowed behind the counters in front of these shelves. Counter clerks stationed there would fetch their purchases for them. It was a labor-intensive system. In smaller stores, a clerk might help a customer with every item on her shopping list. In larger ones, clerks patrolled assigned zones and assisted shoppers with certain types of food items, like meats. The personal attention was nice, but the system was slow, and high labor costs made it expensive for the merchant.

In 1916, in Memphis, Tennessee, Clarence Saunders (1881–1953) introduced a radical innovation when he opened his first Piggly Wiggly market. He removed the counter-and-wall system.

Instead, a customer entered Piggly Wiggly through a turnstile, picked up a shopping basket, and made her way along a one-way route past every shelf in the store, from which she could choose her foods and place them in her basket. The design forced shoppers to view every item Piggly Wiggly had for sale. At the end, they would queue up at the cash register, pay the cashier—cash only, please— and exit. The Piggly Wiggly was the first modern supermarket.

Saunders's new system assigned to customers the work previously done by store clerks—a watershed moment in the history of shadow work. With shadow-working shoppers, Saunders could hire many fewer clerks. The savings enabled him to "slay the demon of high prices," as he promised his customers. Within six years he had opened 1,200 Piggy Wiggly markets in twenty-nine states.

Some upper-class shoppers found self-service degrading, as it made them into workers rather than an elite being waited on by servants. But most did not mind the extra effort and enjoyed the autonomy of self-service. With no clerks attending to them, they could shop at their own pace. Some customers actually felt like they were stealing goods, as only clerks had been allowed to handle merchandise before. But the supermarkets were not putting any special trust in the consumer: Instead of counter clerks, cashiers at the exit turnstiles now ensured that shoppers paid for everything they carried out.

In 1923, the rapid success of Saunders's business attracted the attention of Wall Street. Opportunistic speculators, including some from Merrill Lynch, decided that Piggy Wiggly stock was overvalued. They not only took short positions on it but decided to proactively drive down the stock price, a tactic known as a bear raid. With help from southern banks, Saunders successfully countered the raid by buying large lots of his own stock and driving *up* the price. The speculators then pressured the New York Stock Exchange to alter its rules, arguing that Saunders had gained a corner on Piggly Wiggly stock. The stock exchange caved in and allowed them five days, instead of twenty-four hours, to deliver the shares Saunders had purchased. This manipulation paid off; it cost Saunders $3 million and forced him into bankruptcy. He had no further association with Piggly Wiggly. Nonetheless, it remains an active supermarket chain, with 600 stores in seventeen states.

The visionary Clarence Saunders was decades ahead of his time. He was working on an even more advanced retailing concept, "Foodelectric," at his death in 1953. This was to be a fully automated supermarket, a predecessor of modern self-service checkouts. On entering the Foodelectric store, shoppers would receive a primitive computer. They could slide it into a slot beside any desired item. Glass-enclosed display cabinets then released the chosen purchase and recorded its price on the customer's little computer. At the end of her shopping trip, the customer would hand the computer to the cashier, with her total bill already calculated. Saunders hoped to launch the first Foodelectric market in Memphis, only two blocks away from the site of his original Piggly Wiggly, but unfortunately, the futuristic store never opened.

Meanwhile, in 1930, Michael Cullen (1884–1936), a Kroger (and former A&P) employee in Illinois, wrote a bombastic proposal to the presidents of both chains, suggesting that they back him in scaling up the supermarket concept: large, low-cost stores, self-service, no deliveries, and advertised prices, plus ample parking. Cullen proposed to sell 300 items at cost, pulling in shoppers with "loss leaders." He predicted that the opening of such a store "would be a riot, I would have to call out the police and let the public in so many at a time. I would lead the public out of the high priced houses of bondage into the low prices of the houses of the promised land." Cullen predicted that he could generate ten times the volume and profit of conventional Krogers and A&Ps. Both chains ignored his proposal.

Cullen pushed ahead on his own. He quit Kroger, moved his family to Long Island, and rented a vacant garage near a busy shopping district in Queens. His first King Kullen store opened on August 4, 1930. Advertisements styled King Kullen as "the World's Greatest Price Wrecker" and dared the chain stores to "read these prices and weep." It was an immediate success, pulling shoppers from miles around. Years later, the Smithsonian Institution designated the King Kullen at 171st Street and Jamaica Avenue as "America's first supermarket."

King Kullen's no-frills style and rock-bottom prices proved the right formula for the depths of the Great Depression. Expanded advertising of items and prices enabled consumers to draw up shopping lists with known prices before going to the store. Better-informed customers didn't need to pester store clerks with questions; shadow work transferred the burden of knowledge to the shopper. This helped Cullen pare staff, reducing expenses and helping keep prices low. Eliminating services like delivery (King Kullen operated on a purely cash-and-carry basis) and credit also trimmed costs. Cullen's no-frills approach transferred various types of shadow work to shoppers but also paid off in reduced prices.

Cullen expanded into other large, older buildings, like abandoned factories and warehouses. Seventeen King Kullens were taking in $6 million annually by 1936. That year, at age fifty-two, Michael Cullen died suddenly after an appendectomy, and expansion slowed. Nonetheless, King Kullen remains in business today, operating thirty-nine stores.

Chains like Kroger and A&P that had dismissed Cullen's idea soon jumped on the bandwagon, and by the time he died, there were 1,200 such supermarkets in eighty-five cities; this number had mushroomed to 15,000 by 1950. It took a while for supermarkets to catch on abroad; the English grocery chain Sainsbury's opened its first store in 1950, initially using "hostesses" to guide shoppers around and introduce the concept of handling your own items.

THE GREAT DEPRESSION saw in another innovation that gave supermarket customers more shadow work: the wheeled shopping cart. Sylvan Goldman, a World War I veteran born in Indian Territory (Oklahoma), went into the grocery business with his brother after the war. In 1920, they opened Oklahoma's first supermarket in Tulsa, on the model Saunders had pioneered with Piggly Wiggly. In 1934, the brothers moved to Oklahoma City and bought the Humpty Dumpty chain.

Goldman came up with the idea of a shopping cart on wheels to solve a problem women were having with self-service: Mothers often found it difficult to manage both children and a shopping basket. The mobile shopping cart freed their hands and let them corral youngsters while shopping, without having to worry about their groceries, which waited safely in the cart.

Goldman wanted to make it easier for customers to buy more groceries per store visit. He jury-rigged his prototype cart by placing a basket on a wooden folding chair and fixing casters to the legs. Mechanic Fred Young tinkered with this design and produced a wire frame with upper and lower metal baskets; another mechanic developed an assembly line that could form and weld metal wire into a cart. On June 4, 1937, the first shopping cart rolled out, quite literally, at Goldman's Humpty Dumpty in Oklahoma City. The invention—now called the shopping trolley in England, Canada, and elsewhere—made Goldman richer than groceries ever did. The carts have become ubiquitous worldwide, not only in supermarkets but in other large retail operations, such as Home Depot.

Once the customer has paid for and bagged his groceries, he can wheel the bags to his car. In many American supermarkets, he then abandons the cart in the parking lot. A store employee, typically a teenaged boy, rounds them up and nests them into a long line of carts in front of the store. Other supermarkets provide designated cart-return areas, asking customers to absorb the shadow work of cart retrieval. Most cooperate with no incentive other than conforming to social norms. Returning your cart to the holding pen also lets the supermarket trim teenaged boys from the payroll, or reassign them to other duties.

Throughout Europe and Canada, a coin-deposit system gives customers an additional incentive to bring carts back to a central depot. An arriving shopper inserts a coin (€1 in Europe; commonly 25 cents in the United States) that unlocks a cart from a rack; she receives her deposit back on its return. This system helps prevent damage to parked cars by rogue carts that roll around the lot on their own. It also compels customers to return carts to their point of origin: they must perform this shadow task or forfeit a coin.

IN THE EARLY years of the twenty-first century, self-service checkouts emerged as a new type of supermarket shadow work. Scanning technology, which reads bar codes to instantly record prices at a digital cash register, made this possible, along with the advent of electronic payments. For many years, supermarket cashiers had been scanning groceries for checkout. Why not turn the scanning machine over to the customers and have *them* do that job instead? Voila! The self-service checkout.

Typically, supermarkets set up four or six self-serve scanners at one end of the cashier bank, with a single employee overseeing them. Shoppers with smaller orders who don't want to wait in line for a cashier can instead wait in line for a robot. They'll scan and bag their own purchases, including fresh produce, which they weigh and punch in a code for on the keypad. Credit and debit cards simplify payment, although cash works, too. A robotic voice will occasionally chide the shadow-working customer with commands like "Unexpected item in the bagging area," which has even become a humorous T-shirt slogan. (The "unexpected item" is often a handbag or backpack carelessly placed in the checkout zone.)

Self-serve checkouts have received a mixed reception. The chief executive of Sainsbury's, Justin King, declared, "Self-checkouts are like Marmite [a salty, dark brown food spread made from a yeast extract]: you either love them or loathe them." Furthermore, they may either be the wave of the future or a technology that consumers are rejecting, depending on what reports you believe. A survey in 2014 found that 45 percent of British shoppers always or often need staff assistance with these checkouts, and only 2 percent claimed that they never need help. Just over half (55 percent) opt for a human cashier when buying a few items and when there's a choice between a kiosk and a cashier. Older shoppers (over sixty-five) are far more likely (82 percent) to choose the cashier, while only 42 percent of the eighteen- to twenty-four-year-olds go for the person over the machine.

A 2009 survey by the London-based consulting firm Retail Banking Research Ltd. asserted that there were 92,600 self-checkout terminals in use worldwide at the end of 2008 (80 percent of them in North America) and predicted that the number would more than quadruple to 430,000 by 2014. A 2012 analysis of actual and projected shipments published by the Frost & Sullivan consulting firm pegged the number at the start of 2014 at 194,300, less than half the Retail Banking Research projection but still reflecting an averaged annual growth in revenue of 6.5 percent from 2009 through 2013. National Cash Register (NCR), which manufactures the vast majority of self-checkout kiosks, naturally endorses claims boosting the technology. NCR says the kiosks generate more repeat business for stores and shorten waiting time in lines by 40 percent. In 2011, NCR stated that more than 150 retailers in twenty-two countries had deployed its kiosks, and projected the market to grow by 15 percent annually. However, in a country like Brazil, with low labor costs and strong employee unions, kiosks have proven less popular.

Meanwhile, some supermarkets have removed self-checkouts to enhance their level of customer service. In the fall of 2011, for example, Big Y Foods, which operates sixty-one supermarkets in Connecticut and Massachusetts, announced that it was phasing out self-checkouts. In doing so, Big Y joined other regional chains and some national players, like Albertsons, which operates 217 super-markets in the West and South. In 2011, Albertsons announced it was removing self-checkout kiosks from 100 of its stores in favor of standard or express lanes. "We just want the opportunity to talk to customers more," said Albertsons spokeswoman Christine Wilcox.

Despite their advantages for storeowners and convenience for at least some shoppers, the robotic checkouts pose certain problems (shoplifting, for example) because the devices lack eyes, ears, and brains. Shoplifting is a serious problem in the food business due to the low margins: If a thief steals a single can of beans, the store might have to sell a couple dozen more cans to make up for the loss. And self-checkouts make it easier to steal. In a 2012 survey of

nearly 4,952 shoppers by the British website watchmywallet.com.
uk, almost a third of respondents admitted stealing from stores
when scanning their own items. A common technique was to enter
the code for a less-expensive item of produce, like onions, while
actually weighing and bagging a costlier one, like avocadoes. The
kiosk's scale knows only the weight and the code entered—it cannot see what is actually on the scale.

More blatant theft occurs when shoppers bag items without
scanning them at all. With no cashier present, many find this
tempting. Even celebrities, like British television chef Antony
Worrall Thompson, have succumbed. Security cameras caught him
sneaking wine and cheese past self-serve checkouts at Tesco stores
on five occasions over a sixteen-day span; Thompson received a
formal police caution. Some brazen thieves raise the stakes well
beyond wine and cheese. An electronics store had one man arrested
after he had switched the price tag on a flat-screen plasma television with that of a $4.88 DVD and was trying to take the $2,000
television through a self-checkout kiosk.

Supermarkets have some counters to shoplifting. The staff
member supervising the self-checkout kiosks may spot-check a
random sample of customers to ensure that they are paying for
everything they are taking out. Staff members also observe customers directly as they scan—or don't scan—their items.

Kiosks also have no idea who the customer is. Consequently,
children and teens could be buying age-restricted products like
tobacco and alcohol, and the kiosk is none the wiser. Store clerks
now supposedly check IDs on such purchases but don't always

succeed; eventually a biological technology involving fingerprints or iris recognition may resolve this problem.

Stores can invent cunning incentives to induce shoppers toward self-checkouts. One is to open only two or three staffed checkout lanes beside several self-serve kiosks. This creates longer lines for the human cashier and gives the impression that it will be quicker to scan your own order. This is a form of *wait warping*— distorting consumers' perceptions of waiting time by psychological manipulation. Unless the shopper has only a couple of items to scan, the robotic checkout may not be any faster, in part because professional cashiers and baggers scan and bag items faster than fumbling amateurs attempting the same task. But because those shadow-working shoppers are "actively involved" in the process, they may not mind their own slow-paced work: Time spent *doing* things always seems to pass faster than time spent *waiting* for things to happen. The wait warp bends their perception of how much time has passed.

In recent years, some supermarkets, including the Shop-Rite chain, have experimented with an even more radical form of shadow work. Shoppers with a store loyalty card may borrow an electronic scanning wand that can scan bar codes on all items in the store and record the prices. A couple dozen such wands for customers' use hang on a wall near the entrance. Shoppers wielding a wand scan each purchase as they wend their way through the aisles. They can also bag their own items right in their carts while shopping, sorting them exactly as they desire. When done, these customers simply hand the wand to a cashier and pay the total bill recorded, then leave the store immediately with their already-bagged haul of groceries.

By bringing self-serve scanning right into the food aisles, this mode of shadow work accelerates the shopping trip even more. The wand can display a running total, letting customers monitor how much they are spending as they shop, helping those trying to stay within a budget. In this mode, the customer assumes all the functions of the cashier and bagger except that of accepting payment. In essence, the system realizes Clarence Saunders's vision of a Foodelectric store, seventy years after he propounded the idea.

Ironically, another feature of grocery shopping in the twenty-first century harkens all the way back to the beginnings of the grocery-buying experience in America. Farmers' markets and community-supported agriculture, or CSA, in which customers pay a farmer before the growing season for a share of the crops harvested over the summer, echo the public markets of the colonial era. The technology is low, and farmers' markets remove the layers of middlemen from the food-buying process. These middlemen have become a kind of food chain in their own right. Farmers' markets and CSA delete them by disintermediation.

Farmers' markets and CSA also connect those who grow food with those who eat it. They may reduce the feeling of alienation people get with mass-produced agribusiness food. Generally, farmers' markets operate without shopping carts, checkouts, or digital technology. Carrying one's own basket while perambulating around to the various outdoor stalls might feel like time-travel—going back to shopping as it was three centuries ago—and provide a vacation from some forms of shadow work.

LESSONS FROM THE SUPERMARKET

First, humans evolved as hunter-gatherers, and there is probably nothing more basic to the species than obtaining food. The quest for nourishment has always been both a social and a functional activity. Historically, public markets, general stores, and grocery stores have been places to convene and socialize, as well as acquire food. Over the past century, a purely economic vision of the food market has pared away these social aspects.

Dropping the sociable aspects of shopping, though, has costs for both the community and the store owners. Chances to talk—for example, with staff in supermarkets who give away free samples of a new product—enhance the shopping experience and help draw shoppers back to the store in preference to competitors. Sociability can build goodwill toward the merchant. Retailers in general strive to get customers *into* their stores, and creative ways of recapturing the social dimensions of food gathering may help do this.

Second, work in the grocery store is, to some degree, a zero-sum game: Either staff do it or customers do it. The earlier counter-and-shelf system was highly labor-intensive, as staff handed each item to the customers. Transferring this job to the shoppers meant designing a market that makes it clear where things are, and what they are. Supermarkets had to cultivate an informed shopper. King Kullen pioneered extensive newspaper advertising that let consumers know what was on sale and the prices of items. Such information transfers that knowledge to the customer and means fewer questions for clerks. The store might spend less time on customer service as a result.

Third, simple technologies like shopping carts can increase customer shadow work. Retailers who identify customers' needs (like those of mothers trying to shop with young children) can draw shoppers to their stores with consumer tools that streamline shopping.

Fourth, social norms go a long way toward establishing shadow work. Simply by designating cart-return areas in parking lots, supermarkets can get customers to take over the job of wrangling carts. The innate cooperativeness of most well-socialized adults will do the rest.

Fifth, high technology like self-checkout scanners offers shadow-working customers more autonomy. But these innovations need to be simple and accessible to attract shoppers. Store staff can function as tutors for those having difficulty mastering the scanning kiosk.

Customer autonomy entails certain risks for the retailer, like shoplifting, which becomes easier when the customer controls the entire checkout process, including payment (or lack of same). Countermeasures like spot-checking bags of shoppers at self-serve kiosks make logical sense but risk alienating shoppers.

Sixth, the siloing of customers who deal with robotic kiosks rather than human cashiers may also distance them from the store. Reducing human contact may erode store loyalty. Shopping becomes a less "warm and fuzzy" (that is, human) experience when conducted with robots. Since prehistoric times, food gathering has been at its most efficient, and most enjoyable, in the company of other members of *Homo sapiens*.

five: shadow work on computers and the internet

There's a tendency to totalism, total information, and once you have total information you're making it easier for total control.

—JERRY BROWN

IN THE SPRING of 2014, contractors examining a foreclosed house in suburban Pontiac, Michigan, discovered the "mummified" body of Pia Farrenkopf in the back seat of her Jeep, parked in the garage. Apparently she had been dead for five years. She would have been forty-nine years old. How or why she died still remains unknown.

Farrenkopf had no spouse, children, or pets and had long been out of touch with her family. She had left her job at Chrysler Financial in 2008, so she was not missed at work. Neighbors believed that she frequently traveled abroad on business, which explained why they never saw her around. When the grass grew too high on Farrenkopf's lawn, they were neighborly enough, *USA Today* reported, to mow it for her on occasion. In this way her lawn care actually outlived her by several years.

Strangely, so did her status as a bill-paying consumer. Farrenkopf had set up automatic payments of her mortgage and utility bills, which continued to be deducted from her ample bank account for years. When the money finally ran out in 2013, mortgage payments stopped and the bank foreclosed. Then it hired the contractor who discovered Farrenkopf's body in the garage. Had the mortgage been paid off sooner, Farrenkopf might still be sitting in that Jeep.

From her death until the discovery of her body, Farrenkopf was "a kind of Schrödinger's cat, biologically dead but also, in a way, among the living, paying for her power and her phone, the roof over her head," wrote Carmen Maria Machado in a post for newyorker.com. "Until her body surfaced, Farrenkopf's institutional ties were the only things keeping her 'alive.'" Machado suggests that she had "a kind of institutional doppelgänger, as do we all: a presence that forms as we post on social media, shop online, send e-mails, and use the Internet for paying bills, banking, and dozens of other financial and technological transactions."

Indeed, it does seem that all of us now have two bodies, a biological body and an informational one. The two are certainly related but also quite separate, as Farrenkopf's case proves. Criminals can pull off an "identity theft" of your informational body without ever touching your physical one. (Kidnapping a biological body is *so* twentieth century.) The informational body exists in cyberspace as bits of data stored on computers and in the cloud, and to a great extent it handles your transactions with the financial, institutional, and even social world, as on Facebook.

Illustrations of the human body can single out the circulatory system, stripping away all other flesh, blood, and bone. Vascularization is so complete that blood vessels and capillaries by themselves portray the body's size and form quite well. You might even be recognizable from your veins and arteries alone.

In a parallel way, our informational bodies, composed purely of data, are nonetheless recognizable as ourselves in the economic sense. The aggregate of Social Security and charge-account numbers, medical and credit histories, email, social media posts, and institutional records that trail all adults may not be as singular as fingerprints or retinal scans. Yet it is good enough for paying bills and getting through this world. Furthermore, we receive constant reminders to guard these alter egos vigilantly, lest identity thieves carry them off and exploit them. Meanwhile, the commercial sector constantly prods us for more details on our informational bodies. Economic institutions are far more interested in the cloud of data points we inhabit than in our blood-pumping physical selves, which, as Pia Farrenkopf sadly showed, can be almost incidental.

SEXY DATA CRUNCHERS

In 2009, Hal Varian, chief economist for Google, made a comment to *The McKinsey Quarterly* that instantly upgraded the social status of statisticians. "I keep saying," he declared, "the sexy job in the next ten years will be statisticians."

Yes, those sexy data crunchers, vamping us with their stratified samples, tossing off regression coefficients with insouciant swagger—who can resist them? Not to mention their standard deviations. What's the secret of their devastating sex appeal?

The answer takes us back to Henry Kissinger's oft-quoted remark of 1973: "Power is the ultimate aphrodisiac." Data embody power. Information is the raw material of success. Yet by itself, raw material does little; it has to be processed. The power comes less from the *data* than the *crunching*. The interpretation of information—figuring out what it means and how it applies to the real world—is what adds value. Computers cannot do this job, at least not alone. "To make that data useful is a challenge," said Varian. "It's generally going to require human beings to do it." This is where statisticians come in: They sculpt the clay of facts into recognizable forms, then interpret their meaning. Their crowbars pry loose understandings applied at the fulcrums of power—and yes, there are those who find this sexy.

The emerging phenomenon of Big Data only magnifies statisticians' influence. Big Data involves the assembly and dissection of data sets whose size exceeds the capacities of standard software tools. Technology can now collect and store files measured in terabytes (1,000 gigabytes) and petabytes (1,000 terabytes). But gigantic databases or even skyrocketing computational power isn't the real magic of Big Data. The sorcery involves, in part, linking huge data sets together for a synergistic payoff. And algorithms, those step-by-step rules for making a calculation, distill meaning from these heaps of facts. This is what really unlocks the potential of Big Data.

In the universities, a certain pattern has come to repeat itself, as Gary King, a government professor at Harvard, told Jonathan

Shaw of *Harvard Magazine*. It begins with a group of distinguished experts, reigning authorities in some field. Then an outsider with little knowledge of the discipline shows up, attacks a problem with statistics and algorithms, and unearths an astonishing insight. Algorithms are another tool that democratizes expertise, using the revolutionary power of data to outdo established authorities.

For example, Theodore Ruger, then a law professor at Washington University in St. Louis, and three colleagues ran a contest to predict the outcome of Supreme Court cases on the 2002 docket. The four political scientists developed a statistical model based on six general case characteristics they extracted from previous trials; the model ignored information about specific laws and the facts of the actual cases. Their friendly contest pitted this model against the qualitative judgments of eighty-seven law professors, many of whom had clerked at the Court. The legal mavens knew the jurisprudence, case law, and previous decisions of each sitting justice. The result, published in the *Columbia Law Review* in 2004, was a rout. The algorithm predicted 75 percent of the Court's verdicts correctly; the legal experts, as a group, had them right 59.1 percent of the time.

YET THE WIZARDRY of statistics does not need Big Data or high-powered algorithms. Consider the leverage of a very simple observation known as the Pareto principle. This is statistics at its most basic: a simple percentage. But the power of this percentage is staggering.

In 1941, Romanian management consultant Joseph Juran stumbled on the work of Italian sociologist and economist Vilfredo Pareto

(1848–1923) and extracted an insight now known as the 80–20 rule. The basic idea is that in a wide variety of circumstances, 20 percent of the causes produce 80 percent of the effects. Juran named it the Pareto principle. In his own garden, Pareto had noticed that 20 percent of the peapods produced 80 percent of the peas. As an economist, he found this surprising ratio showing up in much larger contexts. In 1906, Pareto published his finding that 20 percent of Italy's population owned 80 percent of the land. Since then, the 80–20 rule has cropped up in a breathtaking range of phenomena.

In 1992, for example, the United Nations Development Program analyzed the distribution of global income, measured by gross domestic product. The data showed that, worldwide, the wealthiest 20 percent of the population took in 82.7 percent of the income. Businesses make 80 percent of their profits from 20 percent of their customers, while a different 20 percent generate 80 percent of the complaints. Twenty percent of the patients consume 80 percent of healthcare resources. Criminologists have found that one-fifth of the criminals commit four-fifths of the crimes. All these findings suggest strategies for allocating resources. To cut healthcare costs, for example, concentrate on trimming expenses for that 20 percent who run up the huge bills. To make a real dent in crime, focus rehabilitation on that 20 percent who are hardcore, repeat offenders.

In the 1960s, advertising copywriters applied the Pareto principle to selling Schaefer Beer. Market research had revealed that 20 percent of the beer drinkers consumed 80 percent of the beer. The message was clear: go after the guzzlers. The result was Schaefer's celebrated, long-running slogan "Schaefer is the one beer to have when you're having more than one." Quite a few more than one, actually.

STATISTICS MOVE THE world in ways even more important than selling beer. Think about how our social norms regarding tobacco smoking have changed since 1965, when 42 percent of Americans smoked. Smokers then lit up in restaurants and bars, at work, in nightclubs, schools, and sports stadiums, on public transportation, and in all manner of public places. Clouds of smoke hovered above audiences at rock concerts, though this admittedly was not all tobacco smoke. Cigarette machines were ubiquitous in bars, as smoking whetted the thirst for a drink. Even hospitals sold cigarettes in waiting rooms and cafeterias.

Fast-forward to 2014, when the Centers for Disease Control pegged the American smoking rate at 18.1 percent, cigarette machines have all but disappeared, and laws or policies ban smoking in nearly all public places. Data and statistical analysis lie behind this change in lifestyle.

Here's how it happened. In the 1950s and early 1960s, epidemiological studies established the role of smoking in causing cancer, particularly lung cancer. The landmark 1964 surgeon general's report put the U.S. government on record as affirming tobacco's role in disease and death and recommending against smoking. This, combined with energetic public-health efforts to discourage smoking, and sin taxes on tobacco, helped cut down smoking prevalence. Cigarettes took on a new image as a cause of disease rather than as sexy accessories for movie stars like Lauren Bacall and Humphrey Bogart, a heavy smoker who died of esophageal cancer at fifty-seven.

But it was epidemiological research on passive smoking that changed the way we live. Repeated studies of people who inhaled secondhand smoke, such as nonsmokers married to smoking spouses, unequivocally established that taking in tobacco smoke could sicken or kill you, even if you never lit up yourself. Such statistical findings established a beachhead for antismoking groups, who pushed lawmakers to prohibit smoking in places like bars and restaurants. Their legal logic rested on the common-law precept that "my right to swing my fist ends where your nose begins." You may be entitled to destroy your own health with cigarettes, but you don't have the right to take others down with you. An army of scientists, public-health professionals, advocacy groups, elected officials, and ordinary citizens worked for decades to win this war, with statisticians serving as a central battalion in the fight. Data-crunching Davids shot down the Goliath-like tobacco corporations. The stones in their slingshots were correlations and F-tests.

THUS THOSE LOUCHE statisticians attained their sex appeal. The emergence of data analysis as a power center has fueled geek chic, a new wave of esteem for young people with a knack for stats. Students are packing college classrooms to learn statistics and other tools for milking Big Data. In 1997, the College Board introduced an advanced placement examination in statistics. The number of high school students taking it tripled in the decade after 2001, to 149,165 by 2012. American universities conferred close to 3,000 bachelor's degrees in statistics in the 2010–11 academic year, a 68 percent increase from four years before. A Harvard data science course drew 400 students in 2013, not only undergraduates but those from graduate schools of law, business, government, design, and medicine. At the University of California, Berkeley, the number of statistics majors quintupled from 50 in 2003 to 250 a decade later.

Fields of study that strongly attract students like this are an index of what we value, and where society is headed. A 2013 *Wall Street Journal* article, "Data Crunchers Now the Cool Kids on Campus," quoted Richard De Veaux, professor of mathematics and statistics at Williams College. When asked what he did for a living, "even twenty years ago I would try to say something other than statistics," he said. But today, "It's just a great time to be a statistician." Indeed it is. There is a vast appetite for statistical findings, and so much data to feed on. The quest for that data has let loose a surge of shadow work.

THE GRASS ROOTS OF BILLIONAIRES

Though the term "information economy" has become a cliché, few have traced this stream of data to its headwaters. The torrent of information that washes through daily life does have a source. You can see it in the mirror. It is you. The data that institutions seek, accumulate, analyze, and constantly refresh comes largely from their clients. Organizations recognize that people are willing, free of charge, to provide data on themselves. Time spent doing so is shadow work.

Data has emerged as another natural resource, like water, oil, and iron. We are living through the early decades of the information economy, comparable to the first decades of the petroleum boom in the nineteenth century. Underground pools of oil were a naturally occurring resource, just waiting in Mother Earth to be drilled and pumped out—and the oil companies weren't paying her for the petroleum. Their main expense was the cost of extraction.

Similarly, free data now resides naturally in the populace, waiting to be tapped. Organizations need invest only in extraction costs, as they don't pay the shadow-working citizens who provide it. *Their* only payoff may be psychological: Data seekers massage our egos by asking us about ourselves and our opinions.

Social media like Facebook (FB) and LinkedIn serve their members free of charge in order to extract reams of information from them. With more than 1.35 *billion* active users, Facebook has built a gigantic database, which offers commercial entities a huge archive of consumers' names and email addresses, along with rich demographic profiles, preferences in music, movies, gifts, and other things, groups they belong to, apps and games they play, and of course their networks of "friends." Hence Facebook constantly encourages users to post *more* data (words, pictures, and video) and to add more "friends" to their circles. Shadow-working users comply, funneling their twenty-first-century petroleum into Facebook's pool of oil.

For the most part, Facebook users aren't actually performing *work* when they produce the site's content; they are enjoying social recreation. But when Facebook goes to the marketplace with that data, merchandizing its member-produced content, those "recreational" hours start to smell like shadow work. "Their business model is about getting users to create content," Jeremiah Owyang, an analyst with the Altimeter Group, told *The New York Times* in 2013. "It's users who are creating content, liking things, and, ultimately, a brand sees this and comes to deploy advertising dollars. The product is us."

Facebook has the legal right to do this. Users sign over these prerogatives when they accept the boilerplate (never reading it, of course) in the company's 4,000-word terms-of-service agreement. When a member "likes" something on the site, Facebook can even highlight that endorsement in an ad for whatever she liked. The company calls such plugs sponsored stories. Members cannot opt out of them.

Sponsored stories that FB sends to a user's friendship network gain their power from a basic fact of human psychology. We take a recommendation—whether to hire somebody or enroll him in a club—more seriously when it comes from a friend. "Like" something on Facebook, and your friends will credit that endorsement more than they would a television or Internet advertisement. Facebook has told investors that when an ad comes attached to a blurb from a "friend," consumers are 50 percent more likely to remember it.

In 2012, Nick Bergus, a multimedia producer in Iowa City, learned how these sponsored stories play out. On Valentine's Day, he saw an ad on Amazon for an odd product, a fifty-five-gallon drum of "personal lubricant." (The vendor was apparently disintermediating by selling wholesale quantities directly to the consumer.) Bergus found the idea of this gigantic vat of a sexual aid humorous, and so posted the link on Facebook with his comment, "For Valentine's Day. And every day. For the rest of your life," as reported by *The New York Times*. Soon he began seeing this post, along with his name and photo, among advertisements on FB. Facebook had reframed his joking comment as an endorsement, a sponsored story—without, of course, consulting Bergus. He confessed on his blog that he was "mildly annoyed," but added, "I know the costs of using Facebook. It does not cost me money. It uses lots of my personal information." As the Internet-era proverb warns: If you aren't paying for the product, you *are* the product.

When Facebook went public in 2012 (the company had valued itself at $104 billion, though the public offering sold only $16 billion worth of stock), some of its users publicly asked, "Where's our cut?" They recognized that shadow work by the site's users had created the value that founder Mark Zuckerberg and his business partners sold to investors. Unfortunately for those users, they have no claim on the revenue FB generates from their input. Nor are they well organized enough to apply political pressure.

Furthermore, users obviously reap the benefits of Facebook without paying a monthly fee. (There will never be a fee. Facebook's subscribers are its main capital asset, so the company will hardly create a financial barrier to becoming one.) It's a kind of barter arrangement: shadow workers create valuable content for Facebook in exchange for free social recreation.

WE, THE UNORGANIZED citizenry, offer up free content in other ways as well. For example, the Internet has unleashed an avalanche of customer reviews. The basic idea is sound: People who have read a book, eaten at a restaurant, hired a plumber, or bought a tablet computer from Best Buy write a post about their experience. Such reviews have become ubiquitous. Amazon pioneered the technique in the 1990s with reader reviews of books; these lay reactions soon eclipsed the professional ones. Now Amazon offers customer verdicts on all it sells—in other words, nearly everything, from electric toothbrushes to dog food.

Zagat runs a website and publishes guidebooks that consist entirely of user-generated content: customer ratings and reactions to restaurants in eighteen cities. (Restaurants even put up window decals boasting that they are "Zagat Rated," as if it were an endorsement. It is equivalent to a TV show bragging that it is "Nielsen Rated.") Yelp's grassroots critiques ("Real People. Real Reviews") of eateries have expanded worldwide into nightlife, shopping, medical, automotive, and other sectors. Angie's List has enrolled more than two million households, which pay $10 or more annually to access reviews of local businesses in home care, health, automotive, pet, and other services. The Internet presents a barrage of consumer critiques for virtually any product or service.

You won't see professional book reviewers, restaurant critics, or technology writers chiming in at these dish sessions. This is admittedly amateur work. But customers *do* have direct experience with whatever they are praising or panning, and their grassroots nature lends them credibility. Professional critics sometimes

develop cozy relationships with their subjects. But amateurs seemingly have nothing to gain, at least professionally or financially,
from their critiques, so we imagine they are unbiased. Customer
reviews also tap our populist sympathies; as readers, we identify
with our fellow consumers: "These are people like me."

Well, not always. Review sites open their doors democratically
to all, and the reviewers are sometimes the very businesses under
review. Using proxies posing as customers, some proprietors post
rave notices of themselves or harsh ones of competitors. The incentives to do so are certainly there. In 2011, Harvard Business School
professor Michael Luca published a study showing that a one-star
improvement in the average rating on Yelp (five stars is the highest
score) translated into a 5 to 9 percent increase in revenue for a restaurant. One extra star on TripAdvisor, according to a Cornell study,
could mean an 11 percent bump in a hotel's or motel's room rates.

Given this, it was inevitable that some inns and eateries—
typically independent ones facing stiff competition—would try
to game the system. In 2013, Luca and his colleague Georgios
Zervas of Boston University published "Fake It Till You Make It:
Reputation, Competition, and Yelp Review Fraud." They analyzed
316,425 Yelp reviews of Boston restaurants and found that 16 percent were fraudulent, as identified by Yelp's internal algorithm that
flags suspicious posts. Yelp confirmed the study and even raised
the ante, announcing that its filtering software in fact flagged
about 25 percent of Yelp's forty-two million reviews as fakes. Yelp
doesn't completely delete such notices but ghettoizes them as "Not
Currently Recommended" reviews at the bottom of a business's

page and does not factor them into the establishment's star rating. No one knows how many phony reviews escape the algorithm and mingle with the real ones.

Professional forgers are definitely trying. The twenty-first-century term *astroturfing* takes its name from AstroTurf, the original artificial grass used on sports fields. The verb *astroturf* means to artificially simulate "grassroots" support online. For a fee, certain "reputation management" firms will help a business astroturf by fabricating phony reviews. They claim their expert forgeries can slip past the screening algorithms of sites like Yelp.

Not always. In 2013, New York attorney general Eric Schneiderman announced a settlement for $350,000 in fines, plus agreements to cease and desist, from nineteen reputation management companies that had posted ersatz reviews from proxies as far away as the Philippines and Bangladesh. New York's yearlong investigation included a sting operation: One agent posed as the owner of a Brooklyn yogurt shop seeking positive notices. He soon found a company that assured him that it could generate many such posts that Yelp, Google, CitySearch, and other sites would be unable to weed out.

Luca and Zervas determined that fraudulent reviews tend to be more extreme (either positively or negatively) than genuine ones and that restaurants with weak or poor reputations are more likely to post them, especially in highly competitive markets. Consumer critiques matter less to chain restaurants, which rarely fake reviews. The authors concluded that competition and market incentives, not business ethics, drive review fraud.

Researchers cannot directly observe which reviews are fake. Therefore the scholars needed Yelp's filtering algorithm to create their estimate of prevalence. It may be that Yelp's filter—which uses "established," "trustworthy" reviewers as benchmarks to identify, by contrast, suspicious ones—does a good job of filtering out frauds. (Yelp does not publicize details of how its algorithm works, as doing so would simply help cheaters game the system.) But we know even less about the fraud filters, if any, at hundreds of other consumer-review sites, leaving us with the ancient advice of "caveat emptor."

"The screening algorithms take on the counterfeit reviews in a kind of arms race," says Luca. "The gamers are always trying to figure out how to deceive the screening mechanisms, which the review sites keep improving. Overall, the content on Yelp is pretty good. We did a study that indicated that just using Yelp reviews, you could figure out which restaurants to report for health-code violations with a high degree of accuracy. If the review data were junk, you couldn't do things like that." In fact, Luca is using review data to help cities decide which restaurants to inspect. In this way, shadow work by Yelp reviewers is subsuming a task of health inspectors, and perhaps saving municipalities money.

There is also a gray area in which owners of restaurants simply *encourage* happy customers to post favorable notices. Yelp officially advises against this practice, but such reviews are not technically frauds, and the incentives for soliciting them remain in place. New technologies like ordering from restaurant tables with iPads facilitate instant reviewing. "A great time to capture guest reviews is before they leave the restaurant, while details of the experience are top of mind," advised SelfService World, an online organ for self-service technologies and industries. "Willingness to provide feedback is also much greater with this immediacy, since even the most satisfied guests often don't feel compelled to rate their experience later."

Bazaarvoice, an international company based in Austin, Texas, with offices around the United States and in Europe, Asia, and Australia, has a major presence in the consumer-review industry. Its website urges potential clients to "Sell more by encouraging people to review products, ask questions, give answers, and share stories." Bazaarvoice helps its clients transplant reviews from websites of manufacturers like Avon and LG to those of retailers like Walmart. Such efforts can greatly magnify the impact of customer reviews. This process, says Luca, could introduce "a large distortion in the market" by warping perceptions of how random consumers have actually experienced a given product.

CONSUMER REVIEWS ARE voluntary shadow work. As with all shadow work, they do have a payoff, if not a monetary one. Citizen reviewers like getting their opinions off their chests—sharing them, theoretically at least, with the world. Sites like Amazon and Yelp even grant reviewers their own profile pages that not only collect their posts but may provide personal details, location, interests, email addresses, and preferences in food, music, books, and movies. Establishing an identity as a shadow-working reviewer can massage the hungry ego with a bona fide web presence.

The citizen reviewers are not completely self-motivated. Many organizations that publish consumer reviews aggressively solicit them. Angie's List quickly dunned me to review a car mechanic and a plumber whom I had patronized after seeing them praised on that site. In the mail, I received an unsolicited six-page questionnaire from a magazine, *Consumer's CHECKBOOK*, with a cover letter asking for my "ratings of auto repair shops, physicians, plumbers, auto insurance companies, roofers, carpet cleaners, and other local services you have used." Contributing this shadow work would earn me a free issue of my local edition, *Boston CHECKBOOK*.

Some venues even grant prolific or much-read contributors an elite "top reviewer" status. "Designating people as top reviewers is an example of *badging*: giving them some kind of recognition that they are the best," says Sucharita Mulpuru, an analyst with Forrester Research. "There's the ego gratification of having an audience." Those who write mostly favorable reviews are also, indirectly, performing shadow work as marketers, helping to move the website's products. Rewarding them makes sense, even if their intent was not to sell. The incentives seem effective, too. Judging by their colossal number of reviews, some contributors appear to be working at least full-time as critics, logging more hours as shadow workers than professional reviewers do on salary.

There's another caveat: Given an unmoderated forum, the disgruntled are quicker to express themselves than the gruntled. Every single product in the marketplace, no matter how worthy, will receive at least a few blistering criticisms. If there were many customer rundowns on the $400,000 Rolls Royce Phantom (there are very few; Rolls Royce buyers don't rely on consumer feedback), someone would surely be complaining about its low gas mileage and poor cornering. You can report obscenity or abusiveness, but otherwise there is no remedy for this negative bias, as no gatekeepers oversee the traffic.

Consider "Produce59," a reviewer on TripAdvisor.com, who complained that at the Comfort Inn & Suites in Fredericksburg, Virginia, "The heating A/C unit was nice and quiet; however, the thermostat is on the wall, so turning the knobs directly on the unit will not get you any results," as Jim Windolf reported in *The New York Times*. What a drawback—a thermostat on the wall! Regarding a Kentucky Econo Lodge motel, "Tropicandan" observed, "The breakfast was adequate but unremarkable." One has to wonder just what sort of remarkable breakfast this traveler was expecting at the Econo Lodge in Cave City, Kentucky. Windolf concludes that based on review sites, "the American consumer has become a pain in the neck."

THE AMAZON RIVER OF SHADOW WORK

Vending machines once seemed like mechanical, twentieth-century devices, hopelessly decoupled from the digital orbit of the Internet. No more. Newer models connect vending machines to the Internet in imaginative ways. In 2013, the Pepsi Like Machine debuted at a Beyoncé concert in Antwerp, Belgium. (Pepsi and Beyoncé signed a $50 million sponsorship deal in 2012.) This innovative machine invites smartphone users to visit www.likepepsi.com, connect to their Facebook accounts, and "like" the Pepsi Facebook page. It then dispenses a free Pepsi as a reward. Those without a smart-phone can log onto Facebook from the machine's forty-two-inch touchscreen and still get their free soda.

What Pepsi gets in return is a treasure trove of information. For a brand like Pepsi, the "likes" may be trivial, but the connections to Facebook accounts constitute a targeted-advertising bonanza. The Pepsi Like Machine confirms the value corporations now place on collecting customer information: Certain data points are worth giving away product to obtain.

Information translates into money and power, so organizations relentlessly gather data on their clients. The result is a daily outreach through all available channels. Everyone, it seems, wants to know more about you, and institutions aren't even faintly shy about asking. Surveys bombard us online, by telephone, and in the mail, brazenly requesting that we donate our time and information. (The Pepsi Like Machine at least gives you a drink.) Dealing with this information dragnet—including steps taken to dodge it—entails shadow work, often with little or no benefit to the consumer.

Once upon a time, a purchase ended with the exchange of money for whatever you bought. But today, commerce comes with a coda: the survey. Typically, this arrives at your in-box as a "customer satisfaction survey," exploring your experience with the product, service, sales transaction, or customer support. Surveys also appear in hard copies. Inevitably, they include a few demo-graphic items, enabling the firm to profile its customer base. Data crunchers can analyze such information to discover, as one report disclosed, that customer service agents' conversations with women take 1.7 times as long as those with men. "Every time I go to the doctor, or straighten out some billing problem, or buy anything online, I get a damned survey asking me how my experience was," says Hart, a banker in Lakeville, Connecticut. "It's endless. Why do I have to critique everything?"

In mid-2014, Survey Monkey of Palo Alto, California, an online survey platform, processed 2.2 million responses daily, more than double its rate of 1 million in early 2013. Founded in 1999, the company has sent out forty-three million surveys since then. Drafting a survey has become very easy; Survey Monkey even makes a mobile app available to clients who want to cobble one together at, say, the country club after a round of golf.

To take one extreme case, Jeff Ferreira, a Boston-area designer, was inundated with fifteen surveys from a single vendor over only two months. This occurred during a vexing period when he attempted—five times—to have a mirrored console table he'd bought online for $600 delivered in an undamaged state. Each time he called the vendor to complain, "Almost instantly, three customer satisfaction surveys would land in his inbox," *The Boston Globe* reported. "I didn't fill them out," Ferreira noted. "I already spent enough of my time screaming at them over the phone."

Routinely, businesses now ask shadow-working customers to cough up personal information as a way to smooth transactions, or even enable them to buy things at all. To make online purchases, customers open accounts with bookstores, banks, newspapers, utilities, sports teams, apparel vendors, phone service providers, and so on. Everyone wants you to open an account. This means supplying contact and demographic data and then having all transactions tracked, building a personal profile for the vendor.

That profile enables vendors to activate "recommendation engines." Once its algorithms have examined your past purchases, Amazon can recommend books or desk lamps you might like, and Netflix can suggest movies to rent. On my computer, opening Amazon.com brings up thumbnails of books by Bill Bryson, an author whose works I have purchased, and books on pharmaceutical companies, a topic I've browsed. I also see displays of clock radios, pressure cookers, and Egyptian cotton towels—gifts I've bought from Amazon. Personalized ads will show up on many websites where you have done business, or even considered doing so.

In the past, advertisers just hollered out their pitches in cattle-call mode: "Come one, come all." Today, they know who you are and can whisper sweet, personalized nothings in your ear. Purchasing profiles enable *targeted selling;* they let advertisers zero in on people "prequalified" as potential buyers. Such cruise-missile pitches have an improved chance of success.

Furthermore, your profile not only guides advertising to your doorstep but may adjust the price you pay. When you hold a loyalty card for a supermarket chain like Safeway, the store can use its data archive on your past purchases to adjust what you're charged at the register for certain products. If, for example, you are a regular consumer of Snapple iced teas, you may get a lower price to encourage you to buy more of them—by the case, say. The discount kicks in when you scan your loyalty card at the register. You might also get a Snapple coupon for future visits. Your neighbor who hasn't been buying Snapple gets no such price break.

If the supermarket knows that you have a large family (either from demographic information you've provided or from an algorithm that extrapolated this from your purchases of "family-size" boxes of cereal), it might offer inducements to buy larger jugs of laundry detergent or bigger sizes of frozen dinners. Purchase profiles can also target pet owners via their dog-food buys, or new parents from diaper purchases. The data can even help the store react to current events. After a 2012 power failure in Washington, for example, Safeway sent out coupons for frozen foods to encourage customers to restock when power had returned, according to a *New York Times* report.

IN THE RETAIL sector, virtually every supermarket, drugstore, hardware, home-improvement, and office-supply chain encourages customers to carry its loyalty card, proffering discounts and other modest benefits. Each requires an application, usually a brief one, that logs customer data.

The sprawling field of healthcare, situated in the high-stakes arena of life, death, and illness (with their related financial liabilities), records vast amounts of information. Whenever you see a new doctor, if she is not part of your existing healthcare network, her assistant will hand you a pen, a clipboard, and a questionnaire several pages long that asks you to spell out—yet again—your complete medical history, with your past diseases as well as those of your blood relatives, plus your hospitalizations, surgeries, allergies, prescriptions, and reams of other information. Meanwhile, the doctor's staff toils away on mountains of paperwork from health insurers. There is a rage for documentation, because it can help justify any decision—even in court, if necessary. (Of course, documentation can also backfire and be used against you, as many ex-politicians can testify.)

Governments, too, demand gobs of information, generating citizen shadow work. Application forms for building permits, student loans, business licenses, motor vehicle registrations, driver's licenses, and a surfeit of other government documents deluge citizens with shadow work.

Taxation trumps them all. The Internal Revenue Service (IRS) may represent the largest single source of shadow work. (Of course, we have no choice about doing this shadow work, as the law mandates it. But freely chosen or not, tax compliance counts as bona fide shadow work.) In 1998, the IRS estimated that taxpayers "spent approximately 6 billion hours each year on tax compliance activities, such as tax planning, recordkeeping, and form completion," according to a report delivered at a 2004 IRS research conference. As of 2010, the average time burden for those filing Form 1040 (70 percent of taxpayers) was twenty-three hours of shadow work per year.

SLAKING THE RELENTLESS thirst for data has opened the floodgates of a huge river—call it an amazon river—of shadow work. Much of this data collection makes sense: Shipping products obviously requires an address. Yet it's a far different world from the traditional retail store, where you can walk in, pay cash, and leave without even telling the cashier your name. The anonymity of cash bestows a profound degree of privacy (though at a price: Unlike credit cards, cash doesn't offer "cash rewards"). In contrast, credit and debit transactions are thoroughly recorded and traceable. All this documentation, whether by cookies on a server or a video surveillance camera in a convenience store, moves much of what we do from the private to the public realm.

Living under surveillance has some social benefits. When terrorists bombed the finish line of the Boston Marathon in 2013, melting into the crowd before their bombs exploded, one of my first thoughts was, "How are they ever going to catch these guys?" Yet only a few days later, police had identified them, killed one, and arrested the other. The crucial factor was a video surveillance camera near the finish line that recorded the perpetrators planting the bomb.

Even so, most of us also cherish the right of privacy and want to lead our lives without government or corporate oversight. We'd prefer to keep our personal information and preferences private. (For one thing, the more personal info we disclose on the Internet, the more points of attack we offer identity thieves.) Privacy was once the default setting. Your personal data was yours alone. Only if you purposely shared some fact about yourself would it go public. The information revolution has reversed this equation: Maintaining privacy now requires proactive shadow work.

Our "informational bodies" inhabit the public realm. For example, in 2009, when Facebook began allowing users to share posts publicly, its default setting for new users permitted anyone to view them. (Facebook has historically offered complicated privacy controls that let users set separate permissions for nearly every type of item. Under pressure from several directions, FB has strengthened and simplified these controls.)

Every new web account we open asks for an array of contact information, and the computerized auto-fill function makes filling in forms an easy process that takes only seconds. Each account enters another version of your data into another archive, creating both a useful connection and another window of vulnerability. In the widely reported breach of Target's archives before Christmas 2013, data thieves lifted 40,000 credit- and debit-card numbers, plus other personal data for as many as seventy million people. No one knows where hackers will strike next, but the more storage sites there are, the more Targets they have.

The upshot is another tributary feeding the amazon river of shadow work. Protecting your privacy means taking initiatives. This can take a lot of time and money. In an op-ed essay in *The New York Times,* Julia Angwin, author of *Dragnet Nation,* even asked if privacy has become a "luxury good." She detailed how in the prior year she had spent $2,200 "and countless hours" trying to shield her privacy. This involved encryption services; a filter that shields her laptop screen "from coffee-shop voyeurs"; and a monthly service providing disposable email addresses and phone numbers to safeguard against the mining and sale of her personal data. As a specialist in this area, Angwin, a former *Wall Street Journal* reporter who now writes for ProPublica, surely defends her privacy more energetically than most (and her \$2,200 may be tax-deductible), but her efforts highlight the fact that simply keeping personal data personal now means a bushel of shadow work.

NERD SERFDOM

There is a flip side to this coin. While institutions are assembling tons of data on us, we, too, are accumulating archives on our own computers. These files, bookmarks, music downloads and video tracks, photo albums, email messages, applications, and all sorts of stored data demand that we maintain, secure, update, and curate them—and of course back them up. Like it or not, we are all becoming shadow-working nerds.

Digital technology generates data exponentially. One file grows from another. Backups, for example, automatically double the digital footprint of whatever gets backed up. Multiple drafts of documents, or various cuts of videos, build up alongside each other on our hard drives. Files attached to emails replicate themselves as attachments, and the recipient may save or forward the message, cloning more copies.

Consumers have inherited the job of storing and overseeing these immense archives of information. This usually includes a long list of digital keys—usernames and passwords—that open our favorite web portals. Users must update and protect such lists. But if you store a file of passwords on your computer, a hacker who breaks into your machine can instantly enter all your accounts. So we take countermeasures. Some encrypt their passwords in an online "vault" for a monthly fee. My own solution is to print out a list of usernames and passwords and update the underlying digital file on a removable USB flash drive to keep them offline.

Nerd serfdom afflicts us with a modern syndrome, "password fatigue." A 2002 survey in England found that the average Internet user had twenty-one online accounts. That number has likely doubled since then and may be higher in the United States. Nearly all web portals require that users invent new, "secure" passwords and remember them. But we have wearied of these incessant demands: the result is password fatigue. Lazy people—there are many—may use *password* as their personal password; believe it or not, it ranked as the most popular password for two years running, until dethroned in 2013 by the equally ingenious *123456*. A *Consumer Reports* survey in 2010 found that more than two-thirds of users had the same password or a variation of it for all their accounts.

"Billions of times a day, websites prompt us to create or recall user names and passwords for even the most seemingly unimportant tasks," wrote Meghan Keneally in a 2012 essay in *The Berkshire Eagle*. "Passwords are painfully necessary in daily life not only for little secrets but, also, basically for access to your life." (Keneally's statement suggests the degree to which our informational bodies have come to supplant our biological ones; your online life has become "your life.") Yet passwords are a pain. "In addition to the simply overwhelming number of passwords needed on a daily basis," she writes, "another problem arises when every new password stipulates specific requirements (eight–ten characters, punctuation marks, no punctuation marks, capitalization, fake words, no names, no sense!)"

Such demands open a factory of shadow work. The rule of thumb is that the more secure a password is, the harder it is to remember. The online security mavens won't like "tuliplover" and are much happier with "2LiP!LvR." But most of us prefer a password we know by heart to a bizarre string of alphanumeric characters that looks like a tweet from a Martian.

"It's a nightmare," comedian Tracy Ullman told Jacob Bernstein of *The New York Times*. "These passwords just keep getting longer and longer." Writer Paul Rudnick added that tracking down the password to his Time Warner Cable modem "was like a *Bourne Identity* moment." Bernstein summarizes: "The end result: a mind-boggling array of personal codes squirreled away in computer files, scribbled on Post-it notes or simply lost in the ether. Virtually any online user without a computer science degree now seems to be one failed login attempt away from a nervous breakdown."

Password expiration compounds the problem. Harvard University asks staff to invent new passwords annually, but that is child's play compared to corporate environments where passwords expire every ninety days. This pushes employees through the cycle of inventing a new password, remembering it for three months, then forgetting it while devising and memorizing a new one. Some staff throw in the towel and rely on the "Forgot Password" option that emails them a new password on each usage.

Usernames are a separate ordeal. When opening a new account that requires a username, don't even think about anything as easy as your own actual name. With seven billion people roaming the globe, there is no human name that hasn't already been taken. No matter how strange or unique you may believe your moniker to be, get ready for a surprise when you discover that AsdrubalSandomirsky17 is already in use. Just keep inventing other usernames you might be able to remember, and within half an hour or so you could stumble on one that gets clearance from the website. Thankfully, most sites now use email addresses as usernames, as they are by design unique.

Then the next layer of safeguards, the dreaded "security questions," appear. These are fine when they ask what town you were born in, or your mother's maiden name. But they may veer into debatable areas that call for making a judgment, and judgments are slippery. What was your high school mascot? (Well, I went to three high schools, so do you mean the lions, the tigers, or the bears?—oh, my!) What was the name of your first boyfriend/ girlfriend? (Would that be the sweetheart I had in fourth grade, my consuming crush as a high school sophomore, or my first bona fide college romance?)

SOFTWARE UPGRADES RELEASE a steady stream of Shadow Work 2.0, 3.0, and 4.0. Anyone with a computer receives a constant trickle of messages announcing newly released updates to their existing software. Typically free of charge, these don't take much time to install, though they often force you to quit a browser or other application you were using, sidelining your work. In theory, such tweaks improve the functionality or security of your software, though in the vast majority of cases I have not noticed any change in performance from updates; perhaps what counts is something that *doesn't* happen, like a viral attack.

Nonetheless, buying a piece of software isn't exactly like buying silverware. In that case you own it, you keep it, and you use it, period. But the software you *think* you own is really something you share with its developer, which keeps releasing updates. The software evolves, so "your" possession continually transforms itself— the ground keeps shifting beneath your feet. Furthermore, you don't always have a choice about upgrading. If you don't upgrade your computer's operating system for a few years, you will find yourself shut out of many crucial functions, because the web's evolving digital environment "no longer supports" the operating system you bought. It is like being told that you have to buy a faster car with a bigger engine because freeways have improved so much that the minimum speed has increased to eighty miles per hour. Move up or move out. It's certainly a great way to keep selling hardware and software.

The real shadow work comes with upgrades that require re-learning things you had already mastered. This can mean a serious time investment, likely one that will entail teeth-gnashing frustration and loud cursing. And for the most part, as with an insurance claim, the end result will simply be that you can still do what you did before the upgrade. Software developers do not seem to mind that their products' learning curves stick consumers with a sink-hole of shadow work. Like the environmental fallout from bottled water, such costs don't show up on the balance sheet.

In 2012, Microsoft's release of Windows 8, for example, eliminated time-honored features like the Start button for accessing programs and drop-down menus listing their functions. It asks users to relearn things they knew how to do: shadow work. It took Kevin McCarthy, a fifty-nine-year-old New York City copywriter, several minutes simply to work out how to compose an email message with the new system, feeling like "the biggest amateur computer user ever," he told *The New York Times,* which described Windows 8 as having "a stripped-down look and on-screen buttons that at times resemble the runic assembly instructions for Ikea furniture."

PRISONERS OF MADISON AVENUE

Consumers also need to continually sweep out their digital houses. Consider spam. Hardly anyone welcomes spam, that relentless bombardment of your in-box with offers of millions of dollars from deposed Nigerian officials, guaranteed penis enlargement methods, and a raft of other unsolicited offers. Spam was a $200 million global industry as of 2012. Eleven percent of spam recipients actually read the messages.

Spam arrives via email, and in our twenty-first-century economy, few can survive without email. This means identifying and deleting spam. Junk-mail filters can accomplish this automatically (though imperfectly, creating an iatrogenic problem when they divert real messages into the junk mailbox), but no filter is perfect. So spam gets through.

Deleting spam takes time. According to a study by the University of Maryland School of Business, it takes 1.4 minutes per day for the average American adult. That may not sound like much, but it adds up: It means diverting *nine hours* of your waking time each year to an unrewarding and unproductive task. This shadow work, too, merely restores the condition you began with. Some estimates peg spam's prevalence at 50 or even as high as 80 percent of all email, and a 2009 report estimated the annual economic cost of time wasted deleting spam at $21.6 billion. Spammers occasionally offer an "unsubscribe" option to escape their talons. That's nice, but it hands you yet another piece of shadow work: locating the tiny unsubscribe link, clicking it, then perhaps filling in your email address or updating an "email preferences" page. I sometimes wonder whether I am really unsubscribing or only confirming my email address for the spammer.

Junk mail arriving in envelopes also needs disposal, but dropping it in the trash is quicker than unsubscribing from an email list. The overarching point is that we all still have regular mailboxes that fill up with letters, bills, magazines, and ads. But we also have gained one, two, or even more email boxes to tend as well. This simply takes more time, and more shadow work.

The mushrooming number of communication channels spins off another type of shadow work. At one time, to reach a friend, you could send a letter or postcard or phone him at home. Period. Then, as work and personal lives began to overlap more, it became OK to call him at the office, if only for brief chats. Next, email arrived, opening up another means of contact. Then mobile phones, then texting. I won't even bring up Instagram.

With this plethora of channels available, consider what happens if you need to reach your mate, say, on some urgent matter. Perhaps you want to take her to a play, and on the theater's website, you see two choice tickets available. You can see the precise location of the seats, just like selecting your seat on an airline, and they are good ones.

Great, except something else has changed, too. *Everyone else in the world* can see the theater website and take in the same information. Sitting in your study, you are competing with the other *seven billion residents* of Planet Earth. (Thank God we are online, rather than on line, together.) OK, admittedly, not many of the fourteen million people of Dhaka, Bangladesh, will be angling for a Friday night seat for Luigi Pirandello's *Tonight We Improvise* at this particular theater in Cambridge, Massachusetts. Only a handful, at best. But many others *are* angling, which means someone else could snap up those two choice tickets any time. If you want to spend that night in the orchestra section with Larissa, you had better reach her, *pronto*.

What happens next is a fascinating new species of shadow work: the all-media parlay. You phone Larissa's mobile, home, and work numbers, leaving voicemail messages at each. You send emails to her home and work mailboxes. You top it off with a text. You have just composed and sent *six* communications through different channels to get *one* message to *one* person. The good news is that two decades ago, such a multichannel assault was impossible. The bad news is that this electronic D-day landing just gifted you with several minutes of shadow work. And a few more on the other end for Larissa, as she opens, hears, deletes, and, with luck, responds positively to one of the half dozen redundant invitations awaiting her. With more luck, in time to buy those tickets.

WEBSITES BARRAGE VIEWERS with display advertising. It would be convenient just to ignore ads of no interest, but unfortunately it is not quite that simple. Online ads do not behave like print ads in newspapers and magazines, which just lie there. You can absorb print ads if you want to, or skip them and continue reading your story. Web commercials are more aggressive. They emulate the television ads whose audio tracks blare louder than the program you were watching. Many web ads "pop up" off the page in an enlarged version, hiding the content you'd hoped to read and so *forcing* you to deal with the ads. For an even pushier intrusion, some ads leap up and start showing a video—with sound, as usual, several decibels louder than you need. At this point you have to grab the mouse and position your cursor on the X in the upper-right corner to close the ad you never opened. Don't panic in your annoyance and hastily click the ad itself. Doing that will whisk you to the advertiser's home page, and it will take even longer to get back to what you were trying to do before the commercial barged unbidden onto your screen and went into its song and dance.

Consider how reading a newspaper differs structurally from watching television news. Open a newspaper and, as with ads, the choice is yours to read a story—or not—and to decide in what sequence you'll absorb the stories. This remains generally true for online newspapers, depending on their site's design. But the viewer of television news has no such freedoms. *NBC Nightly News* does not present its stories all at once like the *Los Angeles Times*. The telecast offers up one story at a time. A TV news broadcast (impor-tantly, including commercials) unfolds in a linear way, over time, so the only way to ignore a story or ad is to press the mute but-ton on your remote, which at least disables the audio. The news-cast, not the viewer, determines the order of events, and you pretty much have to sit through it. Television's stimulating images and soundtracks come packaged with a loss of freedom.

Similarly, the "free" videos available on YouTube or news websites typically hold you hostage to advertising before showing the video you chose. Two-thirds of those surveyed by *Consumer Reports* in 2014 found this tactic annoying. A commercial will run as a prelude, much as movie theaters now show ads before the feature begins. (Not having to sit through commercials, as you do when you watch television, was once a privilege that came with paying for a movie ticket.) YouTube and theaters have something advertisers love: a captive audience. In one case, I encountered a YouTube video that, as the price of viewing, required me first to answer a multiple-choice question asking which one of five busi-nesses I had seen an online ad for. The survey invaders sometimes hold your desired content as hostage until you comply.

The more user-friendly websites at least allow viewers, after seeing the opening seconds of the ad, to click past the rest and start the video. The basic dynamic, though, is to seize attention: to *make* consumers view those advertisements. Advertisers call it "capturing eyeballs." It's the same bargain that once enabled tele-vision broadcasters, before cable and satellite, to offer programs for free—commercials paid the bills. Decide for yourself whether digesting all these ads constitutes shadow work. (It may cost you money, because if the ads work, you'll end up buying more stuff.)

Some of us genuinely *like* commercials—after all, they have far higher production budgets per second than programs, and many are entertaining and funny. (ESPN's hilarious promotional series "This Is Sports Center" should be collected on a DVD.) Regardless of where you come down, ads, like spam, belong to the medium you are using. And so does the dragnet for user information.

THE DATA GOLD RUSH is under way. It will continue and even ramp up as the information economy grows and technology invents more sophisticated ways to gather facts. There will be mounting demands on you for the shadow work of filling in questionnaires and surveys. At the same time, much data collection will *not* involve shadow work because phones, credit cards, gasoline pumps, supermarket checkouts, cable boxes, and computers can gather it automatically, without your participation. Urban infrastructures like tollbooths record additional data, as do "sensor-equipped buildings, trains, buses, planes, bridges, and factories," as Jonathan Shaw reported in *Harvard Magazine* in 2014. "The data flow so fast that that the total accumulation of the past two years—a zettabyte [one sextillion bytes]—dwarfs the prior record of human civilization."

People at the source points for data often do not know where that data is going or to what uses it will be put. Data from the checkout register at a fast-food franchise, for example, may travel directly to the chain's headquarters, rather than to the franchise owner. Headquarters might compare the franchise's data to the chain's national norms. This can result in an efficiency dictum from the main office: "Your workers are taking too long on their bathroom breaks—averaging five minutes." Most franchisees will go along with this and lay down the law for their employees.

Kiosks that identify users by fingerprints or retinal scans represent the opening act for biometric techniques of assembling data that will come to provide stacks of information to healthcare providers, market researchers, and life insurers. Satellites now track your exact location at any moment via GPS signals from mobile devices. Today, enough smartphones are riding in cars to feed apps GPS data that, when aggregated, can depict traffic density—and identify traffic jams by computing the average speed of cars between, say, exits 13 and 17 of the Garden State Parkway in New Jersey.

The information dragnet promises centralized databanks that store more and more information about each one of us. The vascularization of our informational bodies will fill in with fine capillaries, completing an ever-more-detailed rendering of our economic and social lives. Do not succumb to the naive notion that such databanks just lie there passively as neutral repositories of facts—the myth that "data in itself is neither good nor bad; it's what you *do* with the data that matters." Nonsense. Storing these vast arrays of information is like maintaining a large "neutral" peacetime army: You can be sure that sooner or later, that army will find something to do. Those petabytes weren't built up by accident, and make no mistake: Someone, somewhere is putting them to use right now.

The good news is that the information gathered about you may, in some ways, result in less shadow work, as sensors and electronic pickups record more of it and transmit it to some archive, taking those jobs off your hands. That is also the bad news. Shadow work falls off because you aren't consciously involved in submitting the data, but you also don't know what information you are giving up or where it will land. The information is being collected behind your back.

The incentives behind the information dragnet are too powerful to neutralize completely. Yet awareness is one way to offset its ceaseless demands. Resist if your government tries to *require* all citizens to carry a smartphone, or to keep a GPS transmitter on them. Such policies don't always take the form of laws. They could be no more than judicial indifference when, say, new corporate policies make it very inconvenient to buy gasoline without a credit card.

Institutions have their priorities, and you have yours. As noted earlier, philosopher John Locke argued that labor creates property; taking his view, if your shadow work made some information, it is your possession. In fact, who *owns* your data—your informational body—may some day be as contentious an issue as the ownership of petroleum, water, or any other natural resource.

SHADOW WORK SAGA: Sex, Mating, and Algorithms

For most of human history, there was no dating. Millennia passed when even rich, beautiful people went dateless on Saturday nights.

They coupled in other ways. In prehistory, monogamy was, at best, a tenuous proposition, but humans obviously found ways to reproduce, probably with relatively few amenities. When civilization and marriage appeared, parents took control and arranged matches. Pragmatism ruled. For the upper classes, that meant money, property, even political leverage. For the bootless and unhorsed, physical and mental health, sound character, and, if available, good looks could suffice.

Romance as we know it didn't arise until the Middle Ages. Around AD 1100, troubadours invented *courtly love:* a special magnetism between a man and a woman, mixing erotic desire and spiritual uplift. Traveling minstrels sang poetry celebrating courtly love throughout the picturesque landscape of Occitània, a region that is now mostly southern France.

Courtly love did not involve one's spouse. Love and marriage did *not* "go together like a horse and carriage," as the song has it. They were two separate things—mutually exclusive, in fact. Marriage was a relationship of duty, whereas love was one of personal affinity; thus the two were incompatible. The late-twelfth-century book *De Amore* (English translation: *The Art of Courtly Love*) declared that "True love can have no place between husband and wife."

Over the centuries, courtly love evolved into romantic love—which, with some PR from poets, gradually caught on. The Enlightenment and the eighteenth-century political revolutions sowed seeds of populism and democracy, undermining the authority of those atop social hierarchies, such as parents. In the West, women and men moved toward self-determination, including their choice of mates. Social milieux gradually opened up, allowing young people to connect with peers—in other words, to date.

Traditionally, people met dating partners through family and friends, at work, or through hobbies and social events. Today, various businesses also facilitate linking up. Professional matchmakers introduce their clients for a fee. Printed or online personal ads, singles groups and events (not just drinking and dancing but singles yoga classes, cycling trips, and gardening clubs), and "speed dating" help make connections. The fact that these businesses exist testifies that traditional ways of meeting are no longer getting the job done.

Finding a mate has become complicated. The American divorce rate tripled between 1960 and 1980 and remains high, making single people wary of those vulnerable commitments, even while seeking them—often over and over again. Women have cultivated robust careers, and their financial independence removes what was a powerful motive for marriage before the 1970s. Jobs that involve overnight business travel reduce chances to share time and space with a potential partner. Established mating conventions have fallen away, leaving confusion in their wake. Traditional courtship and marriage may have limited our options, but they also gave straightforward guidance on the mating ritual; when lost in the wilderness, a clear map can be quite welcome.

Amid these developments, singles are using new tools. When I was in college, posters all over the Harvard campus touted Operation Match, a way of finding kindred spirits through a computer algorithm. You just filled out a questionnaire, mailed it in with $3, and six weeks later got a list of matches in the mail. Two Harvard students had cooked up the idea in 1965 at a late-night bull session. Operation Match caught on: It made *Look* magazine's Valentine's Day cover in 1966, and one of the founders appeared on the television game show *To Tell the Truth*. By the time the owners sold the company in 1968, it had data from one million respondents, as Nell Porter Brown wrote in 2003 in *Harvard Magazine*.

Fast-forward to 2014, when online dating has become a billion-dollar industry. The traditional routes of work/school and friends/family remain in play. But meeting online has become the third-most-popular way to find dates, according to a 2013 report in *The Independent* of London. Online dating vastly expands the pool of potential partners beyond those who show up in one's real-world life. There are indeed plenty of fish in the sea, and online services move the fishing grounds from your hometown lake to the Pacific Ocean. Match.com (established 1995) owns thirty other dating sites besides its flagship brand. When, in 2004, the *Guinness Book of World Records* declared it the world's largest, more than fifteen million members were working Match.com's services worldwide. It currently operates in twenty-five countries and eight languages.

FOUR MATHEMATICS MAJORS from Harvard launched OkCupid in 2004 and sold the business to Match.com seven years later. OkCupid calls its questionnaires "quizzes" and also invites users to submit their own quizzes; it had received more than 43,000 of them by 2011, according to a *New Yorker* story by Nick Paumgarten. OkCupid's average user, he reported, answers 300 questions, yielding an archive of 800 million answers. That is quite a pile of data—much of it highly personal, even intimate—that the site can vend to its advertisers.

The strategy of finding a statistically compatible mate by analyzing reams of data departs radically from the past. Yet in a way, it only substitutes hardware for "wetware," or brain tissue. Data about wealth, social status, education, and family of origin have always figured into courtship. But a crucial difference is that your friends and family already *know* your outlooks and tastes extremely well, so they have no need to ask you 300 questions. Your answers are already stored in their brains. They apply their own intuitive "algorithms" when they fix you up with someone. In contrast, OkCupid knows zero about you, so it must trot out the quizzes to compile the same storehouse of information. This begets a serving of shadow work for the user, who must feed the algorithm. It also spins off a nice by-product for OkCupid: a rich harvest of digital info.

Fee-based services like Match.com and eHarmony charge monthly rates. Free services like OkCupid earn their money from advertisers rather than members. (Here again, the maxim applies: If you aren't paying for the product, you *are* the product.) Fee-based or free, online dating services all require customers to cough up data for their formulas. Theories of romance are embedded in these algorithms. The classic advice that "opposites attract," for example, gains few adherents here: The algorithms almost always match people with *similar* outlooks, values, and beliefs, not opposite ones.

Dating-site questionnaires probe views and preferences to build personality profiles. The data archive that shadow-working customers create for free becomes (like Facebook's content) a valuable capital asset that the sites can monetize. In one sense, providing this data is just the obvious ante: You have to pony up information to play the game. On the other hand, it's a task that does not arise when people meet via real social networks rather than virtual ones. In this way it qualifies as shadow work, as the dating site puts it in place.

Dating transforms itself from play into work when it becomes a *project*. And finding a sexual partner, including a potential spouse, has become exactly that for many adults. Remember that work is something we do to achieve a goal, while we play just for its own sake. "I want to find someone to spend the rest of my life with," declared Kara, a thirty-two-year-old marketing consultant in western Massachusetts. "So I am joining a couple of computer dating services, and I will attack this like any other kind of job." The time Kara invests in this "job" is modern shadow work.

Someone seeking a fling need not invest much time in online dating. Apps like Hinge and Tinder import data from one's Facebook profile, simplifying the profile-building process and trimming shadow work considerably. (One advantage Facebook has in Internet commerce is that it helps people avoid the shadow work of entering the same personal data repeatedly on different websites; FB is a clearinghouse of sorts.) The Tinder client can browse photos on her smartphone and make a quick decision on whether to pursue contact. The clients of these apps include many who are looking for serious relationships but prefer to sift through less content and to provide less data. "It's not unlike spotting someone attractive across a bar and deciding to start a conversation with him," says Janice, a graphic designer in Baltimore.

Such apps will match you with "friends of friends"—which, at first glance, mimics the real world. The idea is that you have a better chance of getting along with someone who is a friend of your friend. Sounds good. The catch is that Facebook "friends" are not real-world friends, and people apply vastly different standards for online "friendships" than they do for people they actually hang out with. "I have not found random Facebook connections to be very helpful," says Rachel, a twenty-eight-year-old in Washington, D.C., who has used several online dating services. "My friend Vanessa, for example, can have as a Facebook 'friend' someone she met in a study-abroad program in college—somebody she hasn't talked to in eight years."

A Vassar alumna who works in arts administration, Rachel is looking for a "really substantial" relationship, not a fling. Like many young singles, she favors accessing dating apps on her smartphone. Hence the proper term for what she does is "*online* dating," not "*computer* dating." When she lived in New York City, Rachel worked on dating-app messages while waiting for the subway. The hazard of this, she notes, is that "the programs are always at our fingertips, which is dangerous if we want to limit the amount of interaction, or work, we have on the sites."

Rachel says that "more information is helpful—how people describe themselves, the tone and level of detail." She never sends a flip message like "What's up?" but might mention a book the other user said he liked to open a dialogue: "I put more work into it." If he had answered a question saying he favored gay marriage rights, "I'd stow that away and think it was a point in his favor," she says. She takes on the shadow work of answering more questions for, say, OkCupid, which offers its members incentives to provide more data. "The more questions you answer, the more information it makes available to you," Rachel explains. "I can only see how a guy has answered a question if I have answered it, too. Putting more work into it opens up more information on others. It *does* feel like a lot of work."

The shadow work also involves managing inflow. Most users ignore the vast majority of messages they receive. But they still beg to be opened, or even read, before being deleted. ("You never know.") Members communicate by email messages routed through the dating site. This keeps their identities private in the early stages, as a direct email would identify the user, who might not wish to communicate further.

Messages stream in at all hours. Rachel often responds to this inflow at night after a long day of work, going out with friends, and commuting home. If rapport blooms and progresses to the point of arranging a date, communication switches to texts—and the social convention of answering texts immediately takes the timing out of your hands. Plus, tending to screens keeps us awake. Late-night OkCupid work can mean sleeping less and finding yourself increasingly fatigued by the shadow work of dating. "Typically I would send messages back and forth via the site three times before one of us would suggest exchanging cell phone numbers to arrange a meeting," Rachel says. "Once I had someone's number I would probably exchange another three text messages to decide on a place and time and confirm meeting up."

Then there is the first date. "I think I am an anomaly in this department," Rachel says. "I would tend to have a date of about two hours with a guy once we'd met up in person. I might spend that much time to get a real sense of him, or because it was still interesting to chat even if I wasn't so attracted to him. Many people set more rigid limits for themselves, like having a forty-five-minute coffee date first and ending it then, even if they want to see the person again. I actually enjoyed meeting people regardless, and felt it was a little tricky or rude to dash out after less than an hour or so. I would usually know if I wanted to see someone again after a single date, but I might set up a second date to know for sure."

The site's structure does help Rachel filter out nonstarters in advance. "I at least know they are available and interested," she says. "It does that work for me." There are also many ways, of course, that prospective daters can disqualify themselves. "I would think twice, for example, about bothering to correspond with a guy who explicitly said he never wanted to have kids," Rachel says. "Obviously this is a big question that requires more context and discussion once you're actually a couple—no matter how you met—but I would still see public candor about lack of interest as a bit of a red flag."

At the end of the day, online clients still need to meet in person and decide if they like each other. Then you may discover that the person has "a really annoying voice, or some odd, twitchy habit, or they are only in the city for a summer internship," she notes. "If possible, I'd much rather meet people in the real world."

Communicating with potential partners—by telephone, email, or text—is part of dating and has always absorbed time. "Total hours spent browsing, messaging, setting up dates, and actually going on a couple of two-hour dates a week might have been ten hours," in Rachel's estimate. "Not sure if that's accurate at all—but *ugh,* if so, how depressing! I tried not to think about it."

In one way, the real world reverses the order of events from the dating site. In the real world, you meet the prospective date *first,* and if there is a spark, *then* you exchange phone numbers or email addresses and begin to talk or write. Thus that annoying voice or twitchy habit—and what they *really* look like—all get revealed at the outset. If these are deal-breakers, you can disqualify the person without investing all that time in an extended dialog that leads to a dead end. That's a huge savings in shadow work.

Most single people might share Rachel's preference for the real world over the virtual one. Yet as online dating and its shadow work soak up time and energy and wed people ever more deeply to their screens, the online search can trap them in digital silos. Ironically, this could actually make meeting someone in the real world less and less likely.

LESSONS FROM THE DATING WORLD

First, business and organizations no longer just sell products and provide services: they all are looking to assemble data on their customers. In the twentieth-century world, businesses just wanted your money; today they also want to know who you are.

Furthermore, it does not really matter why people "come in the door"—whether to buy something, learn something, socialize, book a service, entertain themselves . . . or date. OkCupid gladly helps single people date each other, but, as the site charges no fee, what's in it for the company is assembling a massive file of data on each customer. That file, generated by the customer's shadow work, is a capital asset for OkCupid to sell to paying clients—that is, advertisers. Those advertisers will direct well-informed, targeted ads at OkCupid's customers, who then inherit another form of shadow work in dealing with the cupidity of merchants.

Second, because supplying personal background data does take plenty of time, sites like Facebook that can offer their existing data to *other* websites have a big advantage. People just don't want to keep reentering all their information. If they can skip that shadow work with one mouse click that transfers all their data from Facebook, quite often they will. Facebook can bill its fellow websites for this resource: "sign in through Facebook."

Third, try as it might, the digital world does not match the real world very well in certain respects. For example, people add Facebook "friends" much more easily than they acquire real-world friends. So pairing "friends of friends" with each other does not work nearly as well online as it does in reality. The result is that the online dating client can easily find herself going down rabbit holes and following paths that become dead ends.

Fourth, in the digital universe, we deal, by definition, with a narrow channel of information: things that can be encoded in bits. As there are plenty of crucial things bits *cannot* capture, we do a lot of shadow work trying to fill in the picture. We know that the digital stream leaves much out, and we also know that these omitted things—like the timbre of someone's voice or the pace of their conversation—matter greatly. In dating, or just relating, we invest extra time painting in the many blank spaces between the points of light that flicker on the screen.

six: the twilight of leisure

The foundation of all civilization is loitering.

— Jean Renoir

S HADOW WORK WILL grow. It rewards businesses and organizations in ways that are irresistible. No capitalist can refuse a chance to cut those heavy personnel costs by transferring jobs to customers who work for free. As shadow work merges into our daily routines, it will affect social habits, economic patterns, and lifestyles.

It may, for example, rewrite the traditional contract between consumers and corporations. Historically, companies have manufactured and/or provided goods and services for the public to buy and consume: you pay your money and lick your ice-cream cone. But a sales transaction has two phases: *manufacturing* and *distribution.* Shadow-working consumers are making inroads into both.

Regarding distribution, consumers are now *dispensing* what they buy to themselves. Customers pump their own gasoline, draft their own beer, serve their own frogurt, and scoop up bagfuls of basmati rice and then label them, at the bulk-food section of Whole Foods. They fill plates at salad bars and ladle soups, lo mein, mac and cheese, or scrambled eggs from the soup bars, entrée bars, breakfast bars, and other buffets that have sprung up in thousands of food markets and delis.

Consumers have also begun to handle the *manufacturing* phase of commerce. With 3-D printers, they need only download a design to "print out" many objects they would have bought at a store not long ago. This is home manufacturing. When customers build Ikea furniture, or any type of kit, they are taking on the assembly stage of manufacturing. At New Balance kiosks, they can move even further back, to the design phase of the production process, as they fashion the look of their unique pair of running shoes.

Consumers and corporations may forge a new type of relationship. They will become collaborators as consumers take on these more active roles in commerce. Corporations will have to listen more closely to these shadow workers, who happen to also be their customers. Technically, businesses will want to strengthen the intimacy of their feedback loops with customers, probably with innovative digital communications. (In a way, targeted advertising is already doing this.) Customers may exchange messages with companies via Facebook, send photos or videos of products through Instagram to show what went wrong or what they would like to see, interact with customer service departments via texts, or ramp up their use of "live chat" dialogs with company representatives. Such exchanges are, in part, what the insatiable information dragnet is about. The closer bond may help businesses cultivate a consumer base with a friendlier attitude toward corporations, as the two camps develop an informal partnership.

The "Ikea effect" may also strengthen brand loyalty for products that consumers have helped design and build. In many sectors, customers will look for more personalized goods and services—having things their way. They'll assemble end tables and add their own cream to coffee—but will also want input on the design of their clothing, furniture, and bicycles, leading to more individualized products. Crowdsourcing, which taps the creativity of groups, could become a platform for such populist participation. For example, crowdsourcing on the web enables customers to "vote" on potential T-shirt designs. This form of shadow work provides companies with free market research—and essentially guarantees a certain number of sales, as consumers are nearly certain to buy a product they have helped invent, or customized to their preferences.

Disintermediation will also grow as producers sell directly to their customers, eliminating middlemen in venues ranging from farmers' markets to warehouse stores like Costco. Once inside the stores, customers will deploy their smartphones to become their own salespeople, researching products and their prices without bothering the staff. Retail sales personnel may drop out of the equation, as they have already largely done at big-box stores. Internet commerce makes disintermediation effortless: Consumers buy directly from the site without ever seeing the inside of a store. Pictures of products from multiple angles with zoom-in capability and videos now provide abundant information to enable "distance shopping." Younger consumers tend to view shopping at stores as a waste of time ("Old people go to stores," one twentysomething opined); a few mouse clicks can complete the purchase. They will buy clothes and even shoes online and, if they don't fit, send them back; it is still quicker and easier than shopping at a bricks-and-mortar store.

As knowledge becomes more widely accessible, the democratization of expertise will make workers interchangeable in many generic jobs and functions. This could produce a more collaborative, egalitarian society as the collapse of hierarchies brings a leveling trend. Citizens will resist the idea of placing someone "above" them (for example, a doctor or lawyer)—or below them. They'll bus their bagel-shop table without complaint and later that day talk back to their cardiologist. Yet this leveling will first take root *socially*, without necessarily affecting economic realities. Knowledge may be power, but it doesn't always translate into money: Income distribution has become more unequal even as the distribution of knowledge has flattened out.

A complex of economic factors lies behind this seeming incongruity. Without attempting any rigorous analysis, we can elucidate one aspect of this conundrum through an example of shadow work. The medical patient who educates himself about his symptoms and even attempts self-diagnosis by consulting WebMD and Wikipedia is taking advantage of the flattening of the pyramid of expertise. When he sees his doctor, he may be better informed and thus equipped to take a more active role in his treatment. In the abstract, this development has economic consequences, because the patient's shadow work in self-diagnosis apparently reduces the degree of consumer demand for the physician's supply of specialized knowledge. And as such instances play out repeatedly across the society over years, they could chip away at the economic status of the medical profession: If what doctors trade in becomes less scarce, its value—and doctors' compensation—ought to decrease, according to basic economic propositions.

But let's suppose that our hypothetical patient works as a market researcher. Does his shadow work and enhanced medical knowledge actually change his own financial status relative to that of his doctor? At the end of the day, he remains a market researcher, and she remains a doctor. The social and psychological effects of the shadow work are immediate and palpable; the economic consequences, such as they are, will take longer to work through the system.

THE SOCIAL PATHOLOGY OF EVERYDAY LIFE

I once had a job interviewing heroin addicts and other opiate-dependent individuals for a research project funded by the National Institute on Drug Abuse. Not surprisingly, nearly all of them showed evidence of psychopathology. Many suffered from depression or other psychiatric syndromes. Even so, a surprising number of the addicts felt content with their lifestyles. They were neither distressed nor depressed. Their personal reality made sense to them. The only problem was that it didn't overlap much with the one the rest of humanity inhabited.

It is hard to overstate the importance of connecting with the *real world* outside your own mind. Interconnectedness is basic to survival. In a healthy natural habitat, living organisms are interdependent, each playing an essential role. The most reliable way for a plant or animal to ensure its survival is to contribute to the survival of its neighbors. When an organism becomes marginal to the biological community, unnecessary to the vitality of its fellow creatures, it begins to lose its environmental niche and is on its way to extinction. E.M. Forster got it right: *only connect.*

Communication is oxygen. The inability to communicate—to get across to others and to take others in—may be the root of human misery. In prisons, short of torture, the harshest punishment is solitary confinement. People cut off from relationships become dangerous. When a news story breaks about some crazed person who has gone on a murderous rampage, shot up a school classroom, or committed some other barbarity, the backstory reveals, with numbing predictability, that the perpetrator was a loner.

Society doesn't work well when communication breaks down among families, football teams, marketing divisions, or student bodies. People sealed off in individual silos don't coordinate their actions with each other or with the whole. Unconnected units, whether in a defensive backfield or on a board of directors, produce dysfunction and collapse.

Isolation should not be confused with solitude. Spending time alone, whether meditating, installing a window, painting watercolors, playing the saxophone, or relaxing with a book, can be richly rewarding. Solitude nourishes the soul, so we often choose it. Isolation isn't chosen. It gets imposed on us by rejections, failures to connect, our own discouragement, and sometimes institutions. Many things separate people, and not all of them stem from our personalities or social groups. Economic patterns and technologies that are fundamentally antisocial also enforce isolation. These can include shadow work.

THE HUMAN ORGANISM evolved for millions of years in a state of group living. From hunter-gatherer tribes to agricultural communities to feudal villages, people lived in tribes, clans, extended families. Until the eighteenth century, hardly anyone was ever alone. By historical standards, even the modern nuclear family—mother, father, and children in their own house or apartment—represents fragmentation: It's a unit broken off from the extended family of grandparents, uncles, aunts, cousins, and other kin, who in prior centuries lived under the same roof or nearby. (Personally, I was lucky enough to grow up with a version of this older pattern, as nearly all my father's many siblings and their families lived within a few miles of us.)

Yet this ancient pattern of community has been fading away. In recent decades, adults have begun living alone in unprecedented numbers, especially in cities. At least 40 percent of households in Atlanta, Denver, Seattle, San Francisco, and Minneapolis contain a single occupant, and in Manhattan and Washington, D.C., nearly half do. Abroad, the numbers can rise even higher: more than 50 percent in Paris and over 60 percent in Stockholm.

This is good for the housing market, but it also suggests that people simply spend less time relating. In her 2012 book *Alone Together*, Sherry Turkle describes how people are plunging into social media and digital entertainment in ways that disconnect them from each other. "I saw three teen girls walking down the sidewalk alongside each other," says a social worker in Tallahassee, Florida, named Alice. "They were not talking with each other. Or even paying attention to each other. All three had their heads in their smartphones. For my generation, that would be considered rude."

Rather than opening their ears to sound, people now plug up their ears to listen to recorded music while tuning out the rest of the audible world. Earbuds indicate how entertainment technology has evolved to isolate listeners and viewers from each other. Individual experiences of recorded music and movies are replacing the live, communal rite of performance for an audience. I once attended the opening night of Woody Allen's film *Annie Hall* at a crowded, sold-out movie theater in Boston. For an hour and a half, the room rocked with laughter, as Allen's hilarious script and great cast delivered one brilliant punch line after another. I enjoyed it so much that I returned a couple of days later for a weekday matinee. There were only about seven people scattered around the theater. The movie was exactly the same, but hardly anyone laughed at the same great jokes. Laughter, an essential experience for an audience, is contagious. It happens far more easily when you have a few hundred others to share the humor.

Today, instead of collecting in a theater, the movie audience disperses to their individual homes, where each person views a different film on a flatscreen television. Each family has its own home entertainment center. Instead of dealing with the ticket seller, ticket taker, and popcorn vendor at the movie house, we download our movie from Netflix, pay on a Visa card, and microwave popcorn in our own kitchens. We stage the experience entirely with shadow work, performing the jobs of the theater owner (acquiring the film and the place to show it), the box office (paying for it), the projectionist (screening the movie), and the concession stand (making the popcorn). The audience experience is absent.

At work, telecommuting and the ubiquity of computers mean that coworkers interact more with screens and email than by talking, even via telephone or, God forbid, in person. (Conversation—what a time hog!) Cherie Kerr, a public speaking and communications consultant in Santa Ana, California, told Stevenson Swanson of *The Chicago Tribune* in 2005 that she was amazed at how many clients prefer exchanging email to talking on the telephone. "People are just not connecting as much as they did, or as they should," she said. "A lot of people do not want to talk to people anymore."

In this context, the absorption of service jobs like supermarket cashier and gas pump jockey by shadow-working customers and robots weakens communities. Shadow work pushes us toward isolated self-sufficiency. But this autonomy comes at a price. Those daily interchanges, swapping pleasantries and small talk with service personnel, help glue a neighborhood, or a town, together. The 2009 book *Consequential Strangers: The Power of People Who Don't Seem to Matter . . . but Really Do*, by Melinda Blau and Karen Fingerman, vouches for the importance of such relationships—connections that are not strong ones but that still matter a great deal for health, family life, success in school, and the social contentment of community life. Stanford sociologist Mark

Granovetter's landmark 1973 paper "The Strength of Weak Ties" reinforces this point. He demonstrates how, for example, people more often find jobs through relatively distant others—to whom they are weakly related—than through strong ties with friends or relatives. (One advantage weak ties have is that there are so many more of them.)

Yet robots are dissolving this human texture. Those "interactive" kiosks are not really interactive: Robots never talk back. Shadow-working customers control the pace of their transactions at a kiosk. They do not need to adapt to feedback from any living being; instead, they get trained in an autonomous, self-willed mind-set. Siloed in their own bubbles, such shadow workers avoid the give-and-take of even small talk with actual people.

Furthermore, kiosks deal solely with information, banishing sense data and feelings, let alone spiritual aspects, from the interchange. Kiosk users may themselves tend to become robotic: cerebral, unemotional, and enslaved to digital data. This interactive style could gradually become accepted or even become a model of how to deal with humans as well as machines. Robots might instill behavior patterns that produce an epidemic of Asperger syndrome—in essence, creating a nation of biological automatons. For decades, people have been perfecting the art of building robots. The machines may now turn the tables and take over the manufacturing end, using human beings as their raw material.

IN SOCIOLOGY, THE breakdown of bonds in a human community is called atomization. It's a chemical metaphor: People who were once bound together in molecules break up into smaller, unbonded units, or atoms. Atomization sets the stage for serious social pathology—such as *anomie,* a term sociologist Emile Durkheim popularized in his classic 1897 book *Suicide.*

Ultimately, anomie entails the collapse of social norms, those shared values that underpin the social order. It can lead to moral deregulation—an erosion of standards of behavior as well as ethics and integrity. If shared assumptions and values fall away, the newly "atomized" individuals may embrace an every-man-for-himself ethic of self-centered, self-willed actions.

That might sound entrepreneurial, or even echo our archetype of "rugged individualism," but it is something quite different. By definition, an entrepreneur must understand the marketplace, and the true individualist, like Emerson's nonconformist, remains emphatically connected to her community: If you don't know the conformists, you cannot nonconform. Atomization and anomie, in contrast, involve disconnected behavior that ignores the collectivity. This can open the door to an epidemic of sociopathic behavior. Some social analysts, as well as the daily news, suggest that the epidemic may have already begun. Consider the frequent murderous rampages in schools; the barbarities perpetrated by terrorists; the epidemic of bullying by teenagers, which social media only intensifies; the vast wealth appropriated by a tiny fraction of the populace while wages stagnate for all others, with no action taken to redress the balance; the plutocratic domination of national governments in industrialized democracies.

Ironically, in such a scenario of social breakdown, the only well-behaved participants may be the robots.

THE TWILIGHT OF LEISURE

The vanishing of leisure is a mystery of twenty-first century life. It flies in the face of the commonsense view that wealth should mean more leisure. In the past eighty years, the global economy has enlarged its collective gross domestic product by about sixfold. Meanwhile, since 1930, world population has increased about 3.5 times, from two to seven billion people. In industrialized nations, productivity per capita, and per hour, has reached new heights, largely as an outgrowth of technology.

Admittedly, the distribution of this wealth has been anything but egalitarian: The upper echelons have captured the lion's share and then some. Even so, in a robustly expanding economic environment, it is puzzling that people find themselves more pressed for time—especially in the richest countries. Flouting all historical precedents, the wealthiest citizens now seem to be the ones hurting for leisure.

A 2006 paper by Mark Aguiar and Erik Hurst examined five decades of time-use studies and reported that Americans worked a relatively stable number of market hours between 1965 and 2003. (Note that their results differ from those of Juliet Schor of Boston College and Stephen Greenhouse of *The New York Times,* as reported earlier.) They noted that leisure time for men increased by six to eight hours weekly, due to fewer market hours of work, and increased for women by four to six hours a week, due to fewer hours worked at home. The authors translated this into five to ten weeks of additional vacation time annually, based on forty-hour weeks. They also found that the *less*-educated adults experienced the largest increases in leisure and noted "a growing 'inequality' in leisure that is the mirror image of the growing inequality in wages and expenditures."

Despite increased prosperity, many Americans do seem to find themselves in a time crunch. As early as 1970, Swedish economist Staffan Burenstam Linder tried to explain this paradox in *The Harried Leisure Class*. He argued that the scarcity of time had become a pivotal factor in advanced economies:

> What has happened is that in the rich countries all slacks in the use of time have been eliminated, so far as is humanly possible. The attitude to time is dictated by the commodity's extreme scarcity. The day of the sluggard is over. "Personal administration" has become important. We may not be terribly good at it, but we are aware that it is a desirable skill. The pocket calendar becomes our most important book. Its loss causes the owner himself to feel lost. Punctuality has become a virtue that we demand of those around us. Waiting is a squandering of time that angers people in rich countries. Only personal mismanagement, or the inconsiderate behavior of others, will create brief—and highly irritating—periods of involuntary idleness. People are dominated by their awareness of the clock. They are haunted by their knowledge that the shining moments are passing without things having been done.

Linder felt that economists had overlooked a crucial fact: *Consumption takes time.* Economic models, he said, assume that consumption is instantaneous. But it is not. Enjoying a theatrical play, a fine meal in a restaurant, or a European vacation requires time. And time, like money, is a scarce commodity. With increasing wealth, Linder declared, people feel compelled to spend their new income on more goods and services, which take even *more* time to consume. Hence the affluent classes experience a compression of free time—of *leisure*. So much for the leisured classes.

Linder's argument seems self-contradictory in a way: Isn't the consumption of plays, restaurant meals, and vacations what leisure is *for*? Those consumption activities *are* leisure. Well, yes, they can be—if that's what you choose to do. But "free time" means hours you can spend as you like. (The English word *leisure* comes from the Latin *licere*, "to be permitted.") Now, the news flash, which may come as a surprise to some: *You can spend leisure time doing things other than consuming goods and services.* We are not (yet, anyway) required to devote all our nonworking hours to the essentially economic activity of consumption. At leisure, you may take a walk, play with your child, appreciate the garden, luxuriate in an erotic interlude, meditate, read a library book, marvel at the night sky, take a nap. You can even do nothing.

In 1928 John Maynard Keynes wrote "Economic Possibilities for Our Grandchildren," an essay in which he predicted that by 2028, technological progress would make economic productivity so efficient that people would work three-hour days and fifteen-hour weeks, releasing vast amounts of leisure. The main problem would be what to do with all those free hours. Solving this dilemma isn't the cakewalk you might think. Consider the boredom of the idle rich. Those who comprehend "the art of life itself," Keynes wrote, would be "able to enjoy the abundance when it comes."

Keynes was brilliantly prescient in predicting a sevenfold growth in the world economy over the following century, but his bounty of leisure has not arrived. In 2014, Elizabeth Kolbert published a thoughtful essay in *The New Yorker* that reflected on Keynes' forecasts in a review of *Overwhelmed: Work, Love, and Play When No One Has the Time* by Brigid Schulte, a book, Kolbert wrote, that "explores why it is that twenty-first-century Americans feel so swamped."

Schulte advances several theories to explain the disappearance of leisure. One is that leisure has lost its cachet. In *The Theory of the Leisure Class* (1899), sociologist Thorstein Veblen argued that conspicuous leisure, like conspicuous consumption, allowed the privileged to establish, confirm, and announce their elite status. Just as lawns were originally a status symbol proving that a landowner was prosperous enough to devote acreage to merely scenic plantings, conspicuous leisure advertised the fact that the aristocrat could expend hours, even days and weeks, on nonproductive activities like fox hunting.

That status symbol now appears to have been reversed. Members of the elite vie to be "busier than thou." "I asked Samantha if she was free next week for lunch," says Leah, owner of a small gallery in Brooklyn who lives on the Upper East Side of Manhattan. "She told me her first day free for lunch was three and a half weeks off.

Gee, I guess that proves she's busier and more in demand than I am. *Please.*"

Even rich citizens who don't need income still relentlessly work and strive. Perhaps they feel a psychological need to justify their privileged status and find that ceaseless activity does this. From the standpoint of personal pleasure, enjoying the recreational options that wealth affords might seem more rewarding than sprinting through a day hyper-scheduled with appointments. But for the scurrying aristocrats, preserving public image trumps pleasure. They confirm one of Veblen's postulates: The motive of social status routinely outweighs rational self-interest.

Veblen also anticipated Linder's point about how consumption inevitably grows with income. "In the rare cases where it occurs, a failure to increase one's visible consumption when the means for an increase are at hand is felt in popular apprehension to call for explanation, and unworthy motives of miserliness are imputed to those who fall short in this respect," he wrote in *The Theory of the Leisure Class*. "A prompt response to the stimulus, on the other hand, is accepted as the normal effect . . . the standard of expenditure which commonly guides our efforts is an ideal of consumption that lies just beyond our reach."

This indicates where Keynes went wrong. Kolbert cites contributors to *Overwhelmed* who "attribute Keynes's error to a misreading of human nature. Keynes assumed that people work in order to earn enough to buy what they need. And so, he reasoned, as incomes rose, those needs could be fulfilled in ever fewer hours. Workers could knock off earlier and earlier, until eventually they'd be going home by lunchtime." Instead, as Veblen and Linder suggest, with more money, people find more things to buy, which gives them more things to do, and instead of cashing in on a leisure dividend, they find their time getting scarcer.

THE EMERGING PORTRAIT of the future has large institutions taking control of a larger and larger part of human endeavor, funneling more of each individual's time into the essentially economic pursuits of production and consumption. Corporations, governments, labor unions, nonprofits, and the academic world share the agenda of getting people more involved in *economic* activity—things that make money. Work, earn, buy. Create endless economic growth—only good things can come from an expanding economy and more money.

In contrast, leisure, at least the forms of leisure that are free, has no institutional lobby. Leisure pursuits are, by definition, disorganized. (That is one thing that makes them leisurely.) There is no advocacy group in Washington, D.C., promoting the interests of people who nap, read, or walk in the park. The innocence of leisure makes it vulnerable to the predations of organized bodies—and there are many—that have designs on our free time, something they view as a natural resource awaiting their schemes.

IN 1961, ERVING Goffman published a sociological classic, *Asylums: Essays on the Social Situation of Mental Patients and Other Inmates*. In 1955–56, he did fieldwork at St. Elizabeths Hospital in Washington, D.C., the first federally operated psychiatric hospital in the United States, then a century old. It housed more than 7,000 patients when Goffman did his research there.

Asylums opens with a long essay, "On the Characteristics of Total Institutions," in which the author identifies certain features of institutions that take complete control of the humans who populate them. He begins by defining a *total institution* as "a place of residence and work where a large number of like-situated individuals, cut off from the wider society for an appreciable period of time, together lead an enclosed, formally administered round of life." Goffman notes that "prisons serve as a clear example, providing we appreciate that what is prison-like about prisons is found in institutions whose members have broken no laws." Total institutions include the military, convents and monasteries, mental hospitals, institutions for the mentally disabled, and even some boarding schools, particularly in their earlier, single-sex incarnations.

Those inside total institutions do lead an existence that we might describe as "completely institutionalized." For the most part, the controlling organization dictates when inmates go to sleep and wake; when and what they eat; what work they do; what forms of exercise they might take; what medical care they receive; what they wear. Inmates may have little, if any, free time (or too much of it), and they typically spend what time they do have within their compound, confined by its rules.

In the twenty-first century, we may ask whether organizations beyond the military, convents, mental hospitals, and so on have begun to turn society into a total institution without walls. Global corporations, big government, the education establishment, organized labor, mega-healthcare, nonprofits, Big Pharma, Big Data, and their attendants, the ubiquitous news and entertainment media —all are making steady incursions into unstructured time. They aim to seize control of that time, generally for some profit-making purpose, though the end can also be political or involve a social goal like recycling.

Along with work and consumption, shadow work has now emerged as a third force locking in the institutional ownership of our days. Shadow work commandeers a new block of free time and steers it toward institutional designs. In this busy, driven, amped-up theater of modern life, shadow work enters the scene and piles on even more jobs to do. It is a new predator, biting off chunks of time from people whose time is already in short supply.

In this chapter I have sketched out two contrasting dystopias. One sees society fragmenting into millions of atomized, siloed individuals, each doing their work, performing their shadow work, meeting their needs online, and absorbing their feed of digital entertainment without connection to the community, and thus setting the stage for anomie and social breakdown. The other scenario describes a citizenry that is, if anything, *too* integrated with the community. Specifically, it is integrated with social institutions that submerge individuals' own preferences beneath those of larger establishments, as corporations and other behemoths commandeer daily life, funneling nearly all human energy into economic channels and institutionally determined goals.

In advancing these two dark visions, I may call to mind Woody Allen's statement, "More than any other time in history, mankind faces a crossroads. One path leads to despair and utter hopeless-ness. The other, to total extinction. Let us pray we have the wisdom to choose correctly." To make matters worse, these two visions aren't necessarily incompatible: *Both* could arrive simultaneously.

I do not believe any future landscape to be inevitable. Nor do I have a formula to deal with these unsettling prospects. I will, however, share a touchstone that may help ground us in things that matter, now and in the future. I start from the premise that how we invest our time reveals—and determines—who we are.

ULTIMATELY, THE STUDY of shadow work is a study of how we spend our time. No more meaningful choice confronts human beings. "Dost thou love life?" asked the forty-year-old Benjamin Franklin in *Poor Richard's Almanac* in 1746. "Then do not squan-der time, for that is the stuff life is made of."

Naturally, defining squandered time—or squandered money, for that matter—is a subjective call; one man's "squandered" hours might, on another fellow's scorecard, be time very well invested. In 1974, Major League Baseball pitcher Tug McGraw signed a large contract with the Philadelphia Phillies, and soon thereafter a sportswriter asked McGraw what he planned to do with all that money. "Ninety percent I'll spend on good times, women, and Irish whiskey," he said. "The other ten percent . . . I'll probably waste."

Ben Franklin's other dictum, "Time is money," is a philoso-phy more aligned with American values than Tug McGraw's. Two and a half centuries later, money still reigns as America's greatest object of desire. Unfortunately, our obsession with lucre has run off the rails. We have forgotten why we pursue it in the first place: to buy things we need or want. Money is a medium of exchange. It is useful insofar as it brings you goods and services that enrich your life and the lives of those you care for. But money per se is only a symbol; its value lies in what it can buy.

We've lost sight of this. Recall the psychological experiment whose subjects endured harsh noise through headsets to earn chocolates they could not consume, either then or later. The subjects were much better at producing than consuming. They practiced "mindless accumulation" by "stockpiling useless treasure"—much like mindlessly earning piles of money you will never spend. Young investment bankers on Wall Street work 100-hour weeks, hauling in vast sums of money they have neither the time nor energy to use. Typically, they plan to "pay their dues" now and, once they have "made it," dial back their work hours to enjoy their wealth and leisure.

Unfortunately, it rarely works out that way. The young tycoons have bought into a tired American game plan: *Get rich so I can quit working and have the "freedom" to do what I really want.* A few may actually achieve this, and retirees who have planned well can enjoy years of free time without financial concerns, even if they don't wallow in riches. But also recall the sixty-eight-year-old William Gross, who earned $200 million per year but couldn't bring himself to leave the office for an hour to hit golf balls. Fiduciary and professional commitments, along with psychological habits, often stop us from "leaving money on the table" to enjoy free time, even when it's available. If time is money, the exchange seems to go in only one direction. Somehow, we never get around to trading money for time.

We have come to regard time as another commodity, like wheat or petroleum. It is no such thing. Commodities are fungible. Traders can buy and sell them globally because durum wheat is always durum wheat: You know what you are getting. But time is inseparable from experience, so everyone's time is unique and personal. We can sell our time for an hourly rate, but as Coyote, a prostitutes' organization in San Francisco, once proclaimed, call girls aren't *selling* their bodies, they are only *renting* their bodies. On salary, we only rent our time.

Time seems to be a continuum of past, present, and future that we can chop into segments of hours or days. Shadow work has encroached upon these segments. It can "save" time by speeding up some transactions—or act as a thief of time, stealing minutes or hours without compensation. But this is clock time: measurable units exchangeable in the market.

Time as *experienced* cannot be divided up, and it knows neither past nor future. Life happens only in the now. *Real* time, whether spent working for wages, doing shadow work, playing, or sleeping, is not transferrable. Is time really money? Money's value is real yet unquestionably finite. Work has many rewards, both spiritual and material. Time, in contrast, is ineffable, and its value infinite. Time is life. Now abide work, money, time, these three; but the greatest of these is time.

acknowledgements

MY PARENTS, TO whom this book is dedicated, gave me the kind of love any child might wish for. They provided every advantage they could to launch me in life without ever suggesting, beyond their own fine examples, what my life should be. Mom and Dad had the generosity to bestow a gift with no strings attached.

You can choose your friends but not your relatives, they say, though I believe I would have chosen the siblings nature provided. My sister, Nanette Zucker, has proven a lifelong pal and great company; her humor, poise, balance, and unfailingly positive outlook have sustained my spirits for all of our decades together. She also has a great net game. Meanwhile, my brother-in-law, Daniel Zucker, has become essentially another sibling. Batting around either ideas or tennis balls with this fraternal soul is reliably stimulating.

Jeffrey Lambert has taught his older brother many things, mostly by example, including his excellent practice of the art of parenthood. As fellow citizens of Red Sox Nation, Jeff and I have shared moments of exhilaration and pain that only the Fenway Faithful will ever fully understand.

Tom Tiffany, a close friend since college, taught me at least half of what I know about rowing, the subject of my first book. We've shared countless laughs and edifying experiences as the sole members of the International Federation of Sagittarian Coxswains and cofounders of the Sesame Noodle Rowing Club, two of the most exclusive and least-known organizations in the rowing universe.

Peter Desmond has been a pal since we were college freshmen. A fellow writer, Des has brought endless smiles to my days with his wicked humor and gift for arcane philology. Without his sage counsel on taxes all these years, God only knows where I might be now.

Another fellow writer, Charles Coe, has been an unfailing sounding board for ideas on literature and sports, which suggests his breadth. When someone once asked Charles what he, as an African American, had been up to in the Soviet Union in the 1980s, he answered, "Touring as the lead singer of a jazz group." Which he was. What can you add to that?

Phyllis Barajas has long been a delight both to hang out and cook with. Years ago, she appointed herself president of the Craig Lambert Fan Club, and she has performed admirably in that job, whose duties are eased by the fact that she is also the club's only official member.

Nell Porter Brown, a fellow editor at *Harvard Magazine*, has sustained me for years with her understanding and ability to listen. I am grateful for the many ways she helped me work to the highest level of my capacities.

Steve Potter, another friend since college, believed in this book when it was not much more than an idea. With his wife, Kathy Drake, Steve has been a source of bountiful encouragement and support throughout its evolution.

Brad Addison has been a cherished friend since we forged a bond in Harvard's Leverett House Dining Hall, known to initiates as "Lev Dine." Over my years developing, marketing, and writing *Shadow Work*, as with many previous endeavors, Brad has provided unstinting support—as a reliable sounding board, and as a source of encouragement, ideas, critiques, and wise counsel. Our coast-to-coast conversations are filled with laughter, stimulation, and insight: to me, they exemplify friendship at its best.

Lenny Singer is the older brother I didn't have. A true kindred spirit, Lenny has a passion for sports, especially of the Boston and Harvard variety, that, as far as I can tell, is unbounded by time or space. He is also, to my knowledge, the only Jewish, Harvard-educated commercial airline pilot who has ever lived.

Without my longtime friend Tom Vinciguerra, *Shadow Work* might never have come about. An accomplished writer and veteran *New York Times* contributor, Tom introduced me to a *Times* op-ed editor, which led to the publication of my essay on shadow work, the acorn from which this book grew.

Though Jesse Kornbluth was only a year ahead of me in college, we didn't meet until we were both well along in our careers, when he wrote a lovely review of my first book, *Mind Over Water*, for his website. We became fast friends, and years ago I designated Jesse as my "rabbi" in the literary world. He's been my go-to guy for advice on any professional question and has proven reliably smart, savvy, and funny. And even better, *right*. "Jesse the K" ranks at the top of the heap in generosity—with ideas, advice, caveats, and introductions. His peerless email messages are also an art form that rivals haiku in producing the biggest effect with the fewest words.

My literary agent, Julia Lord, showed tenacity in marketing *Shadow Work* and eventually placing it with the distinguished publisher Counterpoint Press. She has been a teammate, sounding board, and resource throughout this project. Julia disproves any and all clichés about inaccessible, uncommunicative agents. And best of all, she is a human off-road vehicle: She'll go wherever necessary, regardless of terrain.

From the start, my editor, Dan Smetanka, understood that "shadow work" was a big idea. Dan has genuinely cared about this book. He has shown the wisdom of an experienced editor, both in what he has done and what he hasn't done—both of which are equally important.

Jim Harrison, *Harvard Magazine*'s ace photographer, did a masterful job of shooting the image that anchors my website. The picture wouldn't have happened without my friend Beth Whittaker, one of Boston's top architects, who served as the model. Anyone as beautiful as Beth has been asked about modeling her whole life long; I am flattered that she agreed to pose for the first time for my photo—and did so, to no one's surprise, with professional aplomb.

Jean McGarry, an old friend and a highly skilled novelist and short-story writer, read my manuscript, chapter by chapter. She provided abundant encouragement and suggestions—made even more credible by the fact that Jean directs the creative writing program at Johns Hopkins.

Danny Klein, a good friend who also happens to be a superb writer and best-selling author, provided unstinting encouragement at every stage of the process. He read the manuscript and set a Guinness record for exclamations of "Mazel!" Danny had a lot of positive things to say about the drafts, and given his literary credentials, I was even inclined to believe him. Danny's wife, Freke Vuijst, at times seemed even more fired up about the shadow work concept than I was. She's a smart, skillful Dutch-American journalist who brought me some European examples of shadow work, helping convince me that it really is a global phenomenon.

Robert and Ilona Bell, a couple who both teach English at Williams College, invested generous amounts of time in reading my chapters. Both helped improve the book. First, simply passing muster with literary minds of their caliber was a validating experience. (Once, after Bob sent me a commentary on *Mind Over Water*, I told him that I had no idea what a good book I'd written until he'd explained it to me.) Ilona is a painstaking reader and brilliant editor; I adopted nearly all of her suggestions, including a recommendation, late in the process, that persuaded me to reorganize the manuscript. Another nice thing is that both Bells are a joy to spend time with.

Lastly, my inamorata, Anne Undeland, has inspired me throughout. Her love, understanding, earthy common sense, and generous spirit have been an amulet through all phases of the work, and her presence and humor have been indispensable.